Readings

OTHER BOOKS BY SVEN BIRKERTS

Tolstoy's Dictaphone: Technology and the Muse, Editor

The Gutenberg Elegies: The Fate of Reading in an Electronic Age

American Energies: Essays on Fiction

The Electric Life: Essays on Modern Poetry

An Artificial Wilderness: Essays on Twentieth-Century Literature

Readings

Sven Birkerts

GRAYWOLF PRESS

Publication of this volume is made possible in part by a grant provided by the Minnesota State Arts Board through an appropriation by the Minnesota State Legislature, and by a grant from the National Endowment for the Arts. Significant support has also been provided by Dayton's, Mervyn's, and Target stores through the Dayton Hudson Foundation, the Bush Foundation, the Andrew W. Mellon Foundation, the McKnight Foundation, the General Mills Foundation, the St. Paul Companies, and other generous contributions from foundations, corporations, and individuals. To these organizations and individuals we offer our heartfelt thanks.

Published by Graywolf Press
2402 University Avenue, Suite 203
Saint Paul, Minnesota 55114
All rights reserved.

www.graywolfpress.org

Published in the United States of America

ISBN 1-55597-283-7
2 4 6 8 9 7 5 3 1
First Graywolf Printing, 1999

Library of Congress Catalog Card Number: 98-84453

Cover design: Julie Metz

Publication of *Readings* is made possible in part through a special partnership with the College of Saint Benedict.

Acknowledgments

The author gratefully acknowledges the editors of the following publications in which the essays listed were first published.

"The Idea of the Internet," *National Review,* July 1997

"Walking after Midnight," *The Oxford American,* June 1998

"Only God Can Make a Tree," *The Boston Book Review,* November–December 1996

"Notes of a Nonpolitical Man," *AGNI,* 1990

"An Open Invitation to Extraterrestrials," *Ploughshares,* 1986; *An Artificial Wilderness: Essays on Twentieth-Century Literature,* William Morrow and Company, Inc., 1987

"Biography and the Dissolving Self," *AGNI,* 1994

"The Grasshopper on the Windowsill," *The Hungry Mind Review,* Spring 1996

"States of Reading," *The Gettysburg Review,* Summer 1997

"Against the Current," *TETYC,* October 1997

"Reading and Depth of Field," *Philosophy and Literature,* Vol. 2, #1, April 1996

"Docufiction," *The Boston Phoenix,* 1986; *An Artificial Wilderness: Essays on Twentieth-Century Literature,* William Morrow and Company, Inc., 1987

" 'Poetry' and 'Politics'," *Margin,* Autumn 1987; *The Electric Life: Essays on Modern Poetry,* William Morrow and Company, Inc., 1989

"Running Out of Gas," *The New York Observer,* October 13, 1997

"Second Thoughts," *The Review of Contemporary Literature,* Spring 1996

"This Year's Canon," *FEED* [www.feedmag.com], December 22, 1997

"When Lightning Strikes," *The Boston Review,* April 1985; *The Electric Life: Essays on Modern Poetry,* William Morrow and Company, Inc., 1989

"On a Stanza by John Keats," *The Electric Life: Essays on Modern Poetry,* William Morrow and Company, Inc., 1989

"Rainer Maria Rilke," *The Threepenny Review,* Fall 1988; *The Electric Life: Essays on Modern Poetry,* William Morrow and Company, Inc., 1989

"Robert Lowell," *The Boston Review,* October 1987; *The Electric Life: Essays on Modern Poetry,* William Morrow and Company, Inc., 1989

"Seamus Heaney," *Wigwag,* December 1990

"Atmospheres of Identity: Elizabeth Bishop," *Conjunctions,* Winter 1997

"The Learning Umbrella: A Reflection on Flaubert," *The Boston Review,* 1987; *An Artificial Wilderness: Essays on Twentieth-Century Literature,* William Morrow and Company, Inc., 1987

"A Gatsby for Today," *The Atlantic Monthly,* March 1993

"Jack Kerouac," *Harper's,* July 1989; *American Energies: Essays on Fiction,* William Morrow and Company, Inc., 1992

"Anne Tyler: Destinies of Character," *American Energies: Essays on Fiction,* William Morrow and Company, Inc., 1992

"Don DeLillo's Underworld," *DoubleTake,* September 1998

Contents

I

II

I

The Millennial Warp

Sometimes my writing students come to me to say that they are stuck or unable to get started or otherwise at a loss, at which point I am compelled to give them some version of my "return to the core" speech. I ask them to get into a meditative mode and then to monitor themselves carefully, to find out where their thoughts go when they are left to find their own level. "Look to those places," I urge them, "because that's where your best subjects and energies will most likely be found."

Physician, heal thyself! I have now spent the better part of a year in the tangles of a project, a very particular sort of memoir, the point of which is not to indulge my recollections for their own sake, but rather to present them selectively in such a way that the reader will grasp my real point, which is that in the past fifty years or so something in the nature of time—or in our experience of it—has changed radically; that, in other words, the shape of the very frame of things has altered. This is not an everyday sort of intuition. Indeed, to remark it is to admit to being in an unbalanced condition. Where do you draw the lines of definition? How do you begin to approach others for correction or corroboration?

I do bring the idea forth—tentatively—to certain people and find a fairly predictable sort of response. Most will concede that there have been astonishing changes on nearly every front in the past half century; that our ways of living have been transformed to an extraordinary degree. Everyone has a fund of available anecdotes on the subject. "I can remember," they begin. Or: "My father can still recall . . ." But nearly all view the process as one of accumulated innovation and cultural and societal acceleration. Brows ascend skeptically when I offer that we may have reached some condition of critical mass, that degree increments have brought us into the first stages of a change in kind. Simply: that our old understandings of time—and, therefore, of life itself—are in many ways useless.

This is my peculiar project. Yet even as I have a concept and an array of corroborating arguments, something in the nature of the topic has me getting lost again and again. I have bursts of local clarity, frequent accesses of new evidence, and these I coax to the page eagerly enough. But the backdrop, the larger point of it all, keeps slipping from me. I cannot easily hold the specific and the general in the right equilibrium. And so, often, much more than ought to be necessary under most writerly circumstances, I make myself heed my own precept. I ease up on the pressure, let the day-dreams in; I look to reconnect with the originating impulse. I walk around in the world and see what thoughts I generate when there is no pressure to produce. The process usually works. I seem to be sufficiently self-consistent to end up once again revolving the same few notions in my thoughts. This must be me, I think, confirmed again. I am able to go back to sifting through the specific memories I have gathered.

But these do not concern me here. Just now I want to confront the sponsoring impulse itself, that special complex of intuitions and anxieties that keeps me fixated on the idea that the human time experience may be undergoing a fundamental mutation. By which I do not simply mean that we feel ourselves to have less and less of it, though this is, of course, part of what is happening, never mind the fact that we are surrounded by laborsaving technologies on every front. But how to present the evidence?

My own way of posing the matter to myself can be figured as a rapid back-and-forth turning of the head—not so rapid as to make me dizzy, but rapid enough to allow the contrast between what I see on either side to be vivid. I am, in effect, looking from one end of my life to the other, from the past that came just before and into which I arrived, suddenly present, to the future, parts of which I have faith I will see, but which will more properly be the time my children will claim as theirs. Rapid shifts of focus, then. On one side, the world of my grandparents and parents—the lore of the old country I absorbed so deeply from their stories, the evidence of their gestures and ways of doing things, and my own awakening perceptions of the early 1950s, a time before television, a time of young stay-at-home mothers and briefcase-toting fathers driving off to work. On the other side, the sound- and image-saturated *now*, my bemusement and unease at the complexly decontextual way the world presents itself, and how confused I am to see my children adapting to it so readily. "Things have always gone so," I mutter to myself, and I wonder, honestly, whether my whole conception of a deep-down renovation of things might not just be the grumpy reactions of aging in a disguised form.

The head-turning operation is, I grant it, dissociative in its very nature: The contrast emerges when the connective tissue has been cut away. But of course we *live* the connective tissue—the whole point of it is *connection*. I am, moreover, skewing things by being so selective in what I view. That is, I look at only those phenomena that will show me something about changes in our time experience. I do not consider the other evidence, the constants—childbirth, say, or the recurrence of irrepressible bonding urges—that might belie my insistence. Besides, one might argue, looking back and forth this way over any fifty-year period is guaranteed to induce time shock. Things change, and they have always changed.

But no. My very point is that the acceleration, the gathering of momentum, over this fifty-year period is something new, that it runs so far in excess of historical expectations of change, and does so on so many different levels at once, that we cannot lay it to rest by calling it just more of the same. If nothing else—and there is much else—this is the first epoch in which all-encompassing shifts in the way life was lived have been recorded—by photograph, by film, by video, by recording machines—and then fed back to us, slowly at first, then as a part of such a cataract of data and imagery that the reflection of life can itself be seen to be one of the most pronounced features of life. It has been in this most recent period, which we are now and perhaps henceforth immersed in, that we finally have seen the creature succeed in swallowing its own tail— this is the first time, ever, that the perceptions of events and the transmission of the perceptions have become as important as the events themselves. It is not enough to say that life has simply evolved and gotten more complicated. Life—the "it"—is now in some crucial ways a new substance, and this basic fact must be contemplated deeply.

When I look back and forth between the early post–World War II years and the premillennial present, I often feel a kind of vertigo overtake me. Much is, of course, the same—people wear clothes, ride buses, eat in restaurants, play baseball—but the sameness is not what is striking. I feel, rather, that the present is a lingering transition moment between that past and a future that offers an entirely unfamiliar aspect to the comparative anthropologist. The elements are still recognizable, but they are part of a momentum that will imminently alter their nature. And time, that grand abstraction, has everything to do with this.

The first thing that any disinterested historian-anthropologist would notice about this period is the astonishing increase and acceleration on all fronts: more people, more things, and rates of activity undreamed of by the most animated of philosophers. It is as if we were all molecules in a liquid that had been subjected to a sudden high heat. One could, I suppose, approach this statistically, citing increases in population, production, consumption, automotive and airline travel, and so on. My impulse is different. I want to grasp at the change subjectively—to remember, admittedly with a child's senses, what it felt like to be in downtown Birmingham, Michigan, on a Saturday afternoon circa 1956, and then to focus in on impressions from recent visits. How else do we study these things—in our souls, I mean?

What I fetch up from them is the inside picture of a very different world. In this quieter, smaller town, people drove their cars right into the center and parked in a metered space on the street. Kids lined up down the block to get into the afternoon movie. Stores—I could almost close my eyes and name them—tended to feature so-called necessities, and these were finite in number. But these are not really the things I remember. What I preserve is an overall feeling, a sense of the essential pace of things. This embraced everything, from the movement of people on the sidewalks to the way adults kept encountering one another and lingering to talk; it also embraced the tempo of transactions, the air given off by shop owners and employees, and—to sound crotchety now—the absence of piped-in music: Many more things seemed to take place against a backdrop of natural ambient noise, nothing more.

Nowadays, returning to visit, I find the place more than doubled in size. Going to town means jockeying to get into a parking lot and adjusting to the sidewalk flow between pricey boutiques; it means, as often as not, laying down plastic for a purchase and having the shopping contact limited to the clerk's rapid-fire verification of the card. I exaggerate—or do I? I am guilty of nostalgia, sure, but to use that word is not to invalidate the perception. The world has speeded up in a thousand ways, and that acceleration has come to comprise a significant part of a person's interaction with society. A change in the rate of interaction is, let's face it, a change in the nature of the interaction.

This molecular agitation, it should be noted, embraces everyone. Even children and the elderly—two groups formerly safe from the ethos of busyness—are now ensnared, racing to clubs, sports, support groups, and lessons. In the collective judgment, expressed through everything from advertisements for pain medication to the gestural inflections of news show anchors, to hold a valid ticket to being, one must be busy.

A direct consequence of this massive systemic speedup is the thinning out, the near disappearance, of the intermediary layer. Leisure, silence, stillness—formerly the stresses of labor were cushioned. There were kinds of time, and the counterpart to busyness was rest. When the sun went down, or the church bells rang, a slowness of the kind we now find intolerable swept in. The entertainment options were fewer: One might read, listen to the radio, play cards. Now the expectation is that entertainment, the right to it, is inalienable. The structure of entertainment—its massive and variegated presence—now fills what were formerly preserves of open time, those often monumentally boring periods when little or nothing stood between the self and the grainy presence of the world. Certainly there was boredom, but there was also nearness to the primary world. Before the great mediation, a person had only to pause in a task or sit calmly in order to be in contact, however fleetingly, with the ground of nature, to feel its rhythms, its essential peacefulness. No longer. We have put between ourselves and the natural world so many layers of signals, noises, devices, and habits that the chance for such connection is very limited. More often than not, a person finding himself suddenly in an uncontaminated natural setting will register a body shock, a tremor of extreme displacement.

Dramatic increases not only in the rate of activity but also in the kinds of activities available—everything from affinity groups to workshops to therapies to lessons to Internet cruising—have naturally affected the way in which we engage events. The more there is to do in a finite period of time, the more likely it is that a person will rationalize the task and divide the time. Indeed, we are now deeply immersed in the perception of life as a set of scheduled events—a kind of actuarial decathlon that has us hitting specific marks at regular intervals through the day as well as at all of the appointed stages of life's way. A vast and intricate grid has been superimposed on our older way of being, and it's hard now to conceive that things were ever really different. Time comes in blocks and everything runs to plan. The awareness is no longer enforced just externally, it penetrates every consciousness. Only young children are—blessedly and, alas, briefly—unaware. The rest of us are completely enshrouded, from the beeping of the morning alarm, to the radio reminders every few minutes, to the giant hourglass that is the urban and suburban traffic pattern; from the opening of offices and shops, to the scheduling of classes, to the programming of our TV shows. We move through the day in lockstep with the clock, far removed from our ancestors—and I don't even mean the cave dwellers—who had no commute, no media, and who, even when they had clocks, were more apt to tune their time awareness to the changes of the light.

The insidious thing is, of course, this internalization, the way we absorb a structure and then bend to its dictates. We have all experienced the vacation syndrome—how the first three or four days of our two-week break find us struggling to escape the hold of habit. We carry the suddenly useless scaffolding with us even as we know we are paying dearly for the privilege of leaving it behind. The longer we work, the more we participate in the societal expectation, the more deeply we absorb a structure that has no organic basis, that was rationalized to serve the interests of commerce. How sad, too, that while it takes so many days to relinquish the work habits, the vacation reflexes disappear as quickly as the taste of brine on our lips.

But it is not simply our relation to time that has been altered here, it is our relation to situation, to event, to life itself. As we become creatures of outward obedience to order and inwardly suppressed impulse, we also take an ever greater role in scripting events, in planning situations so that they will conform to expectation. How indolent and fanciful it seems now that in the era of slower travel and patchwork communications, people would, in going from place to place, get off the grid; could, in effect, wander, or at least proceed without the sense of being enslaved by schedule; could be free of that peculiarly late-modern feeling, call it the "panopticon effect," of somehow always being seen. Or think of the now mythic figure of the flaneur, that unique phenomenon of nineteenth-century Paris, the individual who idled about the urban center in open defiance of the newly minted tyrannies of time.

Or listen to Milan Kundera, who in the opening pages of his wonderfully named novel, *Slowness,* asks: "Why has the pleasure of slowness disappeared? Ah, where have they gone, those loafing heroes of folksong, those vagabonds who roam from one mill to another and bed down under the stars?" Our only contact with this vanished spirit comes during the all-too-infrequent blizzards, which alone, by paralyzing our cars, have the power to overwhelm our planning strategies. Although the radio and TV reports present these events essentially as disasters, a great many people experience them as the only true holidays they have. I can think of few days more liberated and celebratory than those on which the whole neighborhood has been kept from its daily business. Adults appear in the street like bears coming out of caves; children run up and down in packs, alert in every sense to the suspension of routine. But these are the rare exceptions, and their special atmosphere, that electric truancy, is purchased with the internalized expectations of dailyness.

Rhythms have changed, expectations have changed, and so too, with what feels in historical terms like instantaneousness, have the things that people do—the fundamental actions that get performed in the course of an average day. We can contemplate—and this is but a single instance—how many ways in which technological innovations have short-circuited our physical involvement in tasks. From kneading dough to opening the garage door, and from carrying a suitcase to mowing the lawn, there is scarcely a physical operation that has not been simplified, streamlined, or eliminated entirely by some invention. We explain to our incredulous children that telephones once had dials that had to be turned, and that people used to get up from the couch every time they wanted to change the television channel. We do not tell them that there was a time before television even existed.

This technological intervention means many things, among them a worrisome loss of the sense of how things work and, more abstractly, a further change in our understanding of the time of things. For it used to be that the measurement of a task was in terms of how long it took the body to do it. People spoke confidently of a half-day's work, or a week's work, and the centrality of the working self was assumed. Now as tasks are divided and machines are implicated at every level, there is little correlation between the day and the operations one performs in it.

Of the innumerable technologies that have revolutionized our sense of time and our experience of daily life and labor, certainly the computer has had the greatest range of effects. On the most obvious level, the processing power of the microchip and the organizational capacities of software programs have not only transformed how we handle information—transplanting paper and print functions to keyboard and screen—they have changed our relation to information itself. Static print archives—data files—have been rendered potentially dynamic. The drudgery of rote retrieval and transcription, former clerical functions, has yielded to a new ease of access and agency. Energy has been released into the system. Watch individuals at their terminals—at travel agencies, in banks, at service counters—and you can see not only their dependence on the powerful tools they now command but also their delight in working the combinations, at taking part in the dynamic magic of information flow.

Obviously, then, there is much about the arrival of the computer in the workplace that is liberating. The overall change in the relation to information, which these search-and-retrieve operations only hint at, has other kinds of significance as well. For one thing, computers not only put enormous quanta of data into play, but they also, through options of linkage, situate the user in what is a potential infinity. In the blink of an eye, the formerly vast but comprehensible body of information symbolized by banks of paper files has become an incomprehensible totality, an ocean whose shores may never be located—incomprehensible, that is, to the individual, but navigable by technology. And thus we accept the prosthesis, move it into the center of our lives, and grant it the powers we cannot possess. In the process of handing ourselves over, we enact a subliminal self-diminution, tacitly admitting that we no longer have command of the data we manipulate.

This is somewhat general. But haven't we all witnessed the revealing instances, seen how the same agent or teller who at one moment clicks confidently at the keyboard, presiding over some portion of our fate, is suddenly reduced to shakes of the head and dumb shrugs when the mainframe goes down? Take away the prosthesis and the person does not even have the former paper props to fall back on. In the moment of the loss of power we glimpse the differential. Just as when the storm knocks out the power to our houses, we feel ourselves living as in a parenthesis, waiting, unable to carry on with our lives as we know them, never mind that the power we rely on has only been available for the briefest little part of our species' life. The fact is, we not only rely on it practically, we have *defined* ourselves in terms of it; and the same is already becoming true of our relationship with computers. We define our sense of who we are in part through a recognition of what we can do. And our sense of what we can do is being very rapidly altered by the technology we have brought into our midst.

Some will say, "So what?" The fact is that we *have* computers now—they are here to stay—much as we have our circuits, our electricity, and the astonishing know-how that has changed the way we live once and for all. I will propose shortly that the matter is not quite so simple, that such attainments have levied an extraordinary pressure, and that our definitional sense of ourselves may be more than a little affected. But there are certain preliminary implications that need to be considered.

We must consider, for example, that the awareness of the infinite interconnectedness of information made possible by the computer is both literal—is the sensation of potentiality felt by the user

at the terminal—and figurative. That is, we now—owing to computers as well as broadcast media—grasp the world as hypersatu-
rated. Too many channels, too many facts, too many images—too
much that thrusts itself at us. Who does not, now, inhabit a world
at once infinite and absolutely incomprehensible? The once nar-
row aperture defined by place and time, by the cognitive limits of
the unassisted senses—William Blake's "windows"—has been
forced open. Globalness and instantaneity are our new lot. Never
mind that we still live, bodily, in one place and still relate ourselves
to our environment with our bodily senses; that inhabiting, once
the core of our self-conception, our at-homeness in the world, has
become schizophrenic. To simple actuality has been added perpetual possibility. Upon the evidence present to immediacy has
been superimposed an invisible realm of event—the ever-present
awareness of elsewheres and of the impossibly complex ways in
which they impinge on our here and now.

This is not, strictly speaking, an entirely new condition. It has
been with us since the telegraph first breached the barriers of distance and began bringing the news from elsewhere into our lives.
But the momentum that began with the newspaper and intensified with network television has now, just very recently, escalated
past our already overstrained capacities of response. We cannot
avoid it, blinker ourselves as we may, for the movement of the
world all around us is in a thousand ways orchestrated by incessant
global awareness. The moment-by-moment fluctuation of global
financial markets impinges on us whether we own stocks or not.
Everything is connected.

We humans, of course, are not capable of the kind of receptivity and response that a global information environment would
seem to require. As Sigmund Freud astutely suggested, "For a living organism, protection against stimuli is an almost more important function than the reception of stimuli." To put it another way:
The radical refinement of the microchip, measured in generations defined by specific operational capability, is not matched by
the adaptational capacity of the human organism. Yet it is the rate
of evolution of the microchip that is, in significant ways, determining the nature of our information environment.

Human, overwhelmed, we reply to the rapidly mutating conditions of life by editing. We take in what we can, double up our functioning when we need to; we willfully turn away from many kinds of information, of stimuli, because we instinctively grasp that our response mechanisms would be overtaxed. And we flee from saturation—an ever more common sensation—into the decompression of entertainment. The perfect counterbalance to a day spent navigating the perpetual overflow of the present is an evening given over to the mindless absorption of images and music. The spring that is tightened past its natural bent must be allowed to recoil.

This is, I would venture, something new in the world—the overall sense that so many people have of being in arrears; of moving in the midst of data ramified past all true comprehensibility; of living partially with no hope of gaining the ground to wholeness.

Yet, and here is a terrible paradox, at the very same time that the world is felt to be overwhelming, there is also a poignant sense of its limitation. We have created a sphere of endless news, imagery, and information—a sort of world within the world—but the other world, the one that greets our natural senses and imaginations, seems depleted, exhausted. We have eliminated the physical, the geographical, frontiers. There are no more endless tracts or unknown lands to compel the imagination. And what there is of variousness and remoteness is being rapidly stripped of aura and homogenized. Bring the rain forest into the living room enough times and it loses its otherness. Crowd the extremities of earth (what were once the extremities of earth) with Burger Kings and cinemas showing *Die Hard II* and the sense of possibility begins to vaporize. Is it too obvious to note that the two developments are deeply linked, that the infinity of information has in some ways been purchased at the price of the terrestrial unknown and the sense of mystery it once housed? That the sphere of information takes its exponential growth at the expense of the actual, which nowadays appears to be shrinking, losing force?

All of this, of course, relates in specific ways to the human time experience. There is ever less difference between local and global communications—the same near instantaneousness governs both—and this has subjected our older sense of the time of things to a disfiguring pressure. For until quite recently we understood time as being, at least in one sense, in dynamic relation to distance. But when a signal can travel to the other side of the world in a second—easily and cheaply, that is, no longer requiring the voodoo of the long-distance telephone call—then our sense of these two abstractions, once etched so deeply into our reflexes, our very being, must alter. The ground feels different under our feet than it felt to our forebears, as does the distance our eyes gaze into feel different.

These imponderables are what I am finally concerned with—our sense of the ground under and around us, our understanding of what *far away* is, or could be, or what we register when we speak of "long ago" or "tomorrow" or "a year from now." These are, as it were, the bright A-B-C blocks of our being in the world, and they are not the same as they were for so many generations preceding ours. The primary elements—the undercurrents of meaning and the feeling tones—are mysteriously changing.

While I cannot begin to assess what might be the ultimate effects of these subtle alchemizings of the ordinary, it seems clear that they have already wreaked some havoc on our sense of where it is in time we find ourselves. Which is to say, our relation—individually and collectively—to the idea of past, present, and future has been radically modified. A great many people now live with the feeling that both the historical and the personal past exist on the other side of a widening gulf, while the future seems to press down with a palpable urgency. Obviously there is no objective source for such a pronouncement. I take my evidence from talking to people—older people, peers, and students. From the older people I gather that things felt quite a bit different in the past. Although changes came steadily in the old days, too (new inventions, changes in the workplace) and sometimes with unexpected force (the depression, the war), the line of continuity was never ruptured. The idea of tradition still prevailed; the past was felt to be linked to the present as a source, and the future, the perennial unknown, was felt to be a kind of new land that everyone moved slowly into, individually and en masse.

No more. The past, so different from everything we see happening around us—different in kind, not just in degree—appears quaint and irrelevant, fodder for periodic recycling as nostalgia.

At the same time, we feel ourselves hurtling toward the future. Everything feels provisional. No product, no artistic work, no initiative carries any hint of permanence. Rather, we are fixated by the seasonal rotation, the fashion. The music will last for a moment; the computer will be upgraded shortly; and it is cheaper just to throw away the old appliance and get a new one. The idea of repair itself belongs to the past. And the future, the millennium, is the destination. There the time line, the last vestiges of the old orientation, will self-destruct. There, somehow, we will all begin to live in a new configuration. We are pulled inexorably toward that apotheosis.

I will grant that my extrapolations are sketchy and will seem fanciful to some, arbitrary to others. But they are, for better or for worse, the things I keep thinking about; they are what my own experience has thrust into relief. Although I present them sequentially, in my awareness they are all entangled. And I cannot honestly contemplate the future for very long without feeling a swarming sense of angst. Not so much for myself anymore, but for my children. My dread is custodial: I have to wonder what their world, their life experience, will be like. And I ask myself if I should be readying them to adapt to the new order of things, or, contrarily, equipping them with lore about the old. Is the past in this sense a bequest or a burden? It is in asking these very questions that I grasp the profound implications of what we are living through.

Quite recently I had an illumination of sorts. Two very different insights—metaphors, really—from two very different thinkers combined, and all at once I seemed to understand the deeper structure, if not the problem, then at least of my own fear.

The first notion, which reached me only when the lengthy fuse had burned down, came by means of Arthur Danto's recent book, *After the End of Art*. And while the whole book galvanized my thinking about our late-modern circumstance, it was one of its opening passages that figured most suggestively in my thinking:

> At roughly the same moment, but quite in ignorance of one another's thought, the German art historian Hans Belting and I

both published texts on the end of art. Each of us had arrived at
a vivid sense that some momentous historical shift had taken
place in the productive conditions of the visual arts, even if, outwardly speaking, the institutional complexes of the art world—
the galleries, the art schools, the periodicals, the museums, the
critical establishment, curatoriat—seemed relatively stable. Belting has since published an amazing book, tracing the history of
devotional images in the Christian West from late Roman times
until about A.D. 1400, to which he gave the striking subtitle *The
Image before the Era of Art*. It was not that those images were not art
in some large sense, but their being art did not figure in their
production, since the concept of art had not as yet emerged in
general consciousness, and such images—icons, really—played
quite a different role in the lives of people than works of art
came to play when the concept at last emerged and something
like aesthetic considerations began to govern our relationship to
them.

Danto goes on to theorize as follows:

If this is at all thinkable, then there might be another disconti-
nuity, no less profound, between the art produced during the
era of art and art produced after that era ended. The era of art
did not begin abruptly in 1400, nor did it end sharply either,
sometime before the mid-1980s when Belting's and my texts appeared respectively in German and in English. Neither of us,
perhaps, had as clear an idea as we might now have . . . of what
we were trying to say, but, now that Belting has come forward
with the idea of art before the beginning of art, we might think
about *art* after the end of art, as if we were emerging from the
era of art into something else the exact shape and structure of
which remains [*sic*] to be understood.

Danto's idea—that we may now be making art after the end of
art—affected me profoundly. It brought back at least part of the
disturbance I had felt long ago when I understood—grasped vis-
cerally—what Friedrich Nietzsche meant about living after the
death of God. How different was the backdrop—suddenly—
against which all things were seen. So, too, I registered the end of
art as being the end, the expiration, of another way of believing,
as the end of the myth of aesthetic investigation and progress. For
Danto did not mean, of course, that there is to be no more ex-

pressive making, only that individual expressions no longer have a chance of adding up to something larger, something perceived to be substantially related to human experience in important ways. The ground of that mattering, he believes, is gone.

Given the long-standing assumption in many quarters that the deeper expressions of art were bound integrally to the spirit of the times—to the historical moment—one cannot help but wonder whether the end of art might not be consequent upon the end of something in the world itself, something that art had so diversely reflected and drew its fundamental purpose from. An unnerving suggestion, this, but one to which I will need to return.

The other concept, which has steadily haunted me for several years now, and which was, by way of obvious association, brought forth again by my reading of Danto, comes from Bill McKibben's *The End of Nature.* McKibben's idea, or realization, is disturbingly simple. It is that with the growth of world population, urbanization, the spread of mechanization, and, more recently, with the invisible saturation of all airspace with electronic signals, we have effectively eliminated the idea of nature as an entity that exceeds us and to which we belong. Now, and henceforth, we believe and act as if nature belongs to us. All natural environments are either enclosed by or critically influenced by human doings. McKibben asserts:

> When I say that we have ended nature, I don't mean, obviously, that natural processes have ceased—there is still sunshine and still wind, still growth, still decay. Photosynthesis continues, as does respiration. *But we have ended the thing that has, at least in modern times, defined nature for us—its separation from human society. . . .*

> We can no longer imagine that we are part of something larger than ourselves—that is what all this boils down to. We used to be. When we were only a few hundred million, or only a billion or two, and the atmosphere had the composition it would have had with or without us, then even Darwin's revelations could in the end only strengthen our sense of belonging to creation; and our wonder at the magnificence and abundance of that creation. And there was the possibility that something larger than us— Francis's God, Thoreau's Benefactor and Intelligence, Peattie's Supreme Command—reigned over us. We were as bears—we

slept less, made better tools, took longer to rear our young, but
we lived in a world that we found made for us. . . . But now *we*
make that world, affect its every operation.

Why Danto should have called McKibben to mind is easy to see.
The titles alone—*After the End of Art* and *The End of Nature*—signal
their kinship. Both propose the recognition of a core transformation, manifest as the loss of a primary human concept, and both
ask how we propose to live on in what amounts to a new order. I almost wrote "live on bereft," but very likely few people have any
awareness that something may have happened—many, indeed, live
on as if Copernicus had not come along. That is, their conceptions
of art and nature, insofar as they have such conceptions, remain
intact. Nature equates to wooded landscapes and national parks,
art to paintings in museums, full stop. But even the unreflective
must feel at times a sense of great barometric shifts taking place
in the atmosphere they inhabit, and they cannot be entirely un-
anxious about what such shifts may signify.

Danto's and McKibben's scenarios combined in my thoughts
with forceful consequence. No doubt they exacerbated my own
tendency to pessimistic brooding about the future. I know that I
woke one day with a pressing conviction: that if there is any figurative truth to these two assessments, then we must think about the
possibility of a third, a kind of summa. And this would be that in
spite of the fact that various biological constants remain—the human need for food, shelter, and procreation—and despite the
nominal survival of any number of fundamental social institutions,
enough has changed, *is* changing, at a root level to allow us to say
that human life as we have known it and characterized it in our figures of speech, our collective myths, our movies and novels and
advertisements, scarcely exists anymore. We are in a new system, a
new arrangement, one that has become estranged from the defining former norms, even as we continue to look back at them for
orientation and solace.

This is, granted, wide-eyed, and so general as to seem useless,
and anyone who cares to will be able to name enough things that
are unchanged to make the assertion—and its proponent—seem
unbalanced. But might it not, for many others of us, serve to un-

derscore a feeling we share all too often, that something in the fundamental order of things has slipped out of plumb? It won't be the first time a change like this has been noted. Think of Virginia Woolf's famous observation that "on or about December, 1910, human character changed." Did it? Who will say? What criteria will we invoke? The questions are not to be answered. We only know that her words corresponded enough to what many others thought, or felt, that they were much repeated—indeed, became one of the best-known diagnostic assessments of the modern period.

Let this be the spirit and the frame of reference. I am not saying that human life or human possibility has ended, only that the terms are no longer those assumed in our central artistic expressions since at least the Renaissance.

With this strange yoking of Danto and McKibben I have honed in on my own fear, which is that in some way that vitally impinges on the psyche, we are coming to live in an "after the end" period; that the collective sense of the millennium itself may be shaped by this strange apprehension. What does it mean?

To understand "living after the end" we must see that what has ended is not any one thing but the whole ordering—the dynamics of scale and connectedness—that had become the basis of meaning and of our idea of the human. Within that organic complex were woven deep assumptions about time, space, nature, human autonomy, societal connectedness, and a good many other things. These, separately and together, have in a short period of time sustained an unprecedented pressure.

And yet we remain—do we not?—recognizably the same basic creatures. And we persist in holding to the idea of continuity, in refusing the possibility that, in William Butler Yeats's words, "All's changed, changed utterly." That doggedness of refusal may itself be taken as an impulse to cohesion—a conservatism—mightier than any transfiguration. This, too, is an exciting thought: that we may yet prevail as ourselves, even as we move, individually and collectively, into an electronic connectedness that has us sacrificing attributes and reflexes one would have thought absolutely defining. Maybe the citizen of the near future, maneuvering among apparatuses and devoting his day to circulating data through far-flung circuits, is more like than unlike his preelectronic counterpart who moved real things with his hands and inhabited a silence, an isolation, that was deep and resonant. Who will say? And how far would we need to move into the realms of the virtual before that resemblance really changed?

When I was younger I was fascinated by a philosophical riddle of sorts that I had encountered in Miguel de Unamuno's *The Tragic Sense of Life*. There he described a ship that left its home port and sailed around the world. At every port of call, some parts of the vessel were replaced, until, finally, not an original nail remained. Only the name was the same. Was it, Unamuno demanded, the same ship? And if so, why?

I see that I am worrying a similar problem these days. How much change can the fundamental human prototype—whatever that might be—take before we have to retire the old terminologies and come up with something new? Can we sustain indefinitely a divorce from the natural world—its seasons, its creatures, its original wildness—and the breaching of our essential solitude in a condition of dissolved interconnectedness? Can we lose track entirely of the space-time perceptions that were so long believed to be hard-wired into our cognitive engines? Can we mutate endlessly in adaptation to a riot of new forces, moving with each step further from our origins, and still harken to the old paradigmatic images and expressions of the human? Is it silly to be asking these questions?

Let me conclude with two passages drawn from E. M. Forster's hair-raisingly dystopic story, "The Machine Stops," wherein he has imagined a future gone virtual in the extreme. Individuals live in hexagonal cells, their every need secured, and devote themselves almost exclusively to the exchange of information and ideas by means of a peculiar apparatus that can put them into instant contact with others anywhere in the world. The totality of technologies and operations is called "the machine," and although it is known by all to be a human, not a godly, creation, after a time people begin to revere it as if it were, indeed, a deity.

The conflict in the story is between a mother, Vashti, who has become a believer, and her son, Kuno, who alone has rebelled, seeking out the mysteries of the world so long ago transcended. Returning from the aboveground realm to which he has journeyed, Kuno reports:

You know that we have lost the sense of space. We say 'space is annihilated,' but we have annihilated not space, but the sense thereof. We have lost a part of ourselves. I determined to re-cover it and I began by walking up and down the platform of the railway outside my room. Up and down, until I was tired, and so did recapture the meaning of 'near' and 'far.' 'Near' is a place to which I can get quickly *on my feet,* not a place to which the train or air-ship will take me quickly. 'Far' is a place to which I cannot get quickly on my feet. . . . Man is the measure. That was my first lesson. Man's feet are the measure for distance, his hands are the measure for ownership, his body is the measure for all that is lovable and desirable and strong.

Vashti will not accept Kuno's understanding, not until the very end, when the machine—the whole imponderable totality of it— breaks down. Universal horror and anguish ensue. Mother and son, finding one another, burst into tears; they reconcile:

They wept for humanity, those two, not for themselves. They could not bear that this should be the end. Ere silence was com-pleted their hearts were opened, and they knew what had been important on earth. Man, the flower of all flesh, the noblest of all creatures visible, man who had once made god in his image, and had mirrored his strength on the constellations, beautiful naked man was dying, strangled in the garments he had woven. Century after century he had toiled, and here was his reward. Truly the garment had seemed heavenly at first, shot with the colours of culture, sewn with the threads of self-denial. And heavenly it had been so long as it was a garment and no more, so long as man could shed it at will and live by the essence that is his soul, and the essence, equally divine, that is his body.

And this, I believe, is where the line gets drawn, where we deter-mine whether change has been integrated or has led to deforma-tion. Can we differentiate those essences of soul and body from the garment we have woven? I have faith that we still can, though not as naturally and effortlessly as we once may have. If we have a mil-lennial task, it will be to keep the blade of discrimination whetted.

American Nostalgias

When I think, as I increasingly do, about the much-hyped arrival of the millennium, I tend nowadays to focus less on the moment of our official transfer from one chronological construct to another, and much more on what I have come to see as the movement *toward* and the movement *away*. Configuring it in my imagination, I visualize something like an hourglass tipped on its side. I am moving, as are we all, along a narrowing tunnel toward a body-sized aperture; on the other side of it, there when I pass through, is the new world I think of as the future, that strange consummation I've been living toward my whole life without ever reaching.

But this reflection is not about what I feel myself moving toward but rather what remains. It is about my fear that the past may *not* remain—for me and for others—a possession, what Ernest Hemingway called "a moveable feast," in the way it was once expected to. The world is changing more rapidly and completely than it ever has. The changes, many of them more in kind than degree, require sudden new orientations and adaptations. My anxiety is, I realize, irrational, as is all anxiety. But I wonder if by stepping through that body-sized aperture I will not find that I have irrevocably broken the threads binding me to the older way of things, the tradition.

This is not a recent fear; I have been prey to it long before the millennial countdown began, and it has in some way or other underlain much of my thinking about larger cultural concerns. And, I suppose, literary concerns as well. Indeed, it is in the literary realm that I have found one of my anchor points—that of the character of Harry Angstrom, the "Rabbit" of John Updike's tetralogy.

Whether or not he began thus in *Rabbit, Run,* Harry did evolve over the succeeding volumes, which appeared more or less at ten-year intervals, as a representative American male of his generation. This is neither here nor there, except that Harry has been endowed by his author with a powerful nostalgia reflex. As he grows into maturity and then edges into what we sometimes call the fullness of his years, he is increasingly susceptible to eruptions of elegiac fondness, not just for his past, but for a whole way of life that he sees fading before the chaotic excitements of late modernity.

Here, to confine myself to a single instance—and this only to sound the note I need—is Updike describing a reverie Rabbit experiences as he listens to a string of familiar oldies on the car radio:

> Rabbit feels betrayed. He was reared in a world where war was not strange but change was: the world stood still so you could grow up in it. He knows when the bottom fell out. When they closed down Kroll's, Kroll's that had stood in the center of Brewer all those years, bigger than a church, older than the courthouse, right at the head of Weiser Square there, with every Christmas those otherworldly displays of circling trains and nodding dolls and twinkling stars in the corner windows as if God himself put them there to light up this darkest time of the year. As a little kid he couldn't tell what God did from what people did; it all came from above somehow. He can remember standing as a child in the cold with his mother gazing into this world of tinselled toys as real as any other, the air biting at his cheeks, the sound of the Salvation Army bells begging, the smell of the hot soft pretzels sold on Weiser Square those years, the feeling around him of adult hurrying—bundled bodies pushing into Kroll's where you could buy the best of everything from drapes to beds, toys to pots, china to silver.

This seems to me a triumphant passage, a wonderful riff run on the great—or maybe *emerging* great—American theme: What ever happened to the American past? Which is to say: What ever happened to America? Where did a whole great cluster of bedrock certainties disappear to? We wonder, reading Updike, whether the change came about because Rabbit—and we ourselves—grew up, or whether something in fact happened, something more than just the closing of Kroll's, but which that closing, at least in that fictional world, represents.

Come what apocalypses may, there will always be those vocal hardboiled types who get red in the face (and thus belie their own words) and assert that any argument about decline or change is flat-out wrong—that things have always been like this and that they have, in fact, been a good deal worse in the past. Against these citizens there is no arguing, though God knows I have tried. The fact remains, however, that for a great many people, looking from a great many perspectives, life has changed in some anxious-making ways in recent decades. I don't mean in terms of leading economic indicators or anything blandly statistical, but in terms of how things feel, whether experience makes sense, resonates; whether it is possible to believe in a meaningful future; whether there is some essential sense of continuity between past and present. I suspect that a great many Americans, certainly those over the age of forty, feel to some significant degree at sea, lost, living but not fully alive. Increasing numbers of us are suffering time sickness; we no longer understand where we fit—or if fitting is even possible—in the scheme of things. Rabbit's anxious sense of having become lost inside his own skin is our own.

What has happened? Even if we agree that something is different in the world now—that changes over and above the expected changes of societal evolution have taken place—there are a hundred different ways to give account. We have lost the underpinnings of religious faith, succumbed to cultural relativism, entered a global economy, given way to narcissism, allowed ourselves to be overwhelmed by information, surrendered our political will, become enslaved to a consumer ethic, and on and on. Probably all of these explanations can be advanced, and while none of them quite accounts for our impression of a world remade, together they begin to suggest the extent of the transformation.

I would add to this sketchy list another: that we have been carried along, helpless, but also as inadvertent contributing agents, in a large-scale experiential shift, moving from a largely unconscious to an ever more conscious—even "hyperconscious"—relation to reality. We have, and maybe this is another way of saying the same thing, shifted from a simple, direct, unmediated sense of reality to one that is complexly mediated, saturated with information and with the possibility of information. We knew the world with our senses, or at one remove, and now we know it increasingly as a field of data. Our technologies, and our technologically driven employments, have created a secondary world that we inhabit in lieu of the first world that our immediate ancestors, and all of their ancestors before them, inhabited. This original world was determined in many essential ways by the brute realities of nature—by weather, by terrain, by the time required for various processes, and the intervals of long-distance communication. The new reality is significantly cut off from nature, largely unaffected by weather, global in reference, and premised on instantaneous communication. For the real we are substituting the virtual.

This is not to say that we have left the things and procedures of the older world behind completely (we obviously haven't), but we have certainly modified the basic terms of relation—to the natural world, to each other, to our idea of community, country, and culture. Something slippery has been interposed between ourselves and our neighbors. What we do is ever less defining. We consume more and more of the products of the world, but in the process we feel more and more removed from that world. The connection between cause and effect feels like it has loosened. There is a feeling of being in arrears, out of sync with time. We keep making fantastic promises to ourselves, evolve strategies for catching up. We will read those books, relax with our families, reconnect with our friends. Yet even as we make our vows we register the sickly sensation of how it is: We are divided from ourselves as well, our time and attentiveness subtly undermined. By what? Distractedness, too much to do, respond to, feel, control. The pressure of stimulus is itself alienating—we are farther from the things we interact with. And then there is the demon of possibility—it has crept into everything. Suddenly, as never before, we are potentially everywhere, in touch with all information; we are potentially present to everyone. The wires are live with expectation and dread. There is no privacy, no solitude. The phone is silent, but it will ring in an instant. The screen is over there, but it is accumulating messages. We can do so much, but driving through the outskirts of town, with the radio on, we feel as if we are living our lives behind impenetrable glass. The songs are about love, about sensation, and waiting at the stoplight we find we are unaccountably choked up.

To consider that our lives are mediated on nearly every front is dark enough. Darker still is the thought that the systems of mediation are under the control of a few nation-sized corporations, and

that what were formerly distinguished as the various aspects of reality have now been doubly converted, first to information and
then into entertainment. As culture critic Tom Frank has written
(in "Dark Age: Why Johnny Can't Dissent"):

> Business writers understand that the great promise of the In-
> formation Age is not that average consumers will soon wake up
> to the splendor of 100 high-res channels, but that every type of
> human relationship can now be reduced to digital and incor-
> porated into the growing televisual nexus—brought to you by
> Pepsico, of course. What reformed ad man Earl Shorris has writ-
> ten of the early promise of TV may finally be accomplished in
> the near future: "Reality did not cease to exist, of course, but
> much of what people understood as reality, including virtually
> all of the commercial world, was mediated by television. It was
> as if a salesman had been placed between Americans and life."
> TV is no longer merely "entertainment," it is on the verge of be-
> coming the ineluctable center of human consciousness, the site
> of every sort of exchange.

I would only expand the assertion to include all screen-centered
activities, adding net surfing to watching.

Frank's main point, made trenchantly a decade earlier by critic
Mark Crispin Miller, is that the commercial media vanquish all dissent. How? Through relentless irony, and by adopting the pose of
free-spoken rebellion as their own: The icons of protest now shill
happily for jeans, wine coolers, and computer software.

Every bit as frightening as the vaporization of the possibilities
of protest is the dying out of history, that is to say, of historical
consciousness. Invoking Francis Fukayama's controversial manifesto *The End of History,* Frank writes, "While America's arms ex-
penditures triumphed over the Red Menace, its comfortable
consumer banalities triumphed everywhere over local and inher-
ited culture, language, and ideas, literally ended peoples' ability
to think historically."

In part this is the effect of a universalized consumer culture and
in part the creation of a decontextualized and decentralized media stream, a postmodern environment in which all data can be
seen to coexist. A generation of students is growing up without any
sense of temporal perspective. History is a matter of zany costumes

and clumsy accents on made-for-TV movies. It is the juxtaposition by means of mouse clicks of facts about the French Revolution with images from the Broadway production of "Les Mis." Nor are students the only ones suffering the loss of history. We are all implicated. The watershed transformation of life from the real to the virtual, from tangible and comprehensible to mediated and impossibly overdetermined, has so distanced us from everything that came before; it has made everything that happened before high-speed electronics and color television seem equally quaint. Bobby Darin or Roman senators in togas, it scarcely matters—that was all back then.

Frank's summary overview is not sanguine:

> This century's technological advances are often described as victories over the primal facts of nature: hunger, cold, disease, distance, and time. But the wiring of every individual into the warm embrace of the multinational entertainment oligopoly is a conquest of a different sort, the crowning triumph of the marketplace over humanity's unruly consciousness. . . . It is fitting that, as this century of horrors draws to a close, our masters rush to perfect the cultural equivalent of the atom bomb, to destroy once and for all our ability to appreciate horror. With no leader but the "invisible hand," with no elite but the mild and platitudinous Babbitry of the American hinterland, Western capitalism will soon accomplish what the century's more murderous tyrants, with all their poisonous calculation, could only dream of doing: effacing the cultural memory of entire nations.

If we accept that there is a certain truth in Frank's contention—and I do—then our millennial moment presents us with a paradox: on the one hand, the large-scale erasure of historical awareness—indeed, cultural memory itself; on the other, the recrudescence of the time awareness, the presentation of past and memory in works by writers like Updike, as well as in countless films, theatrical productions, and the like. But no, if we look more closely, the paradox dissolves. For one thing, because artists stand apart from the population at large, and it falls to them, as it always has, to manifest and explore the tensions the rest of us largely avoid. But also because no transition so momentous can come about without a struggle, a backlash. As we hurtle into a new culture of images and data, and leave behind the older, slower, more obstacle-laden encounters with reality, it is to be expected that we will feel the surges of loss and the impulse to lament. For our delicate psyches have evolved, down through the millennia, to contend with one kind of reality environment. We cannot expect to saunter into another without some spasms of reaction. What is remarkable, really, is how readily we do succumb, how painless the transition seems to be.

There are reasons for this as well, the main one being that we are not allowed to feel the true shock of the loss of the past and the severance from age-old traditions. Into the gap, or what we would expect to feel as the gap, come the various forms of past re-processed. Here is the bygone done up as something else—as a way of life seen as comfortingly present, part of our ongoing legacy—and it works as a kind of nicotine patch on the ache of our withdrawal. The illusionism of advertising and entertainment persuades us that we can have it all—that we can buy Grandma's homemade lemonade to sip as we hunch in our cubicles before our terminals.

The genius of the entertainment industry has always been to locate our collective cares, and then either play on them remorselessly or else take our minds away, offering fantasy or solace. With prime-time network television, the formula is simple. Apart from sports, game shows, and lightweight comedies, we find, overwhelmingly, shows that feed the night side, the myriad news documentaries that spawn and then intensify our fears about health, product safety, corruption, environmental dangers, and so on, or else high-intensity scenarios about urban crime (*NYPD Blue, Homicide, Murder One*) and hospital operating rooms (*E.R.* and *Chicago Hope*). Or, serving as the ironic counterweight, we note the numberless sitcoms, the basic point of which is to run a laugh track under a steady stream of zingers about the inanities of modern life, simultaneously addressing and discharging anxieties.

The past is not much in evidence on network television—gone are the folksy staples like *Bonanza, Gunsmoke, The Waltons,* and *The Andy Griffith Show.* It surfaces only in high-minded series produced for public channels. There we see, in endless cycling and recycling, documentary programs on the Civil War, Vietnam, the American West, the Depression, baseball. But of course public-television audiences have always been small, drawing as they do on a more educated demographic group.

Hollywood shows a similar split. Blockbuster entertainments are geared to the coliseum mentality. They are lurid, violent, cynical, and feature tornadoes, aliens, venal lawyers, Mafia dons, gouts of blood, car chases and crunching metal, and the pat justification that they are working through the archetypal confrontation between good and evil. It is, again, in the more serious productions that we see the past—that is, the past presented as "culture," as entertainment. In just the last few years we have seen innumerable works of serious literature translated to the screen, including *Jude the Obscure, The English Patient, The Scarlet Letter, Emma, Persuasion, Jane Eyre, Sense and Sensibility, Howards End, A Room with a View, The Age of Innocence, Ethan Frome,* and *The Wings of the Dove.* These films are, almost without exception, scripted for upper-middle-class viewers. There is little comparable fare for everyone else, which is to say, for the bulk of the viewing audience.

What is significant here is not that the general public is not watching film interpretations of highbrow novels, but that neither in film nor on television is that audience asked to confront any images of the past. Whereas, I would venture, screening versions of the past is probably the real point—or much of the real point—of these more artistic efforts. Part of their appeal is, of course, story and part is acting, but certainly viewers who open their wallets are also paying to bask in the artfully arranged mise-en-scène of another time. All of which is to suggest that the thinking people in this country—at the very least, the better-educated people—are moved to confront the vanished past, most commonly the fantasied past of aristocratic England. The films could be said to serve, at some level, like a steam-release valve, showing us what we've lost but at the same time giving the gift of aesthetic experience.

If the past is strenuously and purposefully recycled in our arts— that recycling having become something of a movement itself—it is no less present in the culture of advertising. The point of advertising, as everyone knows, is both to sell specific products and to create a climate generally hospitable to selling. Thus, while ads have no compunction about creating small-scale anxieties of all descriptions—about, say, health and environmental concerns—

their larger mission is to leave the potential consumer reassured about the stability of the order of things. Thus, while some products are promoted for their innovatory capabilities—their newness—many more are situated in a narrative of continuity. Big-ticket items—cars, expensive appliances—are projected in terms of tradition. We are asked to ponder the history of fine craftsmanship, and so on.

But then there is the broad middle range of products and services—foods, medical plans, drugs, drinks—and a great many of these trade freely on nostalgia. "Remember when . . ." the voice intones, while the images deliver the staple associations of small-town or rural life—the picket fence, the craggy, wise pharmacist, the porch swing, children pulling catfish from the old mill pond. Whatever the pitch, there is always a way to forge a link with an imagined American past. We watch, feel a flush of warmth, subliminally identify the sensation with the product, and then, the next time we're shopping, the hand reaches out for Hills Brothers, Pepperidge Farm, Bayer, Dr Pepper.

Television advertising, like most television fare, is pitched at the American middle and below. The more desirable demographic group is either not watching or else is, possibly, tuned in to one of the public channels where there is no advertising. That population, the upper middle class (if there still *is* such a thing) on up, is more reliably reached, perhaps, by way of glossy advertisements in magazines (*Vanity Fair, Esquire, Elle,* Martha Stewart's *Living, Traveler,* etc.) or by way of mail-order catalogs. These last, from pricey fashion and specialty and fine-crafts outlets (L. L. Bean, the Gap, Pottery Barn, Levenger) are identical in their strategy, linking lifestyle, class, fashion, and, implicitly, a fantasied past into what amounts to a daydream of attainment. One can say, reliably, that the higher the class aspiration of the targeted customer, the more vivid will be the images of continuity and tradition. Which is to say, the more emphasis will be placed on the rustic trappings associated with the glory days of a vanished aristocracy—country homes, stone fences, gazebos, horses, open pastureland, sailing regalia, antique decanters, and libraries with leather-bound volumes. The message: What you attain when you arrive at the top is escape from the slightness, distraction, and virtuality; what you gain is entry to the sumptuous world of real things, real places, and peace. The fantasy of the past.

If we assume that the strategies of the advertisers are a kind of lens onto the dream lives of potential consumers, then a careful look at the J. Peterman catalog is revelatory in the extreme. The Peterman approach, of accompanying its illustrations of various wearables with hokey fantasy narratives, an approach that has a campy edge to begin with, has been rendered doubly camp by becoming a staple shtick on *Seinfeld*. Jerry's friend Elaine, formerly a copywriter for the catalog, at one point last season suddenly found herself running the company—the occasion for much drollery. But this should not invalidate any insights that the catalog might yield. Indeed, its appropriation only illustrates how fine the line is in our culture between certain phenomena and their media-alchemized return as self-conscious entities that can only be regarded with irony. The overhyped athlete is a case in point: Watching Michael Jordan or Patrick Ewing or Dennis Rodman playing basketball on television, we find that we cannot see around the notoriety to the player. But this is because there is no pure player to be seen behind the notoriety. And this, in turn, is because there is no separation, as there once was, between sport and entertainment.

In any event, the Peterman catalog is revealing, and the fact that the *Seinfeld* writers picked it up only confirms this. To discover just how it reveals, one need only open it at random. I have before me the "Christmas Edition 1996," subtitled "Easy gifts for difficult people." Page 25:

During the march against the Guardia Civil, her grandfather had been arrested carrying 10 pounds of black powder behind his saddle. (And a hank of fuse.)

He was Ecuador's most celebrated poet, so they placed him in semi-permanent exile on his farm in the high pastures.

Today I'm sitting at a table under a blue sky watching his granddaughter spin yarn for the 7 dozen sweaters I've ordered. Next to her lies a motionless dog; in the distance, a small cloud of dust rises as sheep are released from the night corrals.

Each sweater, before it leaves, is inspected by the 100-year-old
matriarch. In Spanish one says "This is a good strong sweater
that allows no room for being bullied." (Ecuadoran Pullover)

Page 38:

Young again. You've seen this sweater before. You were impossibly young in it once. Could be again.

It travelled in your trunk to Deerfield. You wore it with a pea
coat then. Later with an E-type, racing top-down on cold days.

The last time you had it on, an old girlfriend you should have
married said you reminded her of Alexei Vronsky.

You know, it really wasn't that long ago.

Revert a little.

I am tempted to cite at much greater length, because one narrative bit echoes another and an immersion in the whole sequence
is nearly overwhelming. If it were a Peterman cocktail we were talking about, I would offer the following instructions for mixing. Begin with one time vista, at least several decades, but possibly several
generations, long—long enough, at any rate, to conjure a memory
of better days. Which, for the kind of people who receive and order from the catalog, means when the aristocracy was not yet ex-
pired, when young, romantic, well-to-do people traveled the world
in search of adventure and the rituals of good living. Invoke, as fre-
quently as possible, exotic locales—Ecuador, Shanghai, Pamplona,
Bucharest—and populate them with writers, artists, and the film
stars of an earlier era. Kate Hepburn is a goddess here and so is
Jean Harlow; ditto Hemingway, George Orwell, and Clark Gable.
The fantasy requires picturesque locales within which—or against
which—the clothes make sense. Moody weather, fire-warmed inte-
riors. When you buy J. Peterman you are buying a picture of yourself, and the marketers must assume that the romance—the will to
romance—is stronger than the reflexive irony, the campiness. Indeed, the Peterman writers indulge in just enough winking and
nudging to disarm the opposition. "We know it's over the top,"
they seem to be saying, "so lighten up, for God's sake."

It might seem odd to be directing attention at a gimmicky cloth-
ing catalog, but to sample these descriptions when your thoughts
are focused on the contemporary experience of time is to be

struck by a powerful sense of relevance. These are imaginings about time and the past that are being fed to the famished, and the retailer is betting that fantasy and discretionary income are closely allied in this group. The point is that such a marketing ploy is only conceivable where the fantasy-making conditions are right—that is, in a climate of essential deprivation. We have gained everything in the material sphere, it seems, but we have lost the cultural context that supplies meaning. Therefore, an effort is made by a cynical organization—masking itself as ironic and fun-loving—to inject superdosages into the bloodstream. Not *real* context, mind you, for that would require time and knowledge, but a context of bits and media images.

Of course, the J. Peterman Company hardly has a lock on cynicism, manifested in this instance as the willingness to prostitute fantasies and yearnings for dollars. In "Back to the Future: Disney Reinvents the Company Town," an article in *Harper's,* Russ Rymer narrates the fascinating and revelatory account of the creation, from scratch, of a town—Celebration—by the Walt Disney Company in Florida just outside its Disney World theme park. The cost: $2.5 billion. The point?

The idea for Celebration, Rymer explains, originated in the 1960s, to complement the high-tech dream of EPCOT (Experimental Prototype Community of Tomorrow):

> But where Disney's EPCOT vision was decidedly futuristic, Celebration looks not forward but back. The town's sales brochure begins like a fable: "There was once a place where neighbors greeted neighbors in the quiet of summer twilight," it reads, "where children chased fireflies. And porch swings provided easy refuge from the cares of the day. The movie house showed cartoons on Saturday. The grocery store delivered. And there was one teacher who always knew you had that special something. Remember that place? Perhaps from your childhood. Or maybe just from stories. It held a magic all its own. The special magic of an American home town."

Celebration's "surface attributes," as Rymer calls them, "are those that characterized the more livable American cities before World War II." Except, of course, that instead of growing up naturally around some regional crop or industry, having some geographical reason for being, Celebration would be designed into place by teams of highly paid architects.

Rymer has fun describing a promotional tour he took with his guides:

> Joel and Marlene spelled out the conceptual "cornerstones" of Celebration for me. Two central ones, Community and Place, seemed hard to define; hard to define, that is, without resorting to a frequent reiteration of the phrase "a sense of."
>
> "There's a great need in America for a great community," Marlene told me. "A place where we can get back to family values. A sense of knowing your neighbors."
>
> "A sense of interaction," Joel added, "of participation in their community."
>
> "It's the kind of feeling you get when you go to your grandmother's house," Marlene said.

Celebration is not a theme park, at least not in the usual sense. The idea is that people would buy homes—would pay to inhabit the concept. The Preview Center shows videos, Disney-styled images of kids doing the kinds of things they do in Polaroid and Hallmark TV commercials. Rymer reports that 1,200 people put down a deposit "to qualify for a chance to move into one of 470 homes and apartments being built in Celebration's first stage."

This would be a counterpart to the fantasy offered by Peterman—one that is a good deal more expensive. Instead of buying the clothes that allow you to play an exotic aristocratic script in your head, you buy the home that locates you physically in a collective imagining of an America that time forgot. In both cases, though, you are paying for a ticket out—away from the inconsequential or unromantic or frightening present and into a conjured elsewhere.

The impulse behind Celebration is familiar. The concept follows the lines of a Norman Rockwell painting, and most of us are at some level responsive to charmingly stereotypical images of what must have been a simpler time. The difference between Americana and the Disney project is that the former reflects a mood, a fond retrospection deriving from a sense of loss; the latter is a life choice, an initiative bankrolled to the tune of $2.5 billion. This fact alone suggests that the state of our longings (the longings of some of us, I should say) has attained a critical mass.

Interviewing the first home buyers of Celebration, Rymer finds what we might expect, a desire to escape, "a strong conviction that a rosy past, such as Celebration would re-create, has been betrayed by a brutal present." Young couples seeking to banish urban fears, questing after the elusive feeling of community.

One of the more intriguing—and frightening—features of the Disney project has been the concerted efforts of planners to give the community roots, a soul. "One of the things we do," explains Pete Rummel, president of Disney Design and Development, "is we often create a story, a backstory." Planners tried out various scripted scenarios, before deciding that it would be wiser to imply a history rather than invent one. Rummel confides the vision: "Hopefully someday you'll be able to walk down a street or sit someplace and kind of close your eyes and get some comfort that there are people who have been here before you, that this feels like a place that has a tradition, even though it doesn't." Rymer suggests no awareness of any absurdity on Rummel's part.

As the Celebration project makes clear, the folks up in the paneled offices are beginning to play fast and loose with authenticity. There is a trust in simulation—that is, in people's willingness to accept the staged experience, not because they have been made to believe in it, but because they are willing to live with a substitute, will accept it in a spirit of something better than nothing. In other words, if you can coin the *feeling* of a thing, replicate somehow *a sense of* an experience, then, for many, you have as good as provided the real experience.

This shift, this collective willingness to go with the ersatz, has profound implications. It bears directly on the difference—and the importance of the difference—between the real and the virtual. With growing global population, drastically diminished resources, and the infiltration of the experiential realm by technologies of mediation, fewer and fewer people will be able to bring their lives into accord with their dreams and desires. The world simply won't allow all of us to go rafting down unpolluted rivers or to spend bucolic months in open countryside. Yet the culture of advertising will continue to whet our various appetites. The answer? Virtuality. Fantasy experience. Surrogate living to take the edge off our clamorous needs.

Rymer, addressing the specific phenomenon of Disney, explains the underlying dynamic of the process:

> The genius of Walt Disney was his use of an aesthetic of history to defeat the more troublesome reality of history, just as he created the Magic Kingdom's Main Street as an idyllic replica of the Missouri town where he had endured a dreadful childhood. . . .
>
> Walt Disney was the Louis Pasteur of history, who perfected ways to protect people from the viral effects of memory by injecting it back into them in a denatured form.

Can we really doubt that the global explosion of Disney—the corporation and the concept—is not in deep ways linked to what is befalling us in the postmodern epoch? That as new technologies in alliance with investment capital condition us to new ways of living, creating anxiety, stress, distraction, a sense of fragmentation, our souls—or what passes for our souls—register shock. Small surprise that we should so overwhelmingly look for solace where it is most conspicuously offered to us—in the wonderfully designed entertainments and simulations of a safer, more natural reality. We inject ourselves with sanitized doses of what, in rougher form, is lost to us, and we imagine we are happy.

Nostalgia is no simple thing; it is not to be written off as mere sentimentality. Nostalgia—from the Greek *nostos:* "to return home and survive"—involves us in our deeper emotions. More than merely the longing for what is past, either in a personal or a more general, societal sense, nostalgia is a recognition—pleasant, but not entirely welcome—that the past is home. The past, its places, people, and circumstances, shaped us, in some significant way conferred identity. In longing for it, feeling the sudden call from a memory, a piece of music, a photograph, we are, at some level, harking back to our own beginnings, as if therein lay a greater authenticity than what we know in the present. Perhaps there is a sense that things were more vivid, more on the line.

On a personal level, we are most commonly nostalgic for our younger years. For childhood, for adolescence, or the first years of adulthood. We may, later, feel similar, if less intense, yearnings toward other periods of maturity, specific seasons in the life. Partly we may just feel covetous toward what is gone, a reaction intensified by the recognition that we are getting older. There is the illusion, too, now that we are safely through a time, that the time was essentially safe. We forget that then, as now, we were turned toward an uncertain future. We did not know that we would survive our shoestring life. The fact that we did retroactively bathes everything in the glow of *la vie bohème*.

Private and public nostalgias are different in certain vital respects. Privately we are compelled by specifics—that summer, that lake, that boathouse, that night—whereas collectively we are pulled toward somewhat more generic scenarios. Our fond imaginings of small-town life are, I suspect, fairly similar, very likely because the basic impulses toward retrospection have been artfully manipulated by image brokers—by Currier and Ives, Rockwell, and the advertising geniuses at Hallmark, Kodak, and innumerable other corporations, all of whom know how to play on our primary longings as on an instrument with many stops.

Nostalgia, I once noted in a journal, is "the exhaust of progress." That has a certain epigrammatic ring to it, but it might be more accurate if I substituted *change* for *progress*. For what kindles our longings is mainly the sense that we are moving away from something. And who in our day will use the word *progress* with any confidence?

But everyone will concede, I think, that life is changing rapidly and imponderably. Things feel different than they used to; the contours of events, of public circumstances, are no longer as defined as they once were. Too much, we hear on every front. Too many channels, too much data. We hurry, double up; we break the beam of attention into its component rays. More things are registered, attended to, but the impression any one of them makes is slighter. One result of this is that we feel ourselves as somehow less substantial in the present.

This feeling, then, is part of what underwrites our tropism

toward the past. We are drawn in part to the bygone things—
people, events—and in part to the clarity and gravity that they embodied. An old-fashioned tricycle or wagon is more real than its
molded plastic counterpart, because we feel metal and rubber to
be more substantial than plastic, because the earlier objects,
though mass produced, don't exhibit their uniformity quite as
tellingly, and also because we feel the world those trikes and wag-
ons were made in to be more actual, more palpably about things,
closer to sources. This goes for houses, cars, and commodity goods
of all sorts. The older things had more thingness, and places more
thereness. Some of this skirts the nonsensical. Would we say that
people had more *peopleness?*

Of course not—but wait. We should not brush past the suggestion as if it were utterly and in all senses preposterous. I would suggest, comparing the world of the present to the world of, say, fifty
years ago, that for a whole host of reasons we probably had more
occasion to register the presence of other people. We spent more
time in the company of others, had fewer distracting activities between ourselves and them. People may well have been more *with
us.* At the same time, it is very likely that people were more peculiarly and particularly themselves in times gone by. The leveling
forces of modern life, the homogeneity of lifestyles, the diluting
force of intensified social interaction, had not yet filed the rough
edges from our individuality. People were likely less happy in certain respects, their lives more riddled with what we now recognize
as unhealthy behaviors, but in their unreconstructed person-
hood—maybe—people were more manifestly individuals. The
great drive toward socialized being, which we are just in the first
stages of, had not yet begun.

It seems likely that there are periods that are seen as more
defining—more influential—than others. We see this certainly in
families. Almost every family has what could be called, at least in
collective mythology, its golden age. The real times. When the kids
were home, the parents still young; when the neighborhood was
full of kids; before Dad retired. Somehow *that* was family, and the
later arrangement—kids moved away, parents no longer in the old
house—doesn't count for as much. The later time exists significantly in reference to the earlier.

As for families, so too for society at large. If America had a golden age, a period, or stage, to which many subsequent developments refer, it was the century-plus that saw the burgeoning of the town. The American small town is, perhaps, our most enduring archetype. It is the vanishing point, the place to which most of our nostalgias are directed. In the image of the small town—New England, Midwestern, Southern—the components of our identity, our *fantasy* of identity, are gathered. Thornton Wilder's *Our Town*, Frank Capra's Bedford Falls, Mark Twain's Hannibal, Edgar Lee Masters's Spoon River, Garrison Keillor's Lake Wobegon, *The Music Man*'s River City, television's Mayberry—the place fixed in a hundred *Saturday Evening Post* covers by Rockwell, the formula so laboriously sought after by the planners and architects of Celebration. There is no need to linger on its features, we know them well.

The American small town—the image of it held in the gaze of retrospection—is true north, and we are not likely to just let it slip away. Indeed, as the fundamental nature of life alters in the millennial period, toward complexity, toward data, toward intensely mediated connectivity, that emblematic image will, in some ways, intensify its appeal. More clearly than before, we will understand what we are losing, and we will look to somehow reconstitute its familiar lineaments. Never mind that in doing this we succumb to the virtual, the ersatz. Never mind that in the substitution of commodified images for formerly organic realities we are travestying those realities. Our longing will grow and grow, and we will do what we must to appease it.

Nostalgia, then, is at its root a longing for home, however home is defined. For some it may be a place more of imagination than actual recollection. How many Americans born and raised in suburban tracts don't feel some pull toward, say, a New England town life from the earlier part of the century—never mind that they have never sat on a porch swing or skated on a country pond in their lives? Advertisers and makers of calendars can create their effects so reliably because we all tend to be susceptible to certain fundamental things. We have, I venture, basic feelings about the pace at which life should be lived, the degrees and kinds of private and social intimacy we would like, and what constitutes a right balance between nature and domesticity. And these feelings can be readily mobilized by images and descriptions. It does not matter, in a sense, whether we ever fished in a pond or gathered blueberries in a bucket. Many of us will readily conjure up a wishful picture of what these things are like, and we will endorse a world in which they are still possible. For childhood is not just what we recall from our own younger years, it is possibility itself, the fantasy of what is available.

I wonder if there is not a deep split in our collective psyche. On the one hand, we plunge forward in the late-modern mode of the moment. We buy the appliances, fill the freeways, bombard ourselves with data and images, and the pollsters report that we are essentially content to live thus. Indeed, collectively speaking, we scoff, often, at those who would question or criticize the order of things, finding them cynical, downbeat, or depressing. But in our dream lives, our off-duty lives, we own up to very different things. Talk to people in unguarded moments, privately, when they do not feel that they must represent themselves in any approved manner, and you will find a great many confiding other thoughts and wishes. That things slow down, that life go back to being simpler, more immediate; that people think less about money, status, and consumption; that neighborliness return. My sample is obviously limited, but what I hear from many of the people I talk with is a deep desire not to lose touch with former ways.

Our dream merchants—filmmakers and advertisers—are, of course, very much aware of this split between what we do and what we, at another level, want. And they play on it—skillfully, artistically, but also manipulatively. We consume our buried needs as culture or commodity, as art or kitsch. The difference? Art would be the sincere expression of these feelings in one or another medium. Kitsch would be the heightened presentation of imagery for effect—to identify a bath soap with powerful triggering fantasies of an earlier, less corrupted time. Most of us know instinctively the difference between art and kitsch, but still the bad drives out the good. Despise though we might a cunning advertisement for cookies or butter, we still react to the clips of old-fashioned sleds and covered bridges. And in reacting we discharge the legitimate emotion—some of it—and we begin to suspect all such materials as being of a kind. Any harking back to the past is to be mistrusted, even as it is indulged. And as we are thus cut off from true response, it becomes harder to swerve off what is at every moment sold to us as the bright unscrolling road of progress.

Sense and Semblance:
The Implications of Virtuality

There is now at the Boston Atheneum, a place we might think of as the very cradle of bookishness in this country, an installation by Susan Gamble and Michael Wenyon titled *Bibliomancy*. The display is as unadorned and simple as can be. Entering the large, bare exhibition room, you see arrayed before you, singly, with wall space in between, fifty-four holograms of book spines. Approaching to inspect—and, of course, even the nonbibliophile is compelled to do so—you note various things: how the illusionism encompasses the spine and part of the top of each book, with the rest receding into apparent shadow; how the books themselves seem utterly miscellaneous, ranging from Voltaire's *Correspondance Général, Tome 8*, to *Pursuing the Whale* by John A. Cook. You stand and look and try to ponder, by and by taking note of the images on the right and left walls—the outside faces of several old-style card catalog files, a sight every bit as familiar to most of us as that of the assorted spines. You stand a bit longer, waiting for some revelation to break over you, but it never does. At least not the sort that asks a swift intake of breath. But at some moment, likely, you get the point, and then indeed a shiver of displacement may travel through you: Yes, here you are, standing in a barren room, surrounded on all sides by tens of thousands of books, and you are suddenly—courtesy of holographic technology—able to see things at a slight remove, as if, historically speaking, you had just recently turned your back on a way of being and had taken a step away and were casting a last over-the-shoulder glance back.

A few years ago I wrote an essay called "The Fate of the Book," in which I tried to sort out the deeper differences between print and electronic-information cultures. The premise, which I still subscribe to, was that we are living through a watershed moment, a

42

monumental transition in which the centuries-old print-on-paper paradigm is rapidly being shouldered aside by circuit-driven technologies. As the modes are very different in their fundamental nature, it interested me to speculate on some of the possible consequences of such a paradigm shift. I featured them to myself in terms of a set of crucial oppositions. Let me outline them here.

One: Closure versus open-endedness. Among many other things, the book has always represented to us the ideal of completion. The fixity of the word printed on the page and our awareness of the enormous editorial and institutional pressure behind that fixity, send the message that here is a formulation, an expression, that must be attended to. The array of bound volumes on library shelves communicates that knowledge and understanding are themselves a kind of structure assembled from these parts.

Screen technologies undo these assumptions implicitly. That a work comes to us by way of a circuit means that we think of it as being open—available—in various ways, whether or not we avail ourselves of those ways. The medium not only allows, it all but cries out for links, glosses, supplements, and the like. Whatever one reads, and however one reads, it is never with the totality in view. Reading from a screen is like traveling from coast to coast with only adjoining local maps as guides.

Two: Hierarchy versus the leveling of hierarchy. With print texts, the push to finality, to closure, is also a push for the last word, which is but another way of characterizing the struggle for vertical ascendancy. If intellectual culture is seen as the product, or benefit, of book learning, then it is the Darwinian marketplace of ideas that decides which texts will shape our thinking and our values: the age-old battle of the books.

But now substitute screen textuality, put mutability and open-endedness in the place of definitiveness, and it's easy to see that notions of hierarchy will be very hard to sustain. Many, of course, view this enthusiastically and cheer on the erosion of hegemonic authorship. In the theoretically infinite database, all work is present and available—and, in a way, equal. Where discourse is seen to be woven and, technologically speaking, collective, the idea of ranking dissipates. New systems of search and access are already beginning to render the notion of the enclosed work antiquated.

Three: Historical layering verses simultaneity. The system of print textuality has always promoted the idea of culture as a matter of tradition and succession, with printed works leading back in time like so many footprints. Tracking an idea, an influence, we literally go from newer to older physical texts. The scholar's finger brushes the actual molecules of bygone eras. And historical depth has served us as one of our most powerful metaphors.

Screen technologies work against this supposition. They have the power to transpose the layered recession of texts into a single vast collection of cross-referenced materials. They underwrite the postmodern suspicion of the time line and the continuous narrative. The picture of history that database and screen unroll is one of webs and trees, a field of relations and connections that submerges any notion of story in a vast informational complexity.

Four: The public space versus the private sphere. Book reading, whatever its ulterior purposes, has always been essentially private. The medium is opaque. The word signifies against the dead-endedness of the paper, and in the process of signifying it incessantly enforces the awareness that the communication originated in an individual sensibility, that its inscription was founded in privacy. Whatever we read thus, we understand to be a one-to-one transmission—Henry David Thoreau or Roland Barthes to myself. Reading from a screen, by contrast—and I understand that people do not commonly scroll through longer works on a monitor—automatically invokes the circuit system that underwrites all screen transmissions. On a subliminal level the traditional assumptions are all undone. The words on the screen, though very possibly the same as the words on the page, are not felt to dead-end in their transmitting element. Rather, they keep us actively aware of the quasi-public transparency out of which they emerge. Emphasis on *emerge*. These words are not found in the way that one can thumb forward in a printed text and locate the words one will be reading. No, they appear to arrive, and from a place that carries complex collective associations. To read from a screen—even if one is simply scrolling *Walden*—is to occupy a cognitive environment that is very different from that which we occupy when reading a book.

Five: Expressive versus functional uses of language. A change in our dominant medium of expression will certainly mean a redefinition of our expressive ideals. The way we use language will change—it is already changing—and literary style will be the obvious casualty. Style is not of the essence in screen-to-screen communication; the very premise of this communication is near immediacy. The more we are linked up, the more available we are to each other, the less we need to ponder what Gustave Flaubert called the "mot juste" or exact word. But the fact is that not all truths can be telegraphed and not all insights can find a home in the declarative sentence. To represent experience as a shaded spectrum, we need the subtle shading instruments of language— which is to say that we need the refinements of verbal style. Without them there is a danger that we could condition ourselves into a kind of low-definition consciousness. We should worry not just about dumbing down but also about the loss of subjective reach.

Certainly there were other oppositions to be contemplated, but I stopped with these first formulations. As with anything that remains unfinished, however, the subliminal psyche continued its worrying process. But what I have found, now that I have returned to the subject, has been a discernible shift of emphasis, or perspective. I note that I am less interested now in enumerating significant differences between the technologies—book and electronic—and more occupied with thinking about the kinds of spaces, or subjective cognitive environments, they create, and how these in some way change our conception of knowledge itself. Another small subject.

The matter does bear thinking about. Book space, print space— that which we occupy as we sit turning pages—even though it varies significantly, depending on whether we are reading *Treasure Island* or *Principles of Structural Anthropology,* can still be characterized. Occupying it, we are, or want to be, immersed—which is to say, pledged to a single purpose, refined in our attention. Reading books, we have a clear sense of "ledge," for the immersions are discontinuous from book to book. We know, if only because it is physically enforced for us by the form of the "technology," where the book stops and the rest of the world takes up again. Reading a book, translating the signs into the invisibility of apprehension, we hold the shell, the weight and mass of the volume, as an anchor.

And does this not, I ask parenthetically, form the basis for a profound, if elusive, analogy? That the book, with its concrete exterior and invisible interior—its body and soul—is *like* us in some way? Discrete, laden. Don't we say: "She is a closed book to me," or "I read him like a book"? An analogy to be pursued, but elsewhere.

The space of electronic information is perceived as bottomless. A track ends, not of its own accord, but when one decides to stop following it. There is no clear sense of ledge. Knowledge—or any contents—is not figured as existing in space (on page 68 of the second volume, third edition) but retraceable only as a set of co-ordinates, commands. One does not find things again so much as they are re-created—brought back into being—on demand. Interesting correspondences here with memory theory, the older views supporting the idea of memories as mental contents somehow held in the mind, newer views proposing that memories are created afresh as prompts elicit combinatory responses. Moreover, screen contents—those representing and serving knowledge—are part of the larger stream of all digitized information, adjacent via keystroke (that is: attention shift) to pornography servers, private and corporate Web sites, adjacent to *everything* in a way that the contents of bound volumes simply are not. This adjacency is, of course, merely potential, but the awareness of potentiality has everything to do with how we process information.

With the changing of the processes—the means—of knowledge, do we not also begin to change the definition of what constitutes knowledge?

The transition we are going through is eased—but also complicated somewhat—by the fact that the two processes are right now operating side by side. Most individuals move from page to screen and back, shifting between immersed and open-ended modes. We are nothing if not adaptable, as our large-scale acquiescence to computing demonstrates so clearly. But I would argue that the two-track approach is temporary, a consequence of transition, and that a few decades hence most of our transactions—and conditioned reflexes—will serve the screen and not the book. Books will exist, of course, and they will have their special uses, but they will be like those older roads we find everywhere running parallel to the big interstates. The dominant knowledge environment—or whatever we choose to call it—will be characterized by fluidity, simultaneity, and hypercomplex relationality; it will be non-author centric, nonhierarchical, open to entrance and manipulation, collaborative, significantly unedited; and in its totality, no matter how powerful and sophisticated our search engines and interfaces become, it will be overwhelming. The user will have to contend with intimations of totality that the book user has managed to escape; one book does not suggest all books in the way that a branch in the data trail suggests a network of endless branchings. The idea of this totality—conceptually exhilarating—is likely to seem paralyzing to individual initiatives of the sort that founded and then sustained our intellectual-cultural life for so long. Attainment is, after all, founded partially in hubris, and nothing is so withering to what someone called "the desire and pursuit of the whole" as the unbounded vista of what has already been done. Specialization and teamwork—the game plan of the sciences—will become the procedure of art as well.

But how are we to get at this knowledge question? If we agree, Heisenbergians all, that the regard changes the thing regarded, then certainly we are modifying what we understand knowledge to be as fast as we upgrade the processing power of the microchip. The shift from book to screen may, in its eventual impact on our sense of what knowledge is—how it matters and what its ends are— be as transformative as the shift from Newtonian to Einsteinian physics.

The datum, the fact, the unit of information was once understood—imagined—as fixed, a point mapped to the world, with knowledge seen as a coherent picture made up of points. The same unit is now configured in space subject to relativity; it is in motion, relational, always part of a function. Is this a more accurate picture of the world, or is it that the world simply keeps changing as we modify the rules of looking? By which I mean that there is no picture of the world that stands free of the process of looking. A contemporary cliché, but one worth remembering. In earlier formulations, when knowing was understood differently, knowledge was something one could possess; now it is a relational process that is forever changing—our attempts at apprehension are variables factored into the function.

We are in transit between the habits of the old and the elusive promise of the new. The transformation is inevitable; the new understanding will prevail. Where will it leave us?

A new knowledge system will naturally mean a change in our subjective sense of ourselves. Human agency—and its aims—are being redefined. From this will surely come, in time, a new sense of what it means to be human.

Is it any accident that we are just now hearing on all sides about Steven Pinker's new theories of mind and language—the marriage of the so-called computational model with the precepts of evolutionary biology: mind as highly sophisticated processing system? Or that we are hearing not just about Dolly the sheep—we've already absorbed that—but also about the demiurgic ambitions of Dr. Seed to clone the first human? Nor can it have escaped our notice that *the* word, the buzz concept, of the day is *virtuality*—that which can perfectly seem without in fact being.

The new conversations we are having are suddenly possible because of specific advances in the various sciences, and also because we are allowing a new set of assumptions about the human to invade our thinking. Our resistance has, in certain ways, been lowered. People are less in thrall, so it would seem, to an understanding of being as sacred, as originating from and destined for a place beyond the pale of reason. We proceed, increasingly, on the assumption that rational, if highly complex, systems underlie mind, biological being, indeed the universe around us. The speed and power of the computer have begun to erode former intimations of mystery, reducing what had seemed quasi supernatural to manifestations of mere complexity, potentially comprehensible and reducible. We will fully understand intelligence through reverse engineering, by creating it—so say the high priests of artificial intelligence. And when we have cloned a human being we will in some new way be in possession of the big secret, the platform for so many old notions of deity. Of course, we can only get at many of these former mysteries—mind, DNA—by way of high-speed computation; we can't do it entirely by ourselves. But since we created the computing prosthesis, we accept that its achievements are fully ours.

This assumption of reach and capability—capability so great

that we will, and fairly soon, have mapped the entire human genome—now attends all of our endeavors. Just as we know the power of our automobile even when we creep along at fifteen miles per hour, so we are aware of the power of our computers even if we are merely tracking a simple citation. This sense of potential capability, as I suggested earlier, is now part of our changing cognitive makeup. And having experienced it—the speed of access and the combinatory leverage—we find it ever more difficult to go back to the old technology, even though it surrounds us. The later you were born, the more likely you are to be affronted by the density and difficulty—the obdurate slowness—of the printed page.

To read a book after working with a mouse is to feel yourself paddling upstream. Upstream: where history resides.

A changed sense of potential, a radical increase, alters the nature of our engagement with the actual. When something has ceased to feel necessary, like the only way, we loosen our connection to it, perhaps allow the slightest increment of dismissiveness to inform our attitude.

The past feels slow and stodgy to us because that's how people lived before they knew what we know. The condescension implicit in our bemusement—bemusement whipped to a fine froth on every television screen in the land—is a terrible betrayal of origins.

I am often struck by the following paradox: We celebrate these enormous strides of progress, but it is not as though we had really even begun to exhaust the possibilities of the earlier technology. Content and depth, and understanding, remain largely imprisoned in our pages of print. We never really set them free. We are not really adequate to our radically improved technologies.

I deal with students all the time who carry on their intellectual business seated in front of high-powered computers, but who cannot make their way with any confidence through a relatively straightforward paragraph of literary prose.

One kind of attunement—and aspiration—has been displaced by another. Movement across the vast surface of the grid is favored over immersion in any of its isolated spaces. Correlatively, the knowledge mode now favored in our culture is one that combines externality with a sophisticated awareness of interconnectedness.

Interiority, subjectivity, and the more spiritual resonances are suspect.

As we perfect our lateral sweeps in every direction, flying from node to node, we are also pulling away from language. Language, that is, understood as a process more profound than a mere signal system. We are losing our grip, collectively, on the logic of complex utterance, on syntax; we are abandoning the rhythmic, poetic undercurrents of expression, and losing touch with the etymological variety that has always pointed back toward coinages and, implicitly, the historical perspective.

The near-instantaneous movement of data through circuits has the peculiar effect of charging that data with presentness. The winking cursor is the ledge line, the heartbeat of the present, and whatever words or numbers march across the screen have been recontextualized in the now. The word, formerly static, feels irradiated; it has been changed by its susceptibility to electronic commands.

When we look at the screen, peer into its dimensionless shallows, we locate ourselves in a transpersonal perpetual present—not entirely unlike the time awareness we experience while watching television. This collective present is different from the subjective present we see—experience—when we look around us. The collective element may start to feel safer for some, more like home. When the pressure of self is no longer strong enough to counter the presence of one's surroundings, then one looks—possibly—to merge that self with others.

History, our sense of the layered past, which was represented so clearly by rows and walls of physical books, changes—our subliminal sense of it changes—when we encounter information streaming left to right across a fixed screen surface. When the understanding, the imagining, of history changes, so must our sense of what knowledge is. We cannot simply take up the old inquiry as if everything else but our means of knowing were the same.

For we are not simply augmenting and speeding up the processes of storage, retrieval, presentation, and so on. We are modifying perception. The open vista—an expanse of undisturbed meadow—is not seen in the same way in the era of high-speed travel as it was seen when people got about on foot and horseback.

Never mind that the eye takes in the identical distribution of shapes and colors.

We are just now releasing the genie of linkage—of complex referentiality—from the bottle. The assumption in most quarters is that this can only be to the good. How can more and faster ever *not* be good? More and faster is the mantra of the day, and to question this is to be quaint, if not eventually irritating.

But what if we conceive of knowledge not in terms of quantity—data to be accessed—but rather in terms of a dynamic foreground-background tension, with knowledge always being a function of data in appropriate context?

We have liberated data, but in doing so we have also wreaked havoc on context, which we might think of as the home for data. We live, in George Trow's memorable phrase, "in the context of no context."

A piece of data, of information, only becomes a piece of knowledge when it can be understood as the answer to a question. This is the lesson of Edgar Allan Poe's great story "The Purloined Letter." Poe's detective, Dupin, walked through the same rooms as the other investigators. Lacking a question—which is to say a focused narrative—the stooges could only dismantle the premises in their search for crevices. Dupin understood, as it were, the question to which the letter was the answer, and he therefore was able to pounce on it.

We have filled the world with untethered information, more by many magnitudes than it held even fifty years ago, but for most of us it has become pointless bric-a-brac. The contents of Citizen Kane's legendary warehouses were searched and inventoried, to no avail. No one knew to look for a sled called "Rosebud."

We cannot find answers if we cannot formulate questions; we cannot formulate questions if we cannot grasp context; we cannot grasp context if we try to process more information than our sensoria are equipped to handle.

This is not to say that books themselves do not contain mountains of data, much of it lacking comprehensible contexts. But print culture, through its gradually evolved systems—the standardized formatting of books, the consensual procedures of academia—attained what for some centuries felt like a workable balance. The physicalized text, its location in space, subject to ordering systems, manifested this—multiplicity offset by specificity, the enormous terrain contained as by a map. We should not give all this over too easily.

I still do not feel that I've reached it, the root of my doubt. What *is* it that so disturbs me about the idea that the new human knowledge environment will soon enough become electronic? Am I really against complexity or speed or epically increased access? Surely my attachment to book systems is at least in part sentimentality. The technology can obviously do a great deal more—isn't it foolish not to let it?

Looking for a way to think about this I suddenly recall the advent, not so terribly long ago, of the pocket calculator. How people argued, then, the pros and cons. "The instrument will release us from the drudgery of calculation; it will free our minds for more complex mathematical tasks." "No, it will destroy in users, in students especially, any deeper understanding of the process, the logic of the calculation. When a square root is a button tap, then after enough button taps the concept vanishes; it is simply a thing one does." "But so what? What does this understanding matter now that we have tools that will do the work? Do we still need to know how to milk a cow or skin a deer?"

So it would go. I sided then with the worriers, and I side with them now in this far more critical matter. The underpinnings of my position are essentially the same. To entrust calculation to a machine, useful as it undeniably is, is also to distance oneself from the cipher system of mathematics *and* from the idea of its intrinsic correspondence to reality; it is to impose the abstraction—the mediation—of a mechanical operation on the abstraction of the numbers themselves. Understand, as I say this, that I am arguing on behalf of a concept. If I fly—and sometimes I have to—I prefer that the air-traffic controllers do their calculations on computers rather than scratch pads. Still, the point has to be made. Handing over any function—having an accountant do your taxes (I do), a mechanic fix your car (I do), a service maintain your yard (I don't)—removes you to an obvious degree from the reality, the necessity, of that function. It plants you more deeply in that frictionless secondary environment, the apotheosis of which is virtuality.

Which may be where we are all headed eventually, into lives mediated at every point, where almost no contact is made—ever—with the myriad functions that were once accepted (and often lamented) as our lot.

But this is a matter for another essay. Here I simply want to make the connection between that removal of self from the fundamental processes and what is likely to be the larger personal and collective consequence of rushing into a new knowledge environment. Basically, we are increasingly entrusting to software the various gathering, sorting, and linking operations that we used to perform for ourselves and that were part of the process of thinking about a subject. We have to ask, not just "What does software do, and what does mind do?" but "What *should* software do, and what *should* mind do?" I fear that we will preen ourselves on our astonishing conquest of data, even as we ignore the fact that the better part of any knowing is a grasp of the underlying epistemological principles. Half of any knowing is knowing how knowing works. For every decision, every personal initiative we undertake in the realm of information, reaffirms the system of laws that makes knowledge possible and useful.

In this connection, then, we need to address the question of imagination. For there is a serious danger that that capacity, that muscle, will atrophy from lack of use. Imagination is the means by which we create bridges and connections; it is how the self responds to a gap or an absence—it is a way of creating coherence. But it requires, always has, obstacle and deficit. In the seamless world, the world of point and click, the world of proliferating links and synapses, where every line of thought is seen to connect by branching paths to other lines of thought, there is no void to project toward, no gap to fill. Like children growing up with all desires attended to, we submerge ourselves in the universe of surfeit. And that muscle of imagination, trained ancestrally on barren cave walls, on distances and longings, weakens. Like the great muscle of memory in earlier days, it atrophies, perhaps in a few generations to become vestigial.

Dare I push this a notch further? Dare I say that without absence, without intellectual want, without ledges and baffles and barriers to crash against—without being able to formulate the pressing questions that awaken data from potentiality—we may begin to lose our own sense of boundedness, of definition. Distance and difficulty—yes, and slowness—help confer limit; their lack induces us to feel life as a continuous dream that must, alas, dissolve, for we have not yet schemed a way around mortality. The loss of boundedness is a hallmark of our strange age. We may begin to feel, at first almost imperceptibly, then with an anxious twinge, that we are leaking out into the world around us. When the water is just at body temperature we can't tell anymore where the skin ends.

I pull myself back here. I see now that my thoughts have begun to spiral out too far from their original object—the installation of holographic images. Shaking my head, stepping back a few feet, I can make myself see them again for what they are: straightforward unspectacular illusions, static images of what we still find everywhere in the world around us. Books—vessels of thought and creative impulse—no more noble or sacred, any of them, than what they contain. In the wake of dire imaginings comes the exasperated countering instruction; I tell myself, again, that I must learn to live in the world without worrying quite so much.

The Idea of the Internet

Thinking about the Internet these days, I find myself less preoccupied with the system itself—how it all works, what it can and cannot do—and much more with the importance of the *idea* of the Internet, and in what ways, frontal or oblique, that idea impinges on our cultural life.

The Internet is a phenomenon that in certain ways demands to be treated more as idea than thing. Although for any one user it is always some particular process of sending or receiving information, no transaction happens apart from the core potentiality—the instant linkages possible—of the system.

The pressure, the impact, the implications of this potentiality are what interest me. How has it affected our thinking across a spectrum?

We can take air travel as a partial analogy. Here is a technological innovation that has concrete, practical effects: It gets me from here to there rapidly and allows me a certain range of activity otherwise not available. I can fly to another city, give a lecture, and return without having to cancel a class. But what is, in my view, far more consequential is that the idea of air travel has entirely infiltrated my experience of living in the world, and would have done so even if I never had recourse to flight; has done so because I live in a social world conditioned by an understanding of time and space different from that of generations of forebears. Los Angeles has become a locale that is, in part, a function of access, of the hours it would take to get there (rather than the days, as formerly), even if I never go there. And therefore Los Angeles—the idea of Los Angeles, the idea that cannot be separated entirely from the geographical entity—is different.

This is fairly obvious, but I cannot ignore its bearing on the idea of the Internet.

Before I question in what ways the idea of the Internet changes
the contours of our experience, I need to make certain observations about the arrival of the technology into our collective midst.

Primarily, although the concept itself is somewhat revolutionary,
and is for this reason the subject of a good deal of public attention
and debate, the actual implementation by individuals does not
manifest a revolutionary—or all-transforming—character. By and
large, it functions—like air travel, say—as an augmentation. The Internet is a new thing, a new process, but one brings it into the fold
of habit, makes a place for it, and although life does change, it does
not change utterly. For this reason, we often see the individual response to the media excitement taking the form of a bemused
shrug. Air travel, too, may be a monumental transformation of the
existing, but if we fly twice a year to another city, we will likely not
regard its effect on our lives as being monumental.

Think of it another way, as analogous to global warming. The scientists who study climate are right to be alarmed about the possibility of a temperature increase of two or three degrees over a
period of several decades, even if our local—that is, experiential—
response is a shrug. Climate scientists project the increase systemi-
cally and register a vast array of intertwined consequences, which
in their sum may in significant ways change life as we know it. The
individual, blind to the possibility of systematic consequence, ponders a warmer spring, a hotter summer, perhaps even savors the
thought of less snow on the ground come winter. Two degrees can
be accommodated easily enough.

I have these thoughts when people accuse me of making far too
much of the microchip and the electronic network. But if I sometimes profess a certain alarm, it is at least in part alarm about the
large-scale refusal to contemplate the systemic influence of these
innovations, the fact that our picture of the world is being subtly
but significantly altered.

In what sense do I mean this?

I mean, I suppose, that when a massive electronic nervous system rapidly establishes itself inside the geographical corpus, allowing, as the sketchy preliminary systems like telegraph and
telephone never did, rapid transfer of large quantities of informa-

tion, complex interactivity, and so on, then the idea of connectivity truly becomes part of our sense of things. What high-speed air travel has done to the idea of place, the Internet is, in its way, doing to the idea of individuality and isolated selfhood. It is injecting a new range of possibility into our conception of relation—among other things.

This is not necessarily bad, but it is a significant change and needs to be contemplated as such. There are those like psychologist-technotheorist Sherry Turkle who prognosticate diverse scenarios of liberation. Mediated communication, Turkle believes—and this is the thrust of her recent book, *Life on the Screen: Identity in the Age of the Internet*—will render human boundaries at once more permeable and more provisional; it will encourage the self to morph in diverse ways, slipping in and out of roles in ways that reflect its essential instability. Out of the chaos will arise new systems of relation; we will stand free of the powerful constraints imposed by face-to-face situations.

Thinking in these terms, we begin to consider that the isolated self, the subjective individual, may be less a natural given than a phase in a larger evolutionary process. Is bounded autonomy a desirable characteristic in an age dominated by network communications and mediated (and increasingly virtual) experience?

But we cannot regard such transformation blithely—it is something more than a *Time* or *Newsweek* feature story. For upon our long-standing notions of self (public and private) are predicated our laws, our social customs, our civic institutions, our conceptions of community, of art—of *everything*. It matters greatly how we come to understand the norms and possibilities of interaction. Communication, as the theorist Mikhail Bakhtin understood, is *dialogic*: It always happens between a specific sender and a specific receiver. When the process is transformed, by immediacy over distance, by the possibilities of anonymity and invisibility, and by the sense of endless potential networks running in every direction, we cannot expect anything to remain the same. This, the dissolving of what George W. S. Trow called the "grid of two hundred million" into the subjective space of the self, is the idea of the Internet, and it is an idea now in our midst. The temperature rises by a few degrees and everything changes—ocean levels, currents, vegetation belts. Bring a system of total connectivity—the idea of such a system—forward, and you will feel how a sense of unreality begins to shadow our perceptions. We will no longer stand on the same ground; the atmospheres of relation will have changed. Pundits everywhere will ascribe the new strangeness to the coming of the millennium.

Walking after Midnight

I am not a man bent on gathering souvenirs of my passage through this world, but I seem to have made certain exceptions, including one for Oxford, Mississippi, where I spent two balmy spring days a few years back. I went there to participate in the annual Oxford Conference for the Book. Usually I come back from places with nothing at all to show. From Oxford, I have a coffee cup bearing the wonderfully conventional inscription "You'll Always Come Back!," a photocopied recipe for "shrimp and grits" from a restaurant called the City Grocery, and a cassette of R. L. Burnside's *Too Bad Jim*. I had conceived this as a little reflection about the Burnside, why, apart from its smashing immediacy, I listen to it as often as I do, but it will have to be about everything, for whenever I listen to Burnside—and now that I drive ninety miles each way to a weekly teaching job, I listen often—a whole densely specific set of memories collects around me.

I'm not sure exactly what special combination of factors singled this weekend out in my life. In part, I'm sure, it was the abrupt transition from an ice-locked Boston winter to a place where the warmth and early ripeness of the season were coming like an exhalation from the soil. That, combined with my outsider's fascination with the South, and the knowledge that William Faulkner had taken in and alchemized some of these very same vistas; and the fact that Barry Hannah, whom I knew from a Vermont summer writing program, made Oxford his home. I had heard enough stories from Barry to give the whole surrounding area an aura of faint familiarity.

But even these ties and associations do not get it—Oxford matters to me because it was the site and occasion for a peculiar immersion experience, one that has no obvious connection to the blues of R. L. Burnside but one that I think about every time I play the tape. Indeed, I play the tape to think about the experience.

It was, I think, April, and I was driven down from the Memphis airport by a student assistant, who dropped me at my motel. He had taken me for a loop around the town square—past the famous courthouse, past Square Books—and then, just as I was about to get out of the van, he gave me his last tour-guide tip. With a long leftward inclination of his head, he told me, "Faulkner is buried in a cemetery just down that way—it's a nice walk."

A strange weekend altogether. I was not then (and am only slightly more so now) a veteran of writers' conferences—of their intensities and camaraderies and vinous confessionals. From this one I have stirred together all sorts of nonsequential impressions— spotting an utterly befuddled Andrei Codrescu standing on a street corner; gawking at author photos on the stairway at Square Books, then later—another day—sitting at a signing table upstairs on the store's veranda, next to John Berendt, who did not seem to mind that his line stretched for blocks while I was absolutely free to watch him affix his signature to endless hardcover copies of his book; getting the "behind-the-scenes" tour of Faulkner's house from the curator, Cynthia Shearer, and thinking how terribly confining spaces could seem when there were almost no appliances, when the aspect of the world was almost entirely limited to the vistas that pressed up to the window glass; eating shrimp and grits at the City Grocery with Barry and his wife, Susan, and noting a stir in the room when an old gentleman with a chest full of medals walked in the door. "That's the real Santini," someone whispered—never mind that his son Pat Conroy, technically more famous, was sitting right there by the wall. Of course there was much, much more, but only one part of my visit stands out with a fully contoured clarity.

On my second night, keyed up from bar talk with writers, from drink, I found I was having a very hard time getting to sleep. When I did, at last, sink down, it was short-lived. A car radio, a tailpipe backfiring—something had me up again—and when I consulted the clock (which I should not have done) I saw that it was nearly 5 A.M. There was no point in trying. As my eyes were too tired for reading, and as it was too early to think about finding breakfast, I decided to take a long walk. It was warm enough,

I remember, to go without a jacket, and having come in from New England rigors, I exulted in the feeling of air on my skin. Then, standing in front of the motel, surprised by the absolute silence of the moment, I remembered what my student driver had told me on parting. Faulkner's grave—I would find it.

That stroll, in the very first brightening moments of the day, along whatever side street I had chosen, put me under a spell. I was exhausted, of course, on top of being overstimulated, and maybe still slightly under the influence of the wine I'd been sampling earlier. The streets were profoundly silent—no passing cars, no barking dogs, no birds yet—and, block after block, I heard only my footsteps, the intimate tide of my own breathing. I felt something unusual, a sharpened sensitivity to impressions—or so it seemed—but also an accompanying feeling of connection, of pressing depth. The world seemed very present, charged. I have known only a handful of these moments in my life.

I idled along the sidewalk, right up close to the sleeping houses. Doors sealed against the night, objects—children's bikes, tools, discarded bottles—in their inanimate repose, the upstairs windows now picking up the first strokes of light. At some point I started playing with the idea that I had taken a turn back in time; that this earthly silence, and this aspect of slumbering houses, was just what someone, my doppelgänger, might have encountered walking here thirty or forty years ago.

I tried on the notion as I walked, tried guiding myself backward in increments, and then, suddenly, the line of houses and trees broke and there, across the way, was the cemetery. And I could see that the sun would very soon be coming up over the horizon. But the mood—that feeling I had of being enfolded in another time—held up as I went in through the gates. Now I was among the stones, the names, the dates. Graveyards always provoke contemplation; this one was feeding directly into my preoccupation. I moved along in that same enormous silence, only stopping every few feet, not just to read the names and dates—and what resonant old names some of them were—but to go through that inevitable sequence of projective fancies: This person was once alive, walked these streets, stood at the sweet center of his—of her—life, thought strange thoughts, and knew the world. Perform this maneuver of

the imagination—once, twice, more—and the hold on the present
begins to loosen, which is clearly what happened, because all at
once I had the most peculiar sensation: I felt time to be a medium,
almost substantial, and I somehow grasped that the farther back
into the past we look, the more people could be seen to live in that
medium, in its midst. And I saw that now, in the present, we have
all but lost that sense of immersion, that we move over the surface
like water striders. Characterizing the feeling this way sounds all
wrong—untrue to the event—but I don't know how else to come at
it. The point was simply that people once inhabited their time and
place in ways most of us would find almost impossible to imagine.
I believed, at that moment, that I could feel the difference, feel
how much more condensed and bound, and perhaps poignant,
living may have felt. These streets, these houses, the background
recollection of Faulkner's books, the still transparency of the
morning hour—it seemed to me that, if I only willed it, I could be
in the skin, behind the eyes, of a person living before the inner
form of things was utterly shattered. I could feel the distance as
would a person who mainly walked from place to place, whose life
was deeply circumscribed by locale; feel time as it was felt when
seasons and hours of the day were all determining, when one
stood, waited, and had occasion, always, to observe the look and
movement of things. It seemed unimaginable to me as I stood
there that we had moved so quickly away, that the world inhabited,
until quite recently, not just by our immediate ancestors (maybe
even our parents) but also by the painters, writers, and composers
we revere, no longer really existed. That there was a huge range of
common human experiences, many of the humblest sort, that we
could no longer fully claim. Standing on a road and watching a figure slowly approaching from afar, or hearing a train whistle and
feeling the sweet sorrow of distance, or pining long days for a letter and having it finally arrive . . .

   There, that morning, I finally felt—fully and deeply—what I had
been supposing for a long time: I thought I understood the nature
and the terms of the change. We have freed ourselves significantly
from the confinements of slow time and fixed place—though I
would add that they very likely did not start to seem quite so confining until the possibilities of escape were made available. We are

surrounded as those others, our ancestors, never could be, with diversions of every description for the mind and senses; against boredom we have assembled an arsenal. I thought back to those low-ceilinged, cluttered, yet somehow barren, rooms in Faulkner's house—the antiquated look and feel of everything—and I wondered for an instant how they all coped with time back then. But I was looking with the eyes of the present. Those now-vacated spaces were once, of course, teeming—with talk, innuendo, expectation, history, with all the human elements that render a space intimate. I had an impression not just of the open-window insect buzz of a summer afternoon but also of the lamp-lit intensities that became available when the whole of the larger world was swallowed by night.

Then it was time to go. The immersion sensation was running out—I felt it wearing off like a drug. I hadn't found Faulkner's grave, but I decided I would look for it another time. I thought that if I got back to the motel soon I could still lie down for a bit before the day's events. And without lingering or looking back, I left the cemetery and headed back.

There remains only to close the circle, and this I can do. For as it happened, I had to leave the conference a half-day early. I would miss the last party—much talked up because R. L. Burnside was going to play—which I was, in fact, very sorry about. Not just because I love good blues, but because my entire Oxford experience had been vivid, so full, so right, and it seemed a violation of the charmed rhythm of things to step away before it was all over. It would be like a piece of music—a blues—cut off before resolving back into its dominant chord. But so it went—a round of hasty good-byes, small talk with my driver as the town rapidly shrank away in the sideview mirror. End of event.

Except that one afternoon not long after, the mail brought me a small package, a gift cassette of Burnside's *Too Bad Jim* sent along by Cynthia Shearer. And with that tape came completion. I put on the tape and through some strange sorcery the music at once closed off the weekend, resolved it—and, over time, over many listenings, it has come to contain it. This is peculiar, I know, how the raw slashing redundancy of "Goin' Down South" can hold—and trigger—memories of graveyard reverie, but the logic of association is peculiar, too. It was a long time before I got an inkling of how this connection really worked.

I was off track, I now see, in thinking that my musings about time were one kind of thing, and the syncopations of Mississippi blues another. On the surface, yes, nothing could make for a less likely pairing, never mind that the blues are right at home among tombstones. But one day not so long ago, driving home from a less-than-brilliant day of teaching, and blasting Burnside at thought-canceling volume, it snapped into clarity for me. This music could hold those wispy daydreams because there was, in fact, something kindred between the two. Because the music, not just Burnside but the whole deep tradition of that blues, came straight up out of that prior world, that utterly unmediated life. Listening from one angle, from outside, you hear the rough jangle, identify maybe the traces of Robert Johnson and Lightnin' Hopkins, but when that angle collapses, when insistence suddenly plants you *there,* so that you feel the music around you on every side, an environment of sorrow and release, then you get how this really is news from an older place. This is life lived up to the limit of the skin and no further—the life of the heart, of wanting, getting, and mainly losing—and it is very much, for me, about back then. Odd that a small cassette can call up so many different kinds of memories and that it can so reliably stand for something. After all, it's just one rough-voiced man hammering his version of the age-old blues.

Only God Can Make a Tree

We witness at times in the realm of ideas an intriguing trickle-to-tributary development; a well-timed article in a professional journal, agile responses by a few editors, and an invisible flurry of e-mail yield up other articles and references, and with them the sudden impression that people in different places have been incubating some of the same notions. Then—figure this as a sequence of rapid dissolves—come the panels, the symposia, and the larger conferences, all of them stocked with newly emergent players. The magic happens. The ideas start to get streamlined, and as soon as the pundits can manage it, the whole business gets dubbed a trend and is given a place on the ever more rapidly revolving style-wheel. Then, before those players have even hammered out a coherent philosophy, a flashy and knowing article appears in the *New York Times Magazine*—the water table to which all higher aspirations are condemned to return—and from that point on, whether or not the trend (or "movement") establishes itself in academia, it lodges in the public mind, certainly the portion that watches with interest what thinking people are thinking.

Thus, for the moment, for better or worse, we have a nascent new "ism." Jay Parini's tremblingly sycophantic essay in the magazine of our newspaper of record, titled "The Greening of the Humanities" (October 29, 1995), gave a scatter of tendencies a habitation (a slew of upper-crust institutions, most prominently Middlebury College, where he himself teaches), and a name: ecocriticism. So he referred to it, and that is the word in boldface on a fat new anthology called *The Ecocriticism Reader: Landmarks in Literary Ecology,* edited by Cheryll Glotfelty and Harold Fromm.

From the essay we learn that the movement already boasts a set of gurus, including, is no special order of merit, Middlebury's John Elder ("quietly charismatic," writes Parini, "with a high forehead and steady gaze"), Glotfelty (a "wiry, intense woman with eyes like diamond chips"), David Orr from Oberlin, Lawrence Buell from Harvard, Fromm from the University of Illinois, Chicago, and essayist Scott Russell Sanders.

Easy as it is to name some of the key figures, it is somewhat more difficult to set out exactly what ecocriticism believes or espouses. I do not mean this in any slighting way. Indeed, new disciplines, like new marriages, should be granted honeymoon privileges. They should be allowed to work out their credos away from the glare of publicity. Now that ecocriticism has been exposed, however, it must stand up for scrutiny. And as the Glotfelty-Fromm anthology has all the markings of a foundation document, it is probably the best place to look.

Glotfelty gives us this preliminary definition of ecocriticism in her introduction: "Simply put, ecocriticism is the study of the re-lationship between literature and the physical environment." She then offers an array of sample questions that might suggest the kinds of inquiries that ecocritics might be venturing: "How is na-ture represented in this sonnet?" Or: "Are the values in this play consistent with ecological wisdom?" Or: "In what ways has literacy itself affected humankind's relationship to the natural world?"

The scope, clearly, is broad, and though Glotfelty tries to supply her reader with a basic armature—a tripartite scheme of develop-mental stages—one cannot easily shed the sense of a rampant pro-liferation of perspectives and approaches. Glotfelty borrows her stages from Elaine Showalter's breakdown of the origin and evo-lution of feminist criticism. The first reflects a concern with "rep-resentations"—how nature is represented in literature. Second, there is the rediscovery and reconsideration of antecedent works—the claiming of a heritage. And finally Glotfelty proposes a theoretical phase, for, say, examining "the symbolic construction of species. How has literary discourse defined the human?"

Under the three corresponding section headings, then, and presumably representative of the movement at large, we find es-says ranging from Lynn White, Jr.'s "The Historical Roots of Our Ecological Crisis" (1), to Cynthia Deitering's "The Postnatural Novel: Toxic Consciousness in Fiction of the 1980s" (II), to Vera L. Norwood's "Heroines of Nature: Four Women Respond to the

American Landscape" (III). The writing from one piece to the next is fairly predictable, reflecting here the more empirical locutions of the naturalist, there the cattle-car agglomerations of the career academic.

Metaphors of place spring to mind. Here is yet another new frontier; a land rush is under way; critics and thinkers are staking out their fields, their terrain. There is a bit of that excitement of origins that is found when options are still open, before the power brokers have muscled the first orthodoxies into place. Indeed, the sideline watcher may wonder whether the survival struggle (a natural phenomenon if there ever was one) will play itself out as usual in a discipline that takes the respectful interdependences of the natural ecosystems as a kind of core model. Much will be decided. We are not even sure whether ecocriticism will attempt to be a transformation of literary study, or whether it will become its own bridging endeavor, a link between the humanities and the natural sciences. In the face of so much provisionality one feels a certain speculative license.

I wonder, for instance, whether ecocriticism is to be seen—as suggested in Parini's article—as a reply to and, perhaps, corrective for the perceived irrelevancy of "theory" in recent years. Ecocriticism does seem to have arisen at a moment when text has, in the hands of its exegetical theorists, become a kind of hypothetical cloud formation, too vaporous to offer purchase to the presumptuous demands of sense. Ironically, a sort of comparison can be drawn between the will to specificity of the early New Critics and the drive of the ecocritics to bring the world—at least the natural world—into the literary viewfinder. In all other respects, of course, the disciplines (it feels odd to be calling ecocriticism a "discipline" already) are in fundamental opposition. New Criticism hedged off the text for scrutiny and banished any extratextual awareness of the world. Ecocriticism, by contrast, uses texts mainly as a way to get at the world itself. Ecocritics might, one suspects, ignore any uses of language that are not a direct conduit to the nature they claim such devotion to.

Ecocriticism raises yet again those tiresomely persistent questions. What is the proper sphere—the purpose—of literary study? Which is to ask, naturally, about the nature and purpose of literature itself. Is literature, as some might contend, a dream dreamed alongside our common reality, a symbolic system that trains us, but always indirectly, for life in the real world? Or is it, less romantically, just another part of mucky reality—directly referential, a guide to our moral determinations and our political actions? Or is it something in between?

These are not, finally, questions that can be answered by reasoned analysis. We take positions based not on proof but on the warps and wrinkles of temperament. I can see with perfect plainness the arguments that call for literature to serve in some way the concrete business of living and propose for all art an implicit political role. I can even nod my head to many of the premises, the more so if they are advanced one by one by a nonhysterical individual. But persuade my mind as they may, they are powerless against my intuitive conviction, which I seem to have imbibed with mother's milk, that art bears no instructive relation to life in the world. Reading the ecocritics has, as one might imagine, activated my prejudices, as some of the notions that follow will confirm.

The essays in the Glotfelty-Fromm anthology have convinced me that, before they do anything else, the ecocritics must sort out a crucial terminological confusion. This involves use of the terms *nature* and *environment*. The problem is that *environment* and *nature* are so often used interchangeably that they have become near synonyms. But of course they are not, and the distinction isolates a core uncertainty in this emerging discipline. *Environment* is a capacious term and refers to the whole of the surrounding scape, whether natural, urban, or something mixed. *Nature* is the original given; it is the environment before the transformations wrought by technology.

Ecocriticism appears to be dominantly concerned with nature, though Parini, to be fair, does quote Oberlin's Orr as saying: "Our subject, to borrow a phrase from Alfred North Whitehead, is 'life in all its manifestations.' We study cities as well as forests." But on the evidence, Orr is an exception. Nature and its preservation are what occupy most of the ecocritics. And this imposes a kind of programmatic simplicity on the whole movement, giving it a "crunchiness" that may prove to be a liability. There is, moreover, no great battle to be fought, certainly not among the constituent intelligentsia. Fascism is bad; we must oppose it. The destruction of nature is bad; we must oppose it. The message should go out to those who need to hear it, but academic discourse is the least movable of feasts.

How much more interesting and controversial would be an ecocriticism pledging itself to the more inclusive idea of "environment." For the fact is that most of our late-century environment represents a replacement, a covering over, of nature. Mainly technological, it includes now the myriad invisible electronic transmissions, all of which mediate and warp our contact with the natural world and are changing us significantly into the bargain. Here is a subject on which a debate can be—needs to be—centered: technology, yea or nay? But the ecocritics are nowhere in evidence, and this does not bode well.

After nomenclature, there is another abstract issue, this one involving a more reflective assessment of the idea of "nature." What do we mean, really, when we invoke that most commonplace noun? Generally we refer to the natural world at large or some part of it. We intend land, vegetation, waterways, living creatures, and the ecosystem that allows them all to flourish. But we also mean—or, rather, assume—something else. For nature is a time-honored shorthand for "what is." Nature is, in a sense, the ground of all reference, the origin and end of all organic existence. This is only a problem insofar as ecocriticism tends to isolate, or focus on, nature as phenomenon, and while it does not ignore the underlying process, or the even more basic ontology, it has as its aim the foregrounding of what has always, until recently at least, been the all-embracing basis of being. The ground cannot be foregrounded! It is a vexing paradox. Our culture makes a strong association between nature and the ideal of naturalness. Be natural, be like nature. In other words, be without self-consciousness, be without too much reflection, *just be*. By focusing on nature, by bringing it forth as an object for attention and analysis, ecocriticism makes nature, in effect, unnatural.

We do not know yet in what specific ways the awareness of nature will be brought into the field of literary study—ecocriticism is still inventing itself. But we can glean a few clues, perhaps, from a work that is setting itself up as a staple reference in the field, *Green-*

*ing the College Curriculum: A Guide to Environmental Teaching in the
Liberal Arts,* edited by Jonathan Collett and Stephen Karakashian.
In the "Literature" chapter, written by Vernon Owen Grumbling,
the subject is introduced thus:

> Because literature works through value-laden images and offers
> itself to the interpretation of the reader, its particular value is to
> personalize the moral and aesthetic issues that inevitably arise
> in exploring conservation of biodiversity and sustainable devel-
> opment. Those teaching in disciplines other than literature can
> easily "borrow" a particular literary text as a means of stimulat-
> ing students to respond in personal terms to the environmental
> consequences of attitudes and behaviors. Conversely, the fusion
> of environmental awareness into the study of literature often re-
> sults in unusually lively discussion. Sometimes its students even
> develop an abiding affection for literature itself.

One example of a specific recommendation will have to suffice.
Writes Grumbling:

> By considering the environment as a subtext submerged in set-
> ting, one can infuse discussions of environmental concerns into
> most literature courses, even standard surveys required by gen-
> eral education mandates. With *Huck Finn* [*sic*], for example, one
> may explore the consequences of the steamboat, not only for
> Huck's journey, but for the future of other species—and ask how
> the reader feels about that obviously doomed future. If a text
> does not admit non-human attributes to its environment, that
> fact is itself significant.

Grumbling's suggested approach strikes me as pernicious in the
extreme. Not for nature, but for literature itself. As the opening
passage makes obvious, literature is treated as a kind of means, an
instrument of moral instruction. A text can usefully be "borrowed"
by instructors in other genres—can, in other words, be treated not
as the larger expression it is meant to be, but as an icebreaker, a
way to get students talking about certain nonliterary concepts.
This is no different from using films in order to study fashions or
gender relations. There are obvious uses to these sorts of "readings," but the benefit always comes at the expense of the integrity
of the works themselves. And to have this recommendation com-

ing from inside the camp tells us that we should loft the warning flags.

The second passage, similarly, reveals no compunction on Grumbling's part about using a text—"*Huck Finn*"—as the basis for discussions that ultimately have nothing to do with the novel or its characters. That Grumbling would propose to fellow English teachers that they "explore the consequences of the steamboat, not only for Huck's journey, but for the future of the species" is a sin against the discipline. It is divesting a literary work of its literariness in the interests of an entirely separate agenda. "A more important agenda," one might retort. But that is to put politics ahead of art, an action that presupposes that the two are even remotely comparable operations, which of course they are not.

Not that the future of the planet is not more important than Mark Twain's novel. To be sure, it is. But I have doubts about whether that more important agenda is being served in any meaningful way by the chatter that arises when a professor departs from a text to pursue extratextual themes. Part of the point of literature has always been, through vision, focus, and craft, to give the lie to the easy stances and insights that belong to the sphere of mere conversation. That is to say, the study of literature and conversation about topical matters related to a given book represent two different orders of discourse.

We are back again to asking about the place and purposes of literature. And that these questions should even need asking points as clearly as anything else to a crisis in the humanities. If we keep the inquiry centered strictly on ecocriticism, the question might be posed as follows: Can literature be usefully examined as having some bearing on man and his practical relation to the natural world? And: Can literature—*should* literature—serve as an agency of awareness? Should it be politicized to help advance the cause of the natural environment?

I will speak as a literary purist and assert that literature cannot and should not be used as a pretext for examining man and nature, certainly not more than it is a pretext for examining any other thing or relation. I resist the politicization of literature, though not, as some might suppose, for political reasons. My claim is more philosophical. Literature may be *about* the world, but not in the simple correspondence sense that people often imagine. Wordsworth's or Thoreau's or Twain's settings, however much they appear linked to actual places, are not finally transcriptions of settings in the *out there*. They are independent creations of the world; they are language in the mind. Ecocritics I have read—and Grumbling must be included here, too—very often make the mistake of conflating world and mind, thing and symbol. A critical error.

All of which is to propose that ecocriticism not take the natural world as its core subject, but look instead to man, the most problematic denizen. The true concern, finally, ought not to be with nature and its representations, but with the human being and whatever it is in *our* nature that has led us into crisis. In other words, ecocriticism might want to rechristen itself *ego*-criticism and explore what literature has to say about *human* nature, its avariciousness, rapacity, the will to power . . . this would mean, in some ways, going back to an almost abandoned tradition. But is this necessarily a bad idea? *Huckleberry Finn* studied seriously from a humanist perspective tells us more about the causes underlying the destruction of our environment than does the seemingly more direct—but in fact more oblique—approach that brings to the foreground the characters' interactions with the natural environment. Surely there is more to be gleaned from a study of the assumptions of slaveholding than a tabulation of riverine imagery.

Parini quotes Middlebury's Elder as saying, "It doesn't make sense to have English departments anymore. . . . I've come to prefer a concentric and bioregional approach to learning." By this I understand him to mean that the world is a dense fabric of interdependences and that the proper study of literature—which is ostensibly about the world—ought to be correlatively interdisciplinary. This may be just the ticket for other fields—biology, history, geology, and sociology, say (and of course the Annales historians do something of the sort)—but it is a radical misunderstanding of English, of literature—indeed, or art itself—to insist on cross-pollinating it with more worldly matters.

I feel somewhat guilty about insisting on this separation—about keeping church and state apart, as it were—for I do accept that (A) nothing could be more important that the survival of our natural world and its ecosystems and (B) literature, if it is to matter, must remain relevant, must address the state of things in some meaningful way. But I cannot thereby advocate that literature and literary study be about the natural world. No, literature and all that depends on it must continue to be about what it is in us humans that has brought the crisis about; about what it means for us to confront the evidence of our destructiveness and the likelihood of a severely diminished future; and where in ourselves we might look to find the strength needed to begin to deal with the crisis. Moving the focus anywhere away from the psyche, the soul, ultimately depreciates the art and hobbles it from doing what it does best. We do want to save nature, but we do not need to kill literature in our zeal to do so.

Reflections of a Nonpolitical Man;

or,

Why I Can't in Good Conscience Write about Noam Chomsky

I have a friend who wants me to be more political. He doesn't specify, but I know what he means: He wants me to do things, take conspicuous stances, have a more engaged posture in the world. And he's right. That is, he must be right—otherwise why would I feel such a prickling of guilt whenever he brings the subject up? And these days he seems to bring it up all the time. When he does I naturally become defensive; I scramble toward the familiar silence of not being understood.

This same friend, in an effort to raise my consciousness, has now asked me to write for him an essay on Noam Chomsky's and Edward Herman's latest book, *Manufacturing Consent*. In the face of such sincere concern for the fitness of my soul, I could not think of a way to refuse. I confess, too, that I hoped the book would make a change in me. It's not that I want to be nonpolitical, it's just that I am. I would give a great deal to be able to lay to rest the sickly guilt that moves through me whenever I face up to my own ineffectuality, my refusal to take any direct action against the waste, corruption and oppression that are around us like tethers.

So I read. And I read with care. Slowly, marking passages with a pencil. I paused—sometimes I made myself do so—over statistics confirming one outrage after another. I made every effort to understand, to impress on myself what this really meant in the world beyond the words. And I took pains to track the progress of Chomsky's argument: I marveled at the cool fury of the prose. I could see Chomsky's determination to avoid all rhetoric, to let the facts speak for themselves. Reading, I felt a deep respect for the dedication and will required to wage a campaign for truth in the face of near-universal deafness. I thought, too, about the points I would make and the sections I would cite to push those points home. I read, I marked, I plotted. And when I came to an end of it, I found that I stood squarely before an obstacle in myself: I could not possibly discuss this book, these ideas, in the necessary terms.

Not because I was not persuaded; not because I do not believe that Chomsky is doing a hero's work; not because the information does not need to go out to every person who thinks about anything more consequential than Friday's twilight doubleheader at Fenway Park—but because I was not an adequate vessel for Chomsky's vision. I would have to pretend to a stance or perspective that I could assent to intellectually, but that I had not earned with my heart. Indeed, the more I soaked myself in the information, and the more I thought about the implication of the analysis that Chomsky sets out—how the whole empire of our communications is tacitly and implicitly geared to furthering the vested interests of U.S. imperialism—the more I found myself coiling back upon my own blockage: my inability, unwillingness, to put myself forward in meaningful political action on behalf of anything. The two— Chomsky's thesis and my response—are very separate things, but as I read they became one. The book and its author became in my mind a single emblem of engaged activism before which I was struck dumb.

I faced the difficult fact: I will do nothing overt to further causes I believe in—I will do nothing *political.* An awful admission. Certainly there is no dearth of causes, all of them asking for our most committed support. Greenpeace, Amnesty International, pro-choice mobilization, anti-apartheid organizations, nuclear freeze campaigns. What is wrong with me that I cannot bestir myself to do anything more than sign an occasional petition, write out a small check?

I discussed my sense of handicap with my friend. He suggested that the problem was not mine alone, that it seemed to afflict a great many people, prominent among them the writers, artists and thinkers that one might expect would be closer to such consciousness and involvement. We went back and forth debating possible reasons, considering everything from cultural narcissism to spiritual detachment in the service of art, but we were not able to solve

the matter. I promised him that if I could not write the essay he
had assigned, I would instead set down my reasons for failure.

I would like to write about this inactivity, this political paralysis of
mine, honestly. I would like to write about it without lapsing into
the clever, cynical mode that comes to me so readily when I get defensive. But I am, of course, defensive. Somewhere not all that
deep within I know that the blockage represents a failing. No,
I correct myself: I don't *know* this, I only suspect it. And I would
like to—I *think* I would like to—change myself, to think my way
through to an understanding of things out of which response—
action—would result naturally. For I know that nothing could be
more false, and wrongheaded, than a rash effort on my part to set
things right by simply deciding to *do* something. To go march at
Seabrook, say.

But how to work through this tangle? First, I ought to make a
clear distinction between political passivity (or paralysis) and political apathy. I am not apathetic. Certainly not about the thousand-
and-one ills of the world. If I am apathetic about anything, it's
political process: activity. But no, even that is not quite right. For I
have great admiration for those people who feel the compulsion
to act out their beliefs and who find meaningful ways to do so. I see
newsreel footage of demonstrators being carted away from nuclear
power plants or dumping sites and I envy them. I find myself wishing that I, too, knew my convictions in such a bodily—complete—
fashion. Nothing stops me from joining the march—but I do not
join. I applaud others; I cannot make myself act.

The obvious defense, the first that comes to mind, is that these
activities are ultimately useless, that they will not stay the course of
the world or stop the powers that be from enacting their schemes.
This I can readily discard: for even if the protests availed nothing,
they would still send a signal to those powers that they cannot simply railroad their designs into place; they cannot expect that everyone consents. And this is a necessary statement.

As it happens, such an argument is beside the point anyway.
Protest and activism have brought about a great number of improvements in our collective situation. They hastened the withdrawal of troops from Vietnam; they brought about important

legislative victories for blacks; they have put tremendous social and economic pressure on the South African government to end apartheid policies; they have forced the shutdown of flawed nuclear facilities, and so on. The charge of uselessness will not stick.

So, what stops me from signing up, from going to work on behalf of some cause that is especially important to me? In part, I know, that answer has to do with the sheer complexity of the offenses. I feel that a total situation—I mean a mesh made up of social and economic components, a labyrinth congruent with the deeper structures of society—begs a total response. And a total response is impossible for any individual. I could not give myself wholeheartedly (and what other kind of giving of oneself is there?) to the fight to preserve the snail darter while knowing that apartheid and plutonium dumping were in full swing elsewhere. That is, I could not *psychologically* do this. Logic, of course, protests—one cannot do everything; one should not therefore do nothing. I may not be able to solve all of the problems of the world (which is what I would, with my monstrous egotism, like to do), but I could put my voice and body on the line and do some good on behalf of some small part of the web. Others would be doing the same for other parts—perhaps some collective results could be achieved.

The logic is incontestable, but I remain inert. I must search further into myself. If what stops me from taking action is not apathy—and I believe I am not apathetic—then maybe the culprit is laziness. I squirm a bit as the beam of self-scrutiny probes at the crannies of the soul. Yes, to be sure, laziness is there in the character makeup. Or, to raise it to the dignity of a Deadly Sin: sloth. But pointing the finger there does not bring the matter to an end. For sloth is a disease of the will. And I have to own that I am only slothful in certain areas of my life. When I want or *will* something, I can be tirelessly active. So, my sloth in these political matters must point to some more or less unconscious refusal in myself. I am overtaken by sloth because for some reason I do not want to partake. Why not?

Selfishness? The belief that an expenditure of energy and thought will not net me commensurate return? That I will be giving out more than I get back? Maybe. It's not as though I haven't made those calculations, balancing off the time and caloric output

required just to swell the ranks of a given demonstration by my
humble numerical presence. Couldn't that energy be better spent
elsewhere?

I may be getting closer. That is, I recognize the defensive logic
as one I make use of when guilt afflicts me. I didn't go to take my
stand at such and such a rally because I reckoned my time was better spent doing what I do. I hasten to clarify this. You see, I have to
deem what I do—think, read, write—to be a part of the overall
struggle. Not, perhaps, of the immediate political struggle, but the
larger one, which works to ensure the survival of spirit, free inquiry, humanness—*value*—in a world where these qualities are under threat. There is no way to speak of this without sounding
pompous or holier-than-thou. Trying to be serious about these ultimate things carries that risk.

At any rate, I am aware of making certain kinds of computations
inwardly at times—that the expenditure involved in getting my
body on the line, when set against what I could hope to accom-
plish with the same energy and focus doing what I am most de-
voted to, makes it more practical to continue my work. After all, I
tell myself, I am not greedy of the time because I want to work on
my stamp collection. No, I want to keep on with this business of
thinking and writing.

Oh, but this too is somehow false. Or incomplete. The computation may happen, but it happens on a fairly superficial level. It
does not really touch that level of will. The heavenly powers could
grant me a series of bonus days with the stipulation that they not
be used for reading or writing and I still would not hasten to the
march. No, the deeper part of the business is tightly bound up
with the volitional core, and it is there I must look for my answers.

I do not engage in political activity. I don't march or demonstrate. I give money reluctantly, and for the wrong reasons: to get
the asker off my back. I rarely join letter-writing campaigns for
Amnesty International or PEN; whenever I have written such letters I have had the feeling that I am lying to myself. I may say—I
did say, earlier—that I want to get involved, but clearly I do not. My
will refuses. And insofar as I believe in myself, my experience, I
must trust that resistance; I have to try to understand it. More, I
must consider whether the refusal is not in some way *positive*. What

if I now reversed myself and actually upheld—proclaimed—my inactivity? Not in the manner of the Kantian categorical imperative, as a course for all to follow, but for myself: as the necessary, desirable, optimal position? I blanch to think of doing this. But if I am to stay with my original aim—to be entirely truthful—is this not what I have to do? For if I turn on this in myself, I turn on myself as well. I repudiate a whole pattern of inner evolution that I have followed (or that has been set for me).

Why, then, looking now from the positive side, do I insist on remaining politically passive?

I find two reasons, and they are, in a manner of speaking, joined at the hip. The first is that I do not ultimately believe that there is a division between the political sphere of life and the others, however we might name them. Rather, I see the various levels of perception, action, and consequence as interfused; they form, as does the psyche itself, a continuum. And it is therefore fundamentally—existentially and ontologically—false to mark out one such area—the political—as requiring us especially. Such a view, I realize, does nothing to end apartheid or put food into the mouths of the starving, and it will need further exploration. But let me first spell out the other, linked, reason.

My second belief, put most simply, is that human behavior not only functions along a continuum, with all its parts in relation, it also obeys what might be called hydraulic principles. That is, an excessive pressure at one point must result in diminution elsewhere. Energy given over to *works* is energy withdrawn from the work. Time consecrated to mailing petitions (and it's not just time, it's the energy of the devotion) is time taken from reflection on the larger condition of things. Again, that sounds terribly noble, but the side of me that ponders this dilemma has high-minded aspirations. I speak as one who feels a compulsion to write. I see my job (high-mindedly) as being the recognition and promotion of those values by which we live; or, to put it more conditionally, by which I believe we ought to live. Quite obviously, the goal of political engagement is to fight on behalf of the very same cause, but in immediate, tangible terms. I think that everyone who can should put a shoulder to the wheel and work to rectify abuses. I am trying to explain why I cannot.

I know this all sounds as though I put myself above the struggle, that I claim for myself some exalted, private agenda and urge on others the tasks that I cannot bring myself to do. I do not mean it this way. My point is that even in full awareness of the evils pressing on us from all sides (the evils that activism would address), I find that there is a place for some individuals—those so inclined or driven—to do the more obscure labor of perceiving and processing the larger current shifts, shifts embracing realms outside the political. For in truth, some people are bent in a certain way; they feel a call to filter the world's information in less immediate ways. It does not seem to me possible to do both—to pursue a clear picture of these inchoate weather patterns *and* engage in specified, directed activity. The continuum, the psyche's economy, will not allow it.

My place, then, is at the desk with my books and thoughts. I have to try to do what I can to explore ideas and tendencies. Some part of this activity necessarily impinges upon the terrain of the "political," and insofar as it does I hope that my words promote the humane values, that they exert some small influence on people who do act. But who can say how these indeterminate forces move through the world?

As I write this, I realize that there is a point I have been meaning to make, namely, that the commitment I claim for myself assumes the long view. That is, that I think of these values as continuities, and that I will for myself complete identification with their substance. This, no less than the "processing" I spoke of, calls for an absolute focus of energy and will. I mention this because in the course of thinking about this subject I have more than once looked back to the period of the late '6os. Not only because it was an era of conspicuous and directed political intensity, but also because I now see what happened to a great many members of my generation. Far too many of my peers have gone from vociferous front-line activism ("Free Huey!" and "If you're not part of the solution, you're part of the problem") to careers in the corporate mecca. They are now functionaries in the big machine that runs on only so long as it can exploit a class of have-nots. Well, there's politics, too. They had views and voices, and they gave them over when the prevailing winds shifted. They sold out. And they were able to do so because their convictions, though genuine, though vocally expressed, were shallowly rooted. Have they not undone twice over what they accomplished when they had righteousness in their hearts?

What consequences, then, can I claim for my brand of inactivity? A hard question to answer. I have not put food into one hungry person's mouth. But neither have I knowingly aided any of those who amass their profits by taking it away. (To be sure, I have consumed my share of societal goods and services—I am implicated.) I have not fought to close down any power plants. I have not overtly worked to end policies of apartheid or U.S. involvement in the political process of Central American countries. What have I done? Well, I have tried through teaching and writing to influence the perspectives of others; I have labored through the same channels to expose rhetoric and meretriciousness in writing, and to uphold examples of what is meaningful and sustaining—this in the belief that there *is* a continuum between words and mental processes and actions in the world. I have abstained from giving any comfort or solace to the bureaucrat. I have tried to live through the daily muddle with consistency and mental clarity. I have done everything to follow the promptings of the deeper muse. And all of this has left me very little for politics in the more immediate sense of the word. Probably I am *not* disqualified from urging on others the analysis of Chomsky and Herman, but the assignment happened to give me the pretext I needed for combing out these gnarled thoughts and protestations. They are not every person's thoughts. If they were, there would be little hope for the struggle to better the world. I hope that no one reads me as recommending the kind of stasis I am condemned to. I could not bear it if I somehow abetted the cause of our mutual enemy—the taker, exploiter, liar, polluter, rhetorician . . .

II

An Open Invitation
to Extraterrestrials

I have thought about the matter a great deal, and I am now convinced that one of the few things that could still save our literature, not to mention the deeper life of culture at large, would be evidence—preferably in the form of direct contact—that there is other sentient life in the universe. What else, really, could replenish the sense of mystery that has been leached out of our lives? It is the absence of *that* that has made most everything our artists venture seem inconsequential, vague, and of aluminum lightness. Or is it just midsummer pressing upon my sensorium?

Every newspaper columnist with pretensions to thought has at one time or another dilated on "the greatest single event" or "the most profound transformation" affecting humankind in our age, advancing claims on behalf of the Holocaust, the microchip, the moon landing, and so on. I'm not about to belittle any of these candidates, but it may just be that the claimants are blinded to the most newsworthy story of all. I'm referring to the wholesale alteration—or deformation—of consciousness, individual and collective, by the media: television, radio, print, and photojournalism. So thoroughly (and insidiously) has the metastasis taken place, so utterly saturated are we by the various emanations, that it is impossible to step to one side to see it for what it is. At best, we can try to realize the momentousness of the change. We can consult the memories of our oldest citizens, ask them what life felt like when the airwaves were still empty. "We didn't know so much back then," they say. "Things were slower." And it is astonishing, isn't it, that a few of our countrymen were walking about before the invention of the car and the cathode-ray tube? A person living in 1900 was as close to the civilization in the Tigris-Euphrates region as she was to life in modern L.A.

Life changed on every front, at every level. We know that. The media boom was just one development. But it was, and is, the catalytic one. It fashioned of the myriad changes a picture, or idea, of change and injected it into the culture. Where it now lives. For the first time in history people feel that they are living inside a larger kind of "now," a "now" that they are sharing with people whom they have never set eyes on. And this feeling is not shaped by direct contact with experience, by things as they are; it is entirely a product of things as they are *presented*. Of media. What started out as a tool, a combination package of public service and commercial entertainment, has slipped out of individual control and has taken on a life of its own. Now the image in the mirror moves and the body follows.

When I talk about the "wholesale alteration" of our consciousness, I am not referring so much to the effects on us of the contents, or "messages," of the media as to the changes worked by the process itself. *That,* said Marshall McLuhan, the sage of Toronto, is the message. The frightening thing is that there is no way to gauge what the deluge of secondhand, or "mediated," information and imagery is doing to us. Certainly we are different during exposure—more passive, distracted, impatient, skittish—than otherwise. But now the statisticians tell us that the vast majority of our compatriots have no "otherwise." They are "mediated" (a clever contraction of "media radiated"?) from the first hum of the radio alarm to the last strains of the late-night laugh track. When the car radio goes off, the Muzak in the shopping mall takes over. This collective immersion will not be without consequences, we can be sure of that. Here follow just a few speculative stabs:

1. The media, in the aggregate, are at every second plundering what someone aptly called the stock of available reality. They are, quite simply, demystifying the world. There is no mountain fastness or tropical sanctum (and certainly no indigenous, "primitive" culture) that has not been visited and revisited by the camera crew, the reporter with his notebook, and the stooges with their microphones and sound recorders. There is no mass murderer or creative genius whose secrets have not been exhumed and briskly summarized by one interviewer or

another. Although no one has spelled it out for us in so many
words, we are grasping the fact that our habitat, the world, is finite and knowable—its wonders have all been cataloged and we
are already watching them on reruns, doing our best not to
doze off. Of course, it is a superficial kind of "knowing," but the
point is that the violation of all possible surfaces has ripped
away from everything the sense of uniqueness, the aura. And
everyone knows that once we have glanced at the headlines we
are much less interested in the fine print. Looming before us is
the prospect of a cosmic boredom, a yawn big enough to swallow the universe.

2. Having entrenched themselves, having made themselves entirely indispensable (can we imagine a world without them?),
   the media realize—that is, their executive brokers realize—that
   the serpent is eating its own tail. For the media's continued existence depends completely on their success at holding the attention of the populace. To do this they must be either useful or
   interesting. Unfortunately for the media—and, ultimately, the
   race—the second term has supplanted the first. So great is the
   fear of boredom—indeed, is there anything, apart from illness
   and death (the ultimate condition of boredom, its apotheosis)
   that we fear more?—that every last quantum of ingenuity must
   be exerted in order to outdistance it. News and information
   alone will no longer hold the mass audience. The appetite for
   sensation, for the giddy pacing that suggests that *at last something interesting is really happening,* has forced newscasters and
   publishers to keep one eye fixed on the salability of their "product." (Events as products—property—think of it!)

   Where entertainment is concerned, naturally, this has always
   been the case; and it would have been true in Rome, too, had
   there been two rival Colossea. The public will unfailingly go for
   the latest, fastest, least taxing, most immediately stimulating
   thing. Images and words, words and images. What can be done
   with them to make the thing—whatever it is—seem new and
   fresh? Nothing is new under the sun; subjects are only so many.
   But the "idea men" work through the night to find ways to make
   the ones we have *seem* new.

3. How? By raiding the word hoard, pumping the residues out of language, plundering the arts. They string together adjectives until they fizz like soda in the brainpan. No proportion need be recognized between the thing presented and the words used to present it. Inflate, expand, enlarge—do anything you like so long as it captures the attention. And where there is so much competition for attention, where so many channels and stations and magazines vie for the same dollars, acceleration must set in. Things cannot merely seem new every so often, they must seem so every second, or else Mr. Listener-Watcher-Consumer will turn elsewhere with his precious attention (and checkbook). The Nielsen ratings are a thermometer thrust into the mouth of a dying animal—the devouring disease is boredom.

4. Acceleration of word combinations and images erodes the already-threatened attention span, diminishes further the capacity for interest. This may not have been scientifically proved, but one would have to be a cretin not to know it. The race is on. Which will be exhausted first, the repertoire of possibilities, or the psyche of the consumer? Andy Warhol's pronouncement— that everyone, in the future, will be famous for fifteen minutes— is more prophetic than nonsensical. The fame won't be doled out because of merit, however; it will be because the celebrity machine will soon have used up its celebrities and will start looking elsewhere: at you, at me. Start combing your hair!

I'm getting carried away now by apocalyptic fantasy, sure. But these tendencies *do* exist, they are affecting our lives in ways that we cannot even guess at, and you can be sure that nobody is going to come on television to confirm it for you. Can I prove it? No. There are no facts, no data. Only intuition. And intuition bids me to glance briefly at a not unrelated subject, at that (to me) terrifying cultural phenomenon known as postmodernism.

Do not get taken in by the fashionable sound of that appellation. It is not the "latest thing," the evolutionary advance upon modernism. So far as the arts are concerned, it is the *last* thing. The postmodern sensibility—and I'll characterize it in a moment— represents, in effect, the death of style. By *style* I mean those forms of expression that are seen to characterize a period, and that represent, to their proponents and to the public, something uniquely new, a movement away from the past. Postmodernism is frightening because it is the logical culmination of the processes I have been discussing. It vindicates me, and for once I'd rather not be vindicated. For what it signifies is that the idea of futurity, of progress—the basis for all of our notions of an avant-garde—is defunct; that styles are not advances, but merely shapes on a revolving wheel; and that the wheel has begun to revolve so quickly that all styles look like one.

Postmodernism proposes that from now on the new can only be generated out of combinations of the old, that there is no more new, that history is a rummage sale of effects, that Dr. Frankenstein was right: It *is* possible to bring to life something stitched together from various cadavers. Postmodern fiction (all the arts are infected, but I will restrict myself to one) loots among genres, refurbishing with ironic self-consciousness the documentary, the Western, the pulp, the thriller, the historical novel, the fantasy, and so on. Leading practitioners include William Burroughs, E. L. Doctorow, Joyce Carol Oates, Robert Coover, Donald Barthelme, Gilbert Sorrentino, Evan S. Connell, Don DeLillo, John Barth, John Fowles, Italo Calvino, and Umberto Eco. Of course, not everybody writing at present is a postmodernist. Thank God! But the tendency is very conspicuous and is symptomatic of our deeper distress. A great many of our leading artists are throwing up their hands, are saying by way of their aesthetic choices that there is no more unknown from which to draw new resources. The high seriousness that characterized modernism has been replaced by a wink and a tongue in the cheek. One cannot play mix-and-match with the past without donning the ironic mask. And one cannot come up with a product that is not ultimately trivial.

This may be, as they say, *for real.* In our zealous, unthinking consumption of mediated images and words, in that quest for novel sensation that Americans of recent generations have taken as their birthright, we may have used up the unknown—that is to say, the future. The possibility of nuclear incineration aside, what can we now look for? New diseases and new cures; ecological panic; improvements in computer systems; growing population, longer lives, a gradually diminishing quality of life. This sounds so pessimistic. Why is it that I cannot in all honesty look forward to collective spiritual transformation, or to the appearance of wondrous new works of art and literature?

Because neither, in my view, can come into being where there is no sense of mystery and no significant inner orientation toward the future. Both have been lost, and, ponder as I might, I cannot see how we can regain them. The two potential solutions are so unlikely as to strain credulity. One: that the media conglomerates would get together for their own SALT talks, with the plan of giving over their holdings piece by piece, dismantling their receivers and transmitters and telecommunications systems until the world was finally restored to a pre-Marconi silence, with nothing more than the hometown newspaper for information. The second, a mere fantasy (shared by Steven Spielberg et al.), is the one I mentioned at the outset. If we could, through some extraordinary feat of technology, make contact with extraterrestrial life, it would be an event more significant than the discovery of America. In a flash the night sky would be charged with possibility, with the unknown, with futurity. Leaders and working stiffs alike would quicken with expectancy. And literature . . .

Biography and the Dissolving Self

I have been afflicted with a single strikingly obvious thought about biography these past few months, and the time has come for me to unburden myself. This thought has come to me not as part of a chain of logical connections; it has come instead, if thoughts can, from that part of the night sky through which intuitions pass like comets. The notion is this: that the great flowering of the biography genre that we have been witnessing over these past few decades has been prompted by more than just a happy convergence of cultural and scholarly circumstances. That the public's growing fascination with the lives of the famous and notorious correlates directly with the steadily depreciating sense of subjective coherence many of us are feeling—correlates, that is, in an inverse way. That we turn to biography as compensation, to gather in vicariously what we are losing in the private sphere. Some will object, of course, that our interest in the lives of others has never been anything *but* vicariousness and has always testified to a perceived lack on the part of the reader. To this I can only reply by saying that the situation is more aggravated and a kind of critical mass has been achieved; that the forces that threaten selfhood are pressing on us harder and in new ways, and saying "it's always been that way" no longer makes a sound rebuttal.

Before looking into this, I need to consider the dynamics of reading as they apply to biography. The nonprofessional reader picks up a given "life" for a number of different reasons and the reading unfolds on several levels. There are the obvious motivations, chief among them human curiosity. We want to know about an important or beguiling figure, to know what made him or her "tick." Along with this there is often a historical fascination. The reader seeks to get some purchase on a period through an immersion in the life of an individual. Following the path of Oscar

Wilde or Edith Wharton or Orson Welles or Winston Churchill, we touch the pulse of a milieu, close in upon a historical moment.

But there is another no less important incentive for reading the lives of others, and this is to illuminate facets of our own experience to ourselves. Indeed, this impulse underlies a great deal of reading of all descriptions, though it is too seldom remarked upon. Every genre draws on and reinforces our subjectivity in different ways. We read detective thrillers in order to discharge, but also explore, certain socially proscribed desires. Good literary fiction gratifies our vicariousness and allows us both to surpass and, later, repossess our boundaries. Histories counteract the magnifications of subjectivity by asking us to impose on them a soberingly vast sense of scale.

Biography is especially rich in these secondary incentives. For whatever our ostensible reason for reading the life of Machiavelli or C. S. Lewis, it is inevitable that in the process we will formulate a particular sort of relation between our life and that of the subject. This is second nature. We can't help mapping our experiences to those of others. When a neighbor lays out her woes, we measure them against ours. We cannot scan an obituary without a quick crunching of the numbers. Biography offers a heightened and sustained occasion.

I may be working through the life of a person with whom I appear to have little or nothing in common, but at every point I am making these computations; comparing the pleasures and privations of X's childhood with those of mine; looking to see just how he tempered his youthful idealism and accommodated himself to his vocation; studying how love shaped him, or how he was affected by the deaths of his parents. And then, yes, how did he face his own death? This last may be the deepest question, the one that underwrites our fascination with other lives.

There is, admittedly, a kind of presumption about doing this, never mind that it's more a matter of reflex than willed determination. After all, the subject of the biography has by some consensus attained to greatness, is believed to possess exceptional gifts, at least in certain areas. When a reader—this reader—compares his life with that of, say, Julius Caesar, he is establishing at least some sort of continuum between self and emperor. He has to. And it is along this continuum that the reader plots the points of their common humanity. Genius though Caesar may have been at military strategy, unbridled as his ambitions may appear to have been, he was still, at the core, that recognizably scaled-down thing, a self. Surely he felt some flaring sense of mystery when he looked up at the night sky; surely love came into his life and filled his veins with quicksilver. We base our reading on just such assumptions. And the effect is, finally, as much to raise ourselves as it is to lower, or "humanize," the object of our veneration. We attend to the particulars of the life as we read, but in some essential way we read *past* the defining circumstances and situations to make contact with the common—that is to say "universal"—subject.

Having set out this rudimentary premise, I can return to my original assertion that now, more than in the past, we look to biography for something we lack in our own lives—our lives as we live them privately, but also as the culture refracts to us the idea of what a life is. This refraction changes incessantly, is a historical variable. It is a kind of collective understanding that is constrained by a threshold of expectations. The individual, formerly tethered much more to his place and time, looked around and gathered from others a sense of what life held, what it was. He saw how people supported themselves, gauged the distance to the horizon by their travels, learned what illnesses they contracted, how they died. In the premodern epochs, people by and large partook of the common life—the life prescribed to them by gender, caste, class, and so on.

Now all this has changed. First gradually, then explosively, people bent the bars of place and escaped. Detachment from place is the rule, at least in the urbanized West. Very few people sustain any real continuity with the tribe. The threshold of expectations has been rendered irrelevant by tremendous vertical and lateral mobility and by the huge range of occupation choice. Moreover, speed and stimulus overload and the myriad ills of fragmentation now afflict us all. Our labor is less and less bound to primary societal needs; we give ourselves over to increasingly abstract operations. We are hemmed in on every side by a social and legal bureaucracy that forces us to do things that undermine our sense of subjective individuation. We must register our cars, buy insurance, join health plans, pay taxes, whack away at mortgage debt, enter into the fiscal master-slave relation with credit card companies. The days pass behind desks, behind counters, behind tinted glass, in front of terminals, waiting in lines, sitting in cars. Take everything together and you begin to see how it gets harder for any of us to hold a vivid, compelling idea of "my life." For the idea of a life—one's own life—must stand clear from the jumble of contingent circumstance. It must be coherent, significantly self-directed, charged with a sense of purpose and connectedness. We need to believe in our lives as destinies, as unfolding narratives that take on and manifest meaning, that are distinctive, if not distinguished. And this, I fear, is what we are losing. I have talked with so many people who have expressed the same basic sentiment: that they are living provisionally, "as if," waiting again for the day to come when they will glimpse again what they may have beheld in younger days—a map, a track, a defining sense of how they fit into the world.

More and more we find ourselves living at a remove, with the feeling that life has gone blurry, has lost its singular intensity; we feel our coherence dissipating among needs, obligations, and great troves of competing stimuli. This is not universally true, to be sure, but it is a strong tendency—one of the chief complaints of our age. And this, to me, helps to account for the tremendous surge of interest in biography. Burrowing into a life, the reader experiences clarity and purpose by proxy. It is an exalting baptism. For one thing, the circumstances of earlier times were, if not simpler, then more resonant, and felt more authentic. The vast systems of mediation had not yet fallen like a shadow over the globe. The world *was* a starker, more primary, more clearly defined place. There was more consensus—be it about social mores or public heroes—and perhaps, for most people, a deeper sense of cultural identification. Picking up hints of this as we read, we get a tonic sense of proportion. Things seemed to have density, weight—to matter.

But there is also, of course, the fundamental mode of presentation. Biographical narration itself is premised on coherence and meaning. The biographer almost occupationally views his subject as living under the aspect of a singular destiny, with everything around him contributing to press his experience into its intended shape. Which of us feel some comparable sense of destination about our premillennial lives?

As biography gains in prestige, as there are more and more biographies and readers of biography, the terms of the opposition stand out in ever greater relief: While the subjects of the art loom larger and larger, their lives appearing more purposeful or tragic or grand, our own lives seem to be losing mass and dissolving into ever more nebulous bunches of pixels. The question goes to the biographers of the future: How will the lives of our present, which have lost the heft and distinctness of lives, get written? And, if written, who will want to read them?

The Grasshopper
on the Windowsill

There's a new idea out in the world, and I'm horrified to think that it might be gaining ground. I first got wind of it from my wife, who one day mentioned to me a book by Kenneth Gergen called *The Saturated Self: Dilemmas of Identity in Contemporary Life.* Gergen, as I understood it, was promoting a postmodern redefinition of self, one that allowed for multiple roles and masks and abandoned the anachronism of a core identity. I was still bemusedly shaking my head over this when a student of mine handed me an essay she had written on literary expressions of trauma and adaptation wherein she invoked psychologist Robert Jay Lifton and his idea of the "protean self." Drawing in part on his work with survivors of the Hiroshima bombing, but also integrating insights from his clinical practice, Lifton essentially pronounces a mutating and de-centered self to be a healthy adaptation to the conditions of contemporary life.

At this point my antennae began to bristle. Multiple selves, morphing behaviors untethered by a stabilized "I"—was this William Butler Yeats's rough beast, its hour come round at last? Soon there were other sightings. Looking through a book catalog I noticed that British philosopher Ian Hacking has just published a study called *Rewriting the Soul: Multiple Personality and the Science of Memory;* the descriptive copy noted that cases of that disorder were scarcely known until a very few years ago. But before I got a chance to investigate more closely, I was invited in another direction. Would I review Sherry Turkle's new book, *Life on the Screen: Identity in the Age of the Internet?* And here it was again, only now linked explicitly to computers and to the reinforcement of multiplicity in the self by on-line engagements. We find Turkle citing both Lifton and Gergen as evidence that a serious rethinking of our conceptions of self is under way; she then offers various examples that would seem to underscore the validity of the new paradigm. Writes Turkle:

> The Internet has become a significant social laboratory for experimenting with the constructions and reconstructions of self that characterize postmodern life. In its virtual reality, we consciously construct ourselves. What kinds of persons do we create? What relation do these have with what we have traditionally thought of as a "whole" person? . . . Do our real life selves learn lessons from our virtual personae? . . . Is this a shallow game, a giant waste of time? Is it an expression of an identity crisis of the sort we used to associate with adolescence? Or are we watching the slow emergence of a new, more multiple style of thinking about the mind?

What has all this to do with reading, or with the idea of reading as a potentially subversive activity?

To begin with a general, and perhaps overwhelmingly obvious, observation: The larger cultural practice of reading has always taken place against a shifting historical background. Reading in the early age of print was, for a host of reasons, different from reading in the age of mechanical reproduction; it is different again in the media-irradiated democracy that has followed. Different, that is, in terms of its private as well as its larger societal import. Who can doubt but that in the days when the page of print was still, by virtue of scarcity and novelty, something marvelous, reading imparted to many the exhilarating sense of breaching barriers of solitude and communing at a distance? And by the same token, who would deny that our present-day condition of perpetual inundation has turned our former focal concentration into a grazing operation that is something very different?

As must be clear, I have begun to take this idea of an emerging proteanism seriously. I allow that we may indeed in some gradual and collective way be heading toward a more distributed experience of identity: that, to put it bluntly, our subjectivity might be starting to dissolve, and that the selves of the future could be quite different in fundamental ways from the selves of the present.

The question to ask, of course, is whether the self is a bio/psychological given—hardwired, as they like to say—or whether it is not in various important ways an evolutionary attainment predicated on all manner of conditioning factors. Our twentieth-century notion of selfhood might well be the product of what were our necessary ways of living, and as these change—they are changing with breathtaking velocity—our formerly sacrosanct idea of a centered and self-aware entity might be replaced by this new idea of the self as a kind of federation of personae.

This is, to be sure, extreme. But if one spends some time thinking about the nature of computers and the implications of our growing daily involvement with them, one could, like Turkle, begin to admit this possibility. One could, like digital guru Kevin Kelly, begin to postulate that the life of the not-so-distant future will be a kind of hive life, with the agency that once inhered in the isolated individual taken over by the nonsubjective group agency of myriad connected individuals.

One man's utopia is another man's nightmare. I don't really believe that Kelly's sci-fi scenario will ever come to pass, but I do think that his imagining maps a tendency and that we will, over the next half century, move more toward that kind of connectedness. And that is doomsday scenario enough for me.

But let us return to reading. Only now let us consider not the larger cultural perspective, but the private—and essential—nature of the act. This may help us to better understand a key paradox, which is that although the burgeoning of electronic technologies has endangered the practice of solitary reading, that same practice might yet be what saves many from the unforeseen consequences of technological proliferation. As the poet Friedrich Hölderlin wrote in "Patmos," "Where danger is / there the saving power also grows." It might take the arrival of the electronic millennium to reveal hitherto latent aspects of reading.

We generally think of reading in the transitive sense, as the reading of something specific, the deed then defined or somehow constrained by the thing read: reading the newspaper, reading John Grisham, reading Marcel Proust. I would like to consider reading as an internal act—freed of all its transitive encumbrance—and in so doing expose what may be its subversive possibility.

Probably not much has changed about the basic dynamics of the reading process since people began to internalize language sounds and to gather in sense without enunciating, without even moving their lips. But in former times moving from some worldly activity—working or socializing—to reading involved a switching of the cognitive channel; one moved the beam of awareness from doings in the sphere of the actual to the somewhat differently constituted doings on the page. But now, increasingly, the reading act requires that we *create* the beam of awareness itself. That is, to read we often have to find a way to make ourselves pay attention; we have to make ourselves go against the grain. Living in a late-modern culture, attending to several things at once, we are subject to the constant distribution of our internal energies, and are routinely cut away from the sort of focus that used to be our natural state.

What I will say next is very basic, but I fear that we may be losing sight of it: The objects of our attention matter less than the purity of our awareness. I mean: It is better, more rewarding, to study the grasshopper on the windowsill with full attention than to stand half-distractedly before a painting by Paul Klee or Botticelli. Attention completes the inner circuit, and completing that circuit is everything—at least if we care about the idea of an integral subjective self.

As it happens, reading is one of the very few things that you can only really do with full attentiveness. The act not only requires focus, it sharpens the focus as the reader proceeds with the work (assuming, as I assume throughout, that we are reading something worthy of our capabilities). This is because of the mysterious bond—I won't say identity—between language and cognition: Language is partly projected into the world, partly still embedded in consciousness itself. But let's leave that to the linguists and philosophers. The point is that we can half listen to a piece of music, pay partial attention as we drive, and add up our grocery tab while making love, but when we read we've got to be *reading*—we must be all there, or else the activity is pointless.

And this being *all there* is what we need to look at. For while the reader is, of course, transitively present in the specific world conjured up by Leo Tolstoy or William Faulkner or whoever, he is at the same time intransitively immersed, self-possessed over and above the spell of his reading. I mean: When Levin is scything his

fields in *Anna Karenina*, I am at once fully there *and* most exaltingly myself. Exaltingly, because in my engagement with Tolstoy's
world I am liberated from the contingent entanglement that generally wears me down, that awareness of daily duties and demands
that fragments me and dilutes my sense of having a self. Reading,
even though it proposes an elsewhere, gives me that self—gives it
to me most fully and purely when I am most deeply possessed by
the work.

This is for me the core paradox of reading and is its claim to
philosophical and psychological profundity—and its potentially
revolutionary attribute (though maybe *revolutionary* isn't the best
word to use here). For if the revolution of our times is the electronic transformation of our whole society, then my notion of
reading had better be considered counterrevolutionary.

As we progress toward and then into the circuit-board future,
the dissociation from the core self (yes, I believe there is such a
thing) will steadily increase. All forms of mediation will increase,
and multitasking behavior, already a norm, will become second nature. The protean self—fluid and mutating according to situation
and need—will be taken in many quarters as an acceptable paradigm, a successful adaptation to the forces and stresses of later
modernity. And our individual (and collective) sense of absence,
of homelessness, of being cut off from something vital will grow
stronger too.

The hucksters and quacks, the spiritual snake-oil salesmen, will
flourish, all claiming to have sighted happiness and fulfillment.
Who will remember the grasshopper on the windowsill, that tense,
aggressive stillness sheathed in nothing but the moment? Who will
know what true attention is and how to bestow it? The fate of reading—indeed, of a great deal more than reading—may hinge on the
answer.

States of Reading

In the opening pages of his coy and crafty novel, *If on a Winter's Night a Traveler,* Italo Calvino performs what for any true reader has to feel like a striptease. Or maybe the beginning overtures of what will turn into a full-out seduction. In any event, there is a sense of excited approach, an almost titillating enumeration of the stages by which a reader gets ready to engage a book. "Adjust the light so you won't strain your eyes," he croons. "Do it now, because once you're absorbed in reading there will be no budging you." And: "Try to foresee now everything that might make you interrupt your reading. Cigarettes within reach, if you smoke, and the ashtray. Anything else? Do you have to pee? All right, you know best."

Calvino continues, building tension now by tracking back to the moments just after the reader's purchase of the book in question. Familiar sensations: "You are at the wheel of your car, waiting at a traffic light, you take the book out of the bag, rip off the transparent wrapping, start reading the first lines. A storm of honking breaks over you. . . ."

Then: "Yes, you are in your room, calm; you open the book to page one, no, to the last page, first you want to see how long it is."

And: "You turn the book over in your hands, you scan the sentences on the back of the jacket. . . . Of course, this circling of the book, too, this reading around it before reading inside it, is part of the pleasure in a new book, but like all preliminary pleasures, it has its optimal duration if you want it to serve as a thrust toward the more substantial pleasure of the consummation of the act, namely, the reading of the book." So Calvino guides his chapter to conclusion, the conclusion being, in effect, the reader's excited haste to turn the page to begin. The paradox is suddenly evident: We are reading about getting ready to read, taking part in the tensions of deferral, even as we breached our own deferral pages ago. All of this is clever and could be shown to be more deeply intriguing, but what interests me is not metafictional self-reflexiveness, but something else: simply that all of this tantalization, this spirited foreplay, is possible only where there exists a shared assumption—that the state we achieve when immersed in a novel is powerful, pleasure-inducing, and very nearly hypnotic. ("Adjust the light . . . ," he coaxes, ". . . because once you're absorbed in reading there will be no budging you.")

As striptease can work its thrills only on the understanding that the forbidden fruit, the corpus delectable, is right there, under the shimmer of coverings, so Calvino can toy with us in this way only because we know what a transformation of consciousness a successful—that is, *immersed*—reading act accomplishes.

Reading—and I will speak of it here in its realized mode—is *not* a continuation of the daily by other means. It is not simply another thing one does, like gathering up the laundry, pondering a recipe, checking the tire pressure, or even talking to a friend on the telephone. Reading is a change of state of a very particular sort. And while this can be talked about, it seldom is. Who knows why?

Several things happen when we move via the first string of words from our quotidian world into the realm of the written. We experience almost immediately a transposition—perhaps an expansion, perhaps a condensation—of our customary perception of reality. We shift our sense of time from our ordinary, sequential, clockface awareness to a quasi-timeless sense of suspension, that sublime forgetting of the grid sometimes called duration. Finally, and no less significantly, we find ourselves instantly and implicitly changing our apprehension of the meaning structure of the world.

I would like to explore this transition by looking at the opening passage of Saul Bellow's novel *Humboldt's Gift:*

The book of ballads published by Von Humboldt Fleisher in the Thirties was an immediate hit. Humboldt was just what everyone had been waiting for. Out in the Midwest I had certainly been waiting eagerly, I can tell you that. An avant-garde writer, the first of a new generation, he was handsome, fair, large, serious, witty, he was learned. They guy had it all. All the papers reviewed his book. His picture appeared in *Time* without insult and in

Newsweek with praise. I read *Harlequin Ballads* enthusiastically. I was a student at the University of Wisconsin and thought about nothing but literature day and night. Humboldt revealed to me new ways of doing things. I was ecstatic. I envied his luck, his talent, and his fame, and I went east in May to have a look at him—perhaps to get next to him. The Greyhound bus, taking the Scranton route, made the trip in about fifty hours. That didn't matter. The bus windows were open. I had never seen real mountains before. Trees were budding. It was like Beethoven's *Pastorale*. I felt showered by the green, within.

Bellow's Charlie Citrine goes on for nearly five hundred pages, but I will stop here—not to make any point about the novel, its characters, or conflicts, but to ask: How is my inwardness, my consciousness, different while I'm reading from whatever it was the instant before I began?

Most obviously, the formerly dissipated field of my awareness has been suddenly and dramatically channeled. My attention is significantly, then almost entirely, captured by the voice and what it is telling me. Charlie's confidential tone immediately captures me, replacing whatever cadences I had been thinking in. "An avant-garde writer, the first of a new generation, he was handsome, fair, large, serious, witty, he was learned. The guy had it all." My thought becomes Citrine's, my rhythms and instincts his—I change.

With the shift in momentum and focus comes an alteration in time frame. All the divisions and chronologies of the daily present are submerged beneath the timeless awareness of events unfolding as they must. Reading even a few of Bellow's sentences, we feel ourselves entering the duration world of the tale, the same world that fireside listeners stepped into when the tribal teller began to summon up the other place of the narrative.

Along with this altered sense of time—bound up with it—comes a condensation of reality. Things are linked each to each through association, not physical or chronological proximity. Months, never mind days, are elided in the space of a breath: "I envied his luck, his talent, and his fame, and I went east in May to have a look at him—perhaps to get next to him. The Greyhound bus, taking the Scranton route . . ." Reality—dull, obstacle-laden reality, which moves all too often at the pace of an intravenous dripper—is reconfigured by the imagination—speeded up, harmonized, made efficient—and served back to us in a far more palatable state, appealing in the extreme.

Finally—and my categories are necessarily imprecise—the words, even in so small an excerpt as I have cited, change what I call the meaning structure of the world. To follow Citrine fully, as we long to do, we agree to the core requirement of any work of creative literature that we put ourselves in the hands of a self, a sensibility, that will front life with an original and uncorrected passion, that we will allow this self to dictate its understanding of the world to us. We must adopt Citrine's worldview as our own for the duration of the novel. This acceptance on our part is, I believe, the most important and profound consequence of the literary encounter.

The meaning structure of the world is, for most of us, experienced as an imprecise and mainly unfocused mingling of thoughts and perceptions. Strands of meaning are as if woven through expanses of seemingly unconnected elements—things observed carefully or obliquely, fitfully attended to or ignored. The upshot, unless we feel a powerful call to something higher and possess the discipline to strive constantly toward it, is that we greet the world outside of our immediate sphere of concern as a chaos essentially beyond our grasp, as an event whose meaning will be disclosed to us later, if ever. The constant deferral of significance is the operative principle of most lives: tomorrow, next week—I'll think about it, I'll figure it out—not right now.

The meaning structure of a novel is absolutely different. Using condensation, moving in an altogether different medium of time, the author creates an artifact that is, in certain striking ways, a semblance of life, but with this exception: *Everything* in the novel points toward *meaning*. Every sentence, every meaning observation, every turn of events serves an aesthetic and intellectual purpose. The novel smelts contingency and returns it as meaning.

We can see this distinction, between the outer world of reality and the inner world of the text, even in the act of reading, the way we read. In one of the most famous passages in his *Confessions*, St. Augustine professes his astonishment at seeing St. Ambrose reading a text without moving his lips. Augustine lived from 354 to 430, and his simple observation suggests something essential about the evolution of reading. It has gone inward. Reading aloud is common practice these days, mainly with children, illiterate adults, or those who cannot, owing to some infirmity, read for themselves. To accompany your reading with silent lip motions is to signal that you may have only the most tenuous grasp on vocabulary and syntax.

This transition from exterior vocalizing to silent but perceptible lip movement to an interiority indicated outwardly only by the back-and-forth shuttling of the eyes signifies a considerable augmentation of the power of the reading act. So long as there are still lip motions, there exists a bridge between the world conjured on the page and the exterior realm. But when those motions cease, then the reader simultaneously represents two opposed kinds of presence. One is the physical, the actual—that which occupies space and can be located; the other is the invisible, the unreal—that which happens vividly in the imagination and cannot be fathomed or legislated by any other person. Silent reading, then, is the very signature—the emblem—of subjectivity. The act of reading creates for us a world within a world—indeed, a world within a hollow sphere, the two of them moving not only at different rates, but also, perhaps, counter to one another.

The tension between outer and inner is sharpened by the fact that when readers are fully absorbed in a book and the ulterior world it presents, their awareness of solid reality is supplanted by awareness of what the imagination is experiencing. Then, truly, the stubborn surfaces we live among become figments—a paradoxical transformation, since most of the people who discredit the practice of reading, particularly of novels, do so because the contents of the books are seen to be not-real, mere figments. These reading skeptics mistakenly assume that reading attempts to carry on the business of living by other—suspiciously intangible—means. They seldom consider that reading involves a change of state, that it is a sudden, and at times overwhelming, modification of the quotidian.

Changes of state. I believe increasingly that this, and mainly this, is the core mission of artistic writing. We go to such writing, engage it, not because it is an adjunct or a supplement to our daily

living, but because it allows us the illusion of departure from it. I
am not talking merely about bored commuters losing themselves
in books by Tom Clancy or John Grisham, but of the somewhat
more exalted pattern of departure and return effected by more
serious novels. A work of art has done its deeper work when it
starts to feel like arrival.

Everyone knows that Plato, in Book 10 of his *Republic,* proposed
to banish the poets from the ideal state he was envisaging. At the
conclusion of his argument he has Socrates say to Glaucon:

> we must remain firm in our conviction that hymns to the gods
> and praises of famous men are the only poetry which ought to
> be admitted into our State. For if you go beyond this and allow
> the honeyed muse to enter, either in epic or lyric verse, not law
> and the reason of mankind, which by common consent have
> ever been deemed best, but pleasure and pain will be the rulers
> in our State.

I would agree, I think, that the poet—the artist-writer—poses a
threat to the state, at least to the state as Plato thinks of it—which
is as a republic, or "res publica," or "thing of the people"—but not
on account of emotional persuasiveness. Rather, the artist is a
threat because the effect of art, no matter what its ostensible subject might be, is to alter the relation to experience, to affect a
change of state—and the main point of the new relation is not to
clarify concrete matters in the here and now, but to propose an
understanding that transcends the here and now. The experience
is fundamentally asocial, for it directs preoccupation away from
the *what* and *how* of daily business toward the *why,* the mere asking
of which marks separation from the quotidian, if not yet transcendence. A social order founded on the question *why,* and the relation to things it implies, would not sustain the headlong
consumerism we think of as the only possible option these days.

No matter how I try to come at it, my conception of the aesthetic experience—the reading experience—involves, at its core,
a transfer between subjectivities; not a simple passing of contents
from one subjective "I" to another. Writers are artists precisely to
the extent that they use the transformative agency of imagination

to surpass personality—the contingent attributes of identity—in order to get at what can be said to exist behind the jumble of appearances: some version of truth that results when the artist has disinterestedly reckoned the forces that underlie psychological, social, or other kinds of relationships.

I realize that the critical orthodoxy of our era repudiates this possibility of underlying universals, upholding instead the relativism, the constructedness, of all experience. Yet the reader's self—dare I say, *soul*—and the fact of his engagement with the literary work refuses this version of things. Whether that reader is immersed in Jane Austen, Joseph Conrad, Jane Smiley, or Saul Bellow, the immersion is attained only in part by stylistic power and the presentation of specific situational elements. The true bond is the reader's conviction that beyond all particulars, standing as the very ground and air of the work, is the writer's willing of a supporting world in its entirety. And this willing, which is at the same time an understanding, is achieved only through a complete and possessive act of imagination. It is finally this ability—and determination—to internalize a world that marks the literary artist. Never mind whether it is the world stretching away behind Samuel Beckett's Molloy, Vladimir Nabokov's Pnin, Austen's Emma, or Bellow's Charlie Citrine.

When we begin reading *Humboldt's Gift,* or almost any other novel, we expend an enormous energy. Only part of this goes toward understanding character, setting, and the details of situation. The rest represents an energy of erasure, of self-silencing. We suspend our sense of the world at large, bracket it off, in order that the author's implicit world may declare itself: "The book of ballads published by Von Humboldt Fleisher in the Thirties was an immediate hit. Humboldt was just what everyone had been waiting for. Out in the Midwest I had certainly been waiting eagerly, I can tell you that." Already it begins. The words make a voice, and the voice begins to sound in our auditory imagination, and as we enter the book we move from hearing the voice to listening to it. And to listen is to surrender self-thoughts, impinging awarenesses, and judgments; to listen is to admit a stance, a vantage, a world other than our own. Of course we do not succeed entirely. Of course the author's world bears a number of features that we project from our own irrepressible sense of things. But the interior transfer is profound nonetheless.

Reading, in this very idealized portrayal, is not simply an inscribing of the author's personal subjectivity upon a reader's receptivity. Rather, it is the collaborative bringing forth of an entire world, a world complete with a meaning structure. For hearing completes itself in listening, and listening happens only where there is some subjective basis for recognition. The work is not merely the bridge between author and reader; it is an enabling entity. The text is a pretext. The writer needs the idea of audition—of readers—in order to begin the creative process that gets him beyond the immediate, daily perception of things. In this one sense, the writer does not bring forth the work so much as the work, the idea of it, brings the writer to imaginative readiness. The finished work, the whole of it, then enables the reader to project a sensible and meaningful order of reality, one that might be initially at odds with the habitual relation to things. Writer and reader make a circuit—complete—outside the entanglements of the social contract.

This account of reading is not the majority view. Nor is it in any way self-evident. I don't know if it ever was, but certainly we have trouble thinking this way now. In our time the artistic experience has been compromised on all fronts. For one thing, there is not the belief in art—in literature especially—that existed in previous epochs. We do not, most of us, trust in the transformative power of artistic vision. And lacking the trust, we not only seek it out less, we are less apt to open ourselves to it when there is a chance.

Then, too, there are fewer strong creations—true works of art that arrive on the page for the right reasons, that have not been deformed by the pressures of the marketplace. One can advance all sorts of reasons for this, including prominently the sheer difficulty of creating a world implicitly coherent when our own is so evidently incoherent. True artists—regardless of their subject or its epoch—are still required to grasp the forms and forces that make the reality of the present.

Third—and there are many other factors—is the climate of distractedness that envelops us. The world is too much here, too complex, is transected by too many competing signals. We don't believe in sense, in explanatory meaning, in the same way we once did. We are losing our purchase on time—not just the serene leisure required for reading, but also our vestigial awareness of that other time—unstructured duration time—that is the sustaining element of all art. For it is only in the durational mode that we can grasp that noncontingent relation to experience, the perception that used to be called "under the aspect of eternity"—the seeing of life in a way that acknowledges as its foundation the mystery of the *fact* of existence.

Then there is the effect that electronic technologies are having on writing and reading. This, while indirect, may be the chief one: that these technologies are, in their capacity as mediating tools, dissolving a sense of time that was until quite recently the human norm. Screen transactions not only make possible a fractured and layered and accelerated relation to time, they *require* it. They train us to a new set of expectations, even as the various complex demands of our living remove us further from the naturally contoured day. Reading of the kind that I have been describing cannot survive in such a climate as we are manufacturing for ourselves. The one hope is that reading will, instead of withering away in the glare of a hundred million screens, establish itself as a kind of preserve, a figurative place where we can go when the self needs to make contact with its sources.

It could be, then, that we are just starting to appreciate the potency that reading possesses. It is an interesting speculation: that the cultural threats to reading may be, paradoxically, revealing to us its deeper saving powers. I use the word *saving* intentionally here, not because I want to ascribe to reading some great function of salvation, but because I want to emphasize one last time the ideas of transformation and change of state. The movement from quotidian consciousness into the consciousness irradiated by artistic vision is analogous to the awakening to spirituality. The reader's aesthetic experience is, necessarily, lowercase, at least when set beside the truly spiritual. But it is marked by similar recognitions, including a changed relation to time, a condensation of the sense of significance, an awareness of a system or structure of meaning, and—most difficult to account for—a feeling of being enfolded by something larger, more profound.

Working through these thoughts, I happened upon an essay called "First Person Singular" by Joseph Epstein, wherein he cites Goethe as saying that "a fact of our existence is of value not insofar as it is true, but insofar as it has something to signify." To this Epstein adds concisely: "Only in art do all facts signify." He communicates in seven short words much of what I have been belaboring here: Facts signify whenever one believes that existence is intended, that there are reasons that, as Pascal wrote, reason knows nothing of.

My depiction of the exalted potential of the text and the no less exalted transformation of the reader by the text draws its main energy from spiritual analogy. But I will end by remarking one way in which the analogy breaks down. In religion there is generally a provision made for the afterlife—that is part of its implicit assurance of purpose, the bait on the hook that would capture the frightened soul. Literature extends no such promise. Quite the reverse. With literature we are always at least subliminally aware of the mocking fact that only the work has a claim to living on, and then most likely through others. Within its borders it achieves the poignant eternity that John Keats accords to one of the figures in his "Ode on a Grecian Urn":

> Fair youth, beneath the trees, thou canst not leave
>   Thy song, nor ever can those trees be bare;
>   Bold Lover, never, never canst thou kiss,
>   Though winning near the goal—yet, do not grieve;
>   She cannot fade, though thou hast not thy bliss,
>   For ever wilt thou love, and she be fair!

This is how it is with literary art: Although it can give us no afterlife, within its realm of departure we are made plain to ourselves in a way that feels strangely lasting.

Against the Current

There was a time when I used to be able to read poetry—read it with a zeal and comprehension that quickened my whole life—and now I can't. It's as if the words make a place that I can't quite reach. I feel this as a personal failure, a source of some shame, and I haven't dared confess it to the three or four poets I count as my friends.

When I say "read" poetry, I mean that deeper, maybe *deepest*, kind of reading where the full resources of language become a vessel to sense; where I, the reader, feel lifted as if by a sudden wave by the intensification of consciousness that the language offers. Of course I keep on turning to poems and books of poetry, hoping to find the connection reestablished. And I do read through poems at a serious level of engagement—the same level, say, that I bring to novels and essays that interest me. But having had, at one point in my life, the authentic, scalp-lifting experience, I am very conscious of the shortfall. I am reaching the words, their meanings, but not enough. I am, to offer an analogy, feeling fondly, but I am not in love.

I bring this forward now, not because I think anyone will, or should, care about how it is between me and poetry, but because I believe my condition is partly determined by a larger play of forces, one that has a broader relevance. That is, I link my distancing from the experience of poetry to something I encounter in other forms everywhere I go these days. To take an instance, one of the staple dinner party topics among literary folk these days is the reading complaint. Someone has only to mention a book for the person at the other end of the table to exhale plangently and say—looking up and down for corroboration all the while—"I don't know, I just can't seem to get any serious reading done these days." Assenting murmurs on all sides. Then the grounds of complaint get aired: too much work, too much stress, kids, who has time to even sit down in a chair never mind *read,* must be getting older, can't concentrate like before . . . This, let me repeat, is the complaint among self-styled literary intellectuals, those for whom reading has always been the defining thing in their lives.

I mind these conversations carefully, always with the sense that something absolutely crucial is at issue. I find subtle ways to pose leading questions and then comb the responses, looking for evidence. What interests me is what I don't hear—not in this context or others. That is, while I note a whole list of reasons offered up by the formerly bookish for why they are not reading, I almost never hear the ones that strike me as the *real* reasons. People always act as if *they* are essentially the same, and books and the reading of books are the same as well, that it is just a matter of interferences, of a set of concrete obstacles, and that when these are overcome all things will revert to their former state.

My intuition—and fear—is that things are in fact otherwise: that changes in the way we live are altering our cognitive structure and moving us away, perhaps irrevocably, from former aptitudes. I have said this before, but it is, if true, important enough to repeat: Our movement—steady and not even gradual—into an electronic environment has brought us to a threshold. On one side, the structures and cognitive orientation of print culture; on the other, those of the impulse.

There is a misconception, widely shared, that because words in printed form and words generated by electronic signals are recognizably the same, there is no deeper difference between the media, that the screen is simply a more dynamic and flexible transmission vehicle. I disagree vehemently, and reiterate, with the same droning insistence used by the phrase's originator back in the 1960s: *The medium is the message.* The how of the communication impinges on the what, not by changing the meaning of the message, but by changing the receiver, affecting not only his information context, but also determining the level at which he will engage the message. This second consideration has a great deal to do with my problem with reading poetry, and I will return to it.

But first, what do I mean by "information context," or what I sometimes think of as our environment of signs? Some backtracking is unavoidable here.

All of our reading—or decoding of signs—can be seen to take place in a semiotic environment, and the nature of that environment determines a good deal—though not everything—about how those signs are registered. Contents aside, the inscribed symbol has a certain specific gravity, a ground of implicit significance against which, or with the aid of which, its encoded meaning is received. When Erasmus of Rotterdam famously bent over to read a printed scrap caught in the mud, print was new in the world, and the simple fact that something was *printed* already signified. It was a short step from that sense of signification—if it is printed, it must be important—to the higher level where a more concrete meaning could be extracted.

By vivid contrast, we live in an environment of signs that is utterly saturated. Where so many signs—words—vie for attention, the mainspring of attention itself is spent. Even contents of unarguable importance are diminished, robbed of their due focal claim, by the fact of superabundance.

This should be intuitively obvious to anyone who looks. Less obvious, maybe, is the fact that what I am calling the semiotic environment has not only become saturated, it has begun to alter its fundamental nature. That environment has—and because we tend to see the word, and not always the means of its transmission, this is elusive—shifted from fixity toward fluidity, from stability toward flux. The shift is a direct consequence of technological transformation—the advent of electronic communications media. Formerly that semiotic environment, however dense or thick it was, was composed entirely of stationary elements. Words on billboards, in books, on the sides of cereal boxes, in newspapers. And from that fact we unconsciously derived certain useful truths about the nature of information and our relation to it. Fixed in place, cumulative, information was an accomplished thing. It was there to be found, arranged, annotated, and stored.

Obviously stationary signs are still everywhere around us. But they are in many quarters being superseded by different, younger signs—signs that behave in a fluid manner, mysteriously. Keystrokes bring them into view from some unknown holding place; other

keystrokes vaporize them back. Information, the very *idea* of information, changes. Information now seems to possess agency, motil-
ity. Words are no longer passive elements to be arranged and
sorted; they no longer just lie there. They are now vital constituents
of a process that we sense exceeds us. They move out from, and
back into, a reservoir that is both invisible and infinite (very much
like the child's conception of God). Everything has been recontextualized. Signs have been given a new relational life; the technology makes them sites of possibility. Each word—almost—can be
seen as itself *and* as a potential link, an integral part of any number
of pattern systems, any of which can be rendered active by the
user's decision.

The whole electronic transformation is still in its early stages,
but already it influences how we read and absorb signs. The stationary look of a printed page signifies differently now that the
printed page is no longer the only—or even the main—way of
transmitting information. The page is now value laden in a way it
was not before. In opposition to the fluid presentation of the
screen, the page can be seen to represent immutability, control, a
presumption of finality, of having the last word; there is also about
it a certain datedness, a rigidity, a quixotic determination to arrest
what is most certainly a movable, mutating thing. The page has not
changed its look, but shifts in the larger culture have determined
that it should strike us differently. We project these valuations, of
course, on the most subtly subliminal levels.

Now let me return to reading—my own and that of others. It is
with this underlying awareness of changing cultural paradigms
that I hear the dinner table complaints about reading. I catch
myself thinking, "Yes, you are busy, with children, and getting
older . . ." but then I wonder if these are not the eternal conditions
of adulthood. Were people ever less busy, less put upon? Probably
not, but formerly readers still read, and on the backs of these several hundred thousand committed souls, the literary culture was
carried forward. Something has changed. We don't *have* a literary
culture in the way we once did. What remnant of it survives is in no
way central to our fissured society; it is simply there as one of the
many elements in the great pluralistic stew. Now there are myriad
entertainments, some with serious pretensions, most not. It has

been suggested, too, by many critics, that the quality of reading materials is itself in decline—that there are fewer worthy books. But no, I believe that if reading still delivered as it used to, if an hour or two with a good book were still the easily attained pleasure it once was, I would not be hearing these complaints. I hear them because reading is less and less able to perform its magic, and this is because a fundamental cognitive reorganization is under way.

But this last possibility is the one thing people will not even consider. I have only to suggest it to draw vehement disagreement. People either do not yet see it happening, or else their investment in the tradition they are leaving is deep and laden with complex emotion. As I travel around and speak about what I see as the implications of electronic communications, I encounter the fiercest resistance when I suggest that the human itself may be in some important ways mutating. People are happy to flatter themselves on their own progressiveness—their openness to innovation—only so long as their bedrock faith in the deeper immutable nature of self is intact. But suggest that our so-called progress may result in a loss of connection to Nature, or diminished individualism, or—God knows—a decline of the humanist tradition we all so gladly pay lip service to, and there comes a sharp, often outraged, recoil.

I put it forward nonetheless. These media, print and electronic, are different at the core. They derive from opposing premises. And one cannot, except by performing the most exhausting internal oscillations, serve both. Not adequately. I do not believe the "glass is half-full" types who tell me—and they do, over and over—how they simply take the best of both worlds, using the computer throughout the day and then shutting off and taking up their leather-bound Dickens in the evening. It's not impossible, of course, to do both. What is impossible is switching effortlessly from one mode to another, for they are in no sense adjacent bandwidths.

My sense is that a great many former readers are having trouble with reading these days because they spend too much time in a very different semiotic environment, and because the particular deceleration required by the printed page gets ever harder to perform. And even when the exterior accommodations have been made—when the subject has silence in the house, a good light, a comfortable chair, and her stimulant of choice—it is exceedingly difficult to enter the language at the depth required.

What do I mean by this? Quite simply that language—let's say, rather, sentences put to the page by a subtle literary sensibility—is not a thing that one either grasps or does not grasp, as one can grasp or *not* grasp a string of numbers. Rather, it is always a matter of becoming attuned to the level of consciousness manifested by the words. It is entirely possible to read a page, follow the meanings, and not have the experience. We know this from our own encounters with prose. The same passage that one day just left us with a deposit of sense is, on another occasion, charged with signification. What makes the difference? Our psychological state, obviously, the nature of our attentiveness or distractedness, and, prominently, our ability to get in under the denotational surface of the words.

And *this* is why my current inability to read poetry as I know it needs to be read is so upsetting to me. I feel a sharp pang of loss, for I remember the sensations of immersion. But more vexing still, for me, are the implications. I take my difficulty with the reading of poetry to be an early warning. It signals to me that I am at risk of going out of alignment with language, my medium; that my meditative center, once very attuned to the deeper layers of words—their intimate rhythmic, sonic, and textural properties—is in some key way disrupted.

This complaint of mine may strike many people as a "tempest in a teapot" sort of business, but it has ramifications that are, when viewed in a more general frame, consequential. The crisis I'm addressing—in my case on the level of language—has to do with attention. I cite poetry, but in fact I am talking about a great many things, and I am not training the spotlight just at myself. We are living in a new condition, one of overload and acceleration. Our lives are crammed with stimuli, and the time available for absorbing and processing new information seems to shrink by the day. We respond to this by moving faster, by doubling up when we can (*multitasking* is a term I suddenly hear everywhere), and editing away things that seem superfluous. We prepare dinner at the same time that we punch in the numbers to collect our accumulated phone messages. Just sitting in the park while our kids play on the swings feels like truancy—we find it harder and harder to pull off.

All of which is to say that changes of this order in our way of living daily life are not without effects. We can't expect to accelerate, piggybacking tasks and trimming away our margins of idleness, without experiencing internal consequences. Many people—and we read about this everywhere—have trouble sleeping. Others take medications to counter anxiety and depression, or exercise compulsively. Or, or—it would be easy to compile quite a long list of the morbid symptoms of late modernity.

The large-scale emergence of sleep difficulties interests me because it affords a ready analogy. I know well the intense frustration that comes when the desire and need for sleep are powerful and yet the mind will not slow itself down. There come the maddening moments when I feel that I'm just on the brink, about to subside, but then the next agitating surge kicks in.

The sensations are, in some ways, quite similar to what I experience when I stare at a poem by, say, Thomas Hardy, and find that while I can with perfect alert competence read the lines, I cannot bring the receiving mind into the condition of attentiveness I need, the condition I once took for granted as a kind of cognitive given. This attentiveness represents not only clarity and intensity of focus, but also a particular kind of calm patience. When I had it, I could not only take the full impression of the word, the phrase, the line, but I would then be able to register the echoes, the aftertones, the nuances that never disclose themselves immediately. Now, far too often, I feel myself balk. I read the line, the stanza, but I cannot, to use the sleep analogy, subside. What could be more frustrating— knowing that a finer order of sensation awaits, but finding oneself unable to pass through the needle's eye?

How do I account for this? I do not use a computer, even for writing; I have no e-mail, and am in no sense of the word "on-line." But this is my point. Whether I sit at a terminal or not is, in some ways, immaterial. As a citizen of my times, I am condemned (yes, and privileged, too) to inhabit the same environment of signs as everyone else, and it is that environment that has not only become saturated, but that has, as I suggested, changed its basic nature. It is to this fact I ascribe my difficulty. I see my problem with engaging the deeper life of words as my own psyche's way of marking the shift from print to electronic paradigms.

I would normally hesitate to make broad generalizations from what are finally private encounters and experiences, but the whole issue seems to me so important that I will take the risk. Basically: I fear that a great many of us—and in numbers ever increasing—are losing the ability to pay attention. I don't mean necessarily to a task, a set of workplace commands, but to life itself—to the slow-moving phenomena of the natural world, to the lowercase encounters that fill up the lives of children and the elderly (our attention specialists), and to the layers and layers of implication alive in great works of art. For just as there is a shiver-inducing intensity available in the full experience of poetry, so we can find the most profound resonances in painting, music, indeed in all of the expressive arts. But we cannot find them—ever—on the fly. Meaning, experiential meaning of the sort that actually gives us something, only yields itself to the right sort of receptivity.

But so what? Isn't it also true that by living at a different rhythm, by taking on more and more stimulus, by doing more, we are testing our potential in other directions? Are there not gains to counteract the loss of what we might think of as the subtler undertones?

I can imagine—have heard—many people arguing that there are, that what we give over from the more meditative side of the spectrum, we gain back in the form of excitement and complexity. After all, the world changes, as it always has, and we must change along with it.

I would respond to this with a great caution: namely, that by turning our backs on the fruits—the proceeds—of that finer attentiveness, we are in fact risking the loss of what is our very claim to uniqueness. That is, to inwardness. Without focus and reflection—which is to say, without a certain relation to time—we cannot sustain that delicate atmosphere compounded of thought, feeling, and perception.

And where this—the stuff of our various arts, the plasma of our culture—is missing, we have to ask how our subjective notions of meaning and purpose can survive. Without a clear awareness of meaning and purpose—I take this as axiomatic—we are lost.

From my private problems with poetry to the grand universal questioning of human purpose—this is quite a stretch. But not an impossible one. Indeed, I would suggest that it is precisely by way of such private disruptions that we often learn about the possible influence of larger societal tendencies on our lives.

Although I am skeptical in many ways of our societal love affair with the computer, I am not blaming that technology entirely for our endangered attention patterns. Electronic information processing has a role to play, of course, but so do many other factors, including economics, education, and the broadcast media. It is the momentum of late modernity itself that is sweeping us forward and renovating our subjective selves. The idea of stopping, or even slowing, the juggernaut is laughable. Which leaves us with the single pressing question: What is to be done?

I cannot speak for others, only for myself. I have lately come to believe that a great deal depends for me on my being able to recover that endangered attentiveness. In fact, the need for clarity—and for poetry, for the deeper sense of self it certifies to me—is so powerful that I find myself making all sorts of sacrifices to gain it back. I am making what I think of as a concerted movement against the current; I am beginning to practice upstreaming. I do things, daily—or whenever I can—to counter the time- and labor-saving strategies that are being sold to me. Taken one by one, the choices seem silly and the impulse crudely contrarian, but I know that taken together they have begun to make a difference. Although it takes me longer, I write most of my letters to people by hand. I like the feel of it. I like the reminder of distance and separateness that the feel of the scratching pen provides. Often, too, instead of driving to the post office to mail them—and never mind that there are a thousand things I could be doing with the time—I take the extra half hour and walk. The to-do list gets longer, but never mind. I get an unexpected purchase on my thinking. I see things by the roadside. The world feels momentarily sorted back to its basic elements.

And reading? I am trying hard to fence out stimuli, to curtail inessential information. I make generous places in the day for slow reading—reading of the sort that lingers, tarries, modifies the heart rate and changes the ions in the air around me. I get less done, but I feel a different kind of strength building in its stead, a strength for rejecting many of the wares that are hawked on all sides; a doggedness. One explanation—I cannot rule it out—may be that I'm picking up the first real crochets of middle age. But I'd rather believe that I'm slowly finding my way back to poetry, that one day I'll lower myself into slow language and reestablish an ancient circuit, the only circuit I finally care about.

With that final little flourish I had believed myself done with my essay on reading against the current. But as things turned out, the idea was not quite done with me. And thus I am compelled to fasten on, like a caboose, this additional bit of autobiographical reflection.

As it happened, just a few days after writing the last pages of that essay, I found myself waking up in a strange motel room—but of course all motel rooms are strange—and feeling the sharp dissociation that occasionally afflicts me after an unsettled sleep in a faraway place. I was sitting on the edge of the bed, waiting for the minuscule coffeemaker to brew my allotted cup, when I suddenly visualized a very specific image: I was looking down into one of those tidal pools that are—if you stare into them—like nothing so much as jewel boxes, with every detail somehow gilded and magnified into hyperclarity, with every stone or mollusk or ribbon of sea grass held in an aura, suspended in visual resonance.

And I thought—dimly—as I pictured this to myself, for who knows what reason—what a shame. That is, what a shame that the elements of this little world cannot retain that particular numinosity as they are fetched up into the air. I suppose I was remembering a time when I lived by the ocean in Maine, a time when I haunted those rock pools and succumbed over and over to the desire to carry some special thing into the light. But then, also suddenly, and in a way that seemed fraught with larger relevance, I thought: The truth of those shells and stones and bits of weed is not in the daylight gaze, it is *there,* under the water. To see that truth—to possess that vision—you simply need to inhabit its element.

Does this make sense? It did to me just then, as I listened to the hissing suck of air at the end of the brewing cycle. I thought: The water is language, and those tantalizing shapes represent the world as art discloses it to us. Dailiness and distraction do not mount an argument against that world, they merely deprive us of it.

From this it was but a short leap of association to a certain memory. It is the mid-1980s and I am—though no poet—auditing Derek Walcott's poetry seminar at Boston University. On this one occasion, Walcott is being what seems to me curiously insistent, making us repeat a single line from Keats: "The hare limp'd trembling through the frozen grass." He speaks the line and figures the rhythm with his fingers gathered into a kind of salute. "The hare limp'd trembling through the frozen grass." And then, yes, I get it. All at once I am not monitoring the sense of the words from without, but I am inside. I feel the rhythm—the perfect hesitation of "limp'd trembling" and the harsh barrier of "frozen grass." The rhythm, word sounds, and sense converge—three vectors finding their apex somewhere in my plexus. Poetry.

And now, back in my motel room, I understand the point of the memory, its import. This, the experience, the real point of the poet's—writer's—art is the very thing that in our haste and distractedness we miss altogether. And if ever there were reason to read against the current it would be this—to catch the grace of things that only attention can reveal.

Reading and Depth of Field

I have the idea that much of what we think of as literary reading involves the animation of an interior space—a kind of supporting world for the narrative elements—and that the logistics of this phenomenon are in some way comparable to the way we create depth of field when we look at a naturalistic painting. The painter creates the effect through very specific techniques, which include placing the vanishing point and setting up a complex balance between forms and colors. The writer, apart from the deployment of actual descriptive elements—pictorial indicators that make a scene in the reader's mind—manages his evocation more subtly, perhaps even less consciously. This supporting world exists in the imagination of the writer, and it comes to exist, however differently, in the mind of the reader. What interests me is the transfer, which takes place right from the threshold, even where the language is not deliberately descriptive or evocative.

In part, I would argue, the process depends not on a meeting of minds or sensibilities, but on a meeting of the wills. At the root of the writer's endeavor is the will to convey an entire interior world to the reader. So, too, the true impulse behind reading is the reader's will to bring another world inside his own. Without this wanting-to-give and wanting-to-receive, both writing and reading acts are inert. Of course, none of this can be measured, and unless one falls into a Heideggerian idiom the process is very difficult to discuss. Still, we need to be aware that the transfer happens—ideally—between two charged poles.

Between the writer and the reader there are only the words on the page. What is striking, if seldom remarked, is the process of the transfer. What essentially happens is that the black marks not only are converted into a sensible narrative—if we are reading a novel, say—they also elicit in the reader the surrounding impression of a world that is strong enough to sustain the narrative line, that gives it credibility.

This transfer, for the sighted reader, takes place by means of the collusion of eye and ear. The sight of the word creates the hearing memory; though we are moving our eyes we are, in a sense, listening, and it is fundamentally as listeners that we furnish that interior space. Indeed, could it be that in reading we recapitulate origins, returning to the orality that predated literacy? If this were so, then one could perhaps locate in the reading act a kind of fundamental friction: between the imperatives of literate prose and the vestiges of oral conditioning that control our primary sense-making operations.

But remember, when we read with the eye we are not actually hearing—the tympanum does not vibrate—we are listening in memory. Which means that it's not the physical ear, but the metaphysical *mind* that is engaged. And maybe this holds a clue about the mysterious sensations reading can sometimes unleash: the fact that body (the ear) and mind are joined by the strand of memory for the duration of the act.

We hear in memory—more and less sharply. The more sharply we hear, the more intense will likely be our reading experience. Or, at least, the more vivid. This sharpness of hearing has to do, in part, with the focus and will that we are able to direct at the words on the page, and in part with the author's ability to reward our attentiveness. The Coleridgean model of a "willing suspension of disbelief" is too simplistic and too passive. Indeed, it figures the primary act of will in reading as a will to be passive, to neutralize oneself before the expression of the author.

I see the receptive will as far more active and creative. For one does not merely absorb—hear—the conscious and unconscious components of the author's work; one instantly sets about bringing to life that interior scape. Reading performs an energetic hearing—a *listening.* This listening begins with the very first words, and the greatest expenditure of conscious and unconscious deciphering energy is directed initially. It takes more to found a world than to sustain it. The most charged moments of any reading act—the most revealing—are the first.

I began by citing an analogy with painterly depth of field. How does a reader, over and above tracking the sense of the narrative, bring into being the world that will enfold that narrative and make it matter? Will, attentive hearing, yes. But these are only of use where there is something they can act on.

My claim is that syntax—and linked to syntax, diction—serves a function comparable to the painter's use of vanishing point and the structural balance of shape and color. Moreover, in reading we heed these unconsciously (liminally) while our conscious sense-making aptitudes contend with the more denotative aspects of the language. Further, it is only when the full reading register is active that we are able to summon both the narrative circumstance and the less tangible context—the supporting world—that allows it to matter. Where the full register is not active—whether because of our own inattentiveness or the author's failure to bring the components of his expression together—the reading experience is at best partial.

Syntax and diction, then, are every bit as important to literary expression—and reception—as the seemingly more salient narrative contents. Reading is, at root, auditory. Syntax is the author's arrangement of auditory elements on the page. The syntax is the structure, the scaffold, the architectural principle itself, and it signifies no less than do the signifying words.

What I'm saying here is not entirely new, but the emphasis perhaps is. So, too, the idea that diction and syntax, absorbed subliminally, are vital to the reader's creation of that supporting world, which sustains the narrative—which *is*, in effect, the interior space in which we locate the narrative—a world that we require even as we seldom give it our focused attention.

A pair of examples might make my point more obvious. The first is a portion of the opening passage of Henry James's *The Portrait of a Lady:*

> Under certain circumstances there are few hours in life more agreeable than the hour dedicated to the ceremony known as afternoon tea. There are circumstances in which, whether you partake of the tea or not—some people of course never do,—the situation is in itself delightful. Those that I have in mind in beginning to unfold this simple history offered an admirable setting to an innocent pastime. The implements of the little feast

had been disposed upon the lawn of an old English country-house, in what I should call the perfect middle of a splendid summer afternoon. Part of the afternoon had waned, but much of it was left, and what was left was of the finest and rarest quality. Real dusk would not arrive for many hours; but the flood of summer light had begun to ebb, the air had grown mellow, the shadows were long upon the smooth, dense turf. They lengthened slowly, however, and the scene expressed that sense of leisure still to come which is perhaps the chief source of one's enjoyment of such a scene at such an hour. From five o'clock to eight is on certain occasions a little eternity; but on such an occasion as this the interval could only be an eternity of pleasure.

How do we begin fashioning an interior world from this? (For I would argue that we do begin from the very first words.) Of what is this passage informing us apart from what it purports to be informing us?

The passage—and the novel—opens on a note of leisurely indirection, not only naming the ceremony proper to a particular class, but doing so by means of a rolling period that, by holding its true subject—"afternoon tea"—for the last, implants in readers their first sense of pace, scale, and the larger consequentiality of ritual. The diction, of course, is that of the educated upper classes, and the delayed gratification enforced by the syntax signals not only authorial playfulness but also the implicit conviction that the readers, themselves unharried, will allow the authorial sensibility to announce itself as it chooses to. That the passage itself is in part about delay—about pleasure being greater in anticipation—imparts a retroactive rightness to this first sentence, making it a kind of structural signal not just for the opening but, it could be asserted, for the whole work. That does not concern us here, however.

The reader will then notice how the syntax and diction, in interplay with the sense of the first two sentences, enact a logic of discrimination. We begin with the first delimitation—"Under certain circumstances . . ." that will be, of course, the circumstances soon unfolded before us—and then, with the following sentence, receive a further refinement: "There are circumstances . . ." The effect is of moving from the general—and for a certain societal echelon "universal"—to the somewhat more specific, for now there

are people implicated—takers and refusers of tea—*and* the circumstance has become a "situation," which is to say it is very nearly
concrete. The third sentence narrows the aperture further—there
are people that the narrator has "in mind"; and the fourth, citing
"the implements of the little feast" and the specific setting of "the
lawn of an old English country-house," nearly lands us in the event.
It is the most tarrying of paces, yet there is strong purpose behind
it. The impression of slow, easeful motion at once informs us of a
"universal" societal order and uses that as the backdrop for the introduction of the various specific elements that will figure so vividly
in the telling. A subliminal sense of balance is established, a part-
to-whole harmony, in which what follows is in accord with the
larger system of assumptions already laid out.

The second part of the passage—now moving from generaliza-
tion to the more concrete business of setting, of place and time
and weather—fulfills a similar discriminatory process. We are
placed in "the perfect middle of a splendid summer afternoon"
and then led, by careful stages, to bring our attention to rest on a
brightly illumined part of the stage—the brightness the more precious for the sense we have, literal and figurative, of encroaching
shadows. The general societal distinctions made in the opening
sentences are reinforced—subliminally amplified—by the concrete correlatives of light, shadows lengthening across the lawn,
and highlighted radiance. Thus, and by his discreet authorial self-
insertions—"Those that I have in mind" and "what I should call
the perfect middle"—James makes coextensive the narrative sensibility and the world it sets forth. The narrative voice—its man-
ners, civilized paraphrases, strategic delays—maps exactly the
rhythms and behavior patterns of the subject society. Our confidence in the concord between how and what allows us to postulate
the terms, the order, of that world before we have even passed
through the first gateway. James has told us next to nothing, but
he has informed us of a great deal.

Now here is the opening paragraph of Ford Madox Ford's *The
Good Soldier:*

This is the saddest story I have ever heard. We had known the
Ashburnhams for nine seasons of the town of Nauheim with an

extreme intimacy—or, rather, with an acquaintanceship as loose and easy and yet as close as a good glove's with your hand. My wife and I knew Captain and Mrs. Ashburnham as well as it was possible to know anybody, and yet, in another sense, we knew nothing at all about them. This is, I believe, a state of things only possible with English people of whom, till today, when I sit down to puzzle out what I know of this sad affair, I knew nothing whatever. Six months ago I had never been to England, and, certainly, I had never sounded the depths of an English heart. I had known the shallows.

Looking at Ford's opening, directing once again the beam of our attention more at the subliminal elements of the passage, we register an impression quite different from that created by James. As in the former passage, a particular and privileged societal segment is set before us, but now the cues combine to configure another order altogether. The subtext of the James passage was, in a sense, the immemorial fixity of the world of the old English country house. James impressed upon us that the people we should soon meet were representative members of a larger set, a class, and that the discriminating observations and asides were the linguistic mode best suited to giving their account. Subtext: reliability and rightness; the world is everything that is the case, provided that the case be this.

Ford, by contrast, brings the narrative "I" into the front foreground and by having that "I" venture certain immediate distinctions—having him struggle to make them—directs us to found a very different supporting world. Where James begins on a note of pleasure, showcasing the tea ceremony as the joyous summit of a pyramid built on order, good sense, and manner—all of this implicit in mode of presentation—Ford invokes a subjective extreme. "This is the saddest story I have ever heard." We credit the sentiment, even as we hold out the possibility that it may be hyperbole. We read on, and with the very next sentence, that suspicion of hyperbole is translated into an impression of unsteadiness and unreliability. (Ford's Dowell is, as you know, the classic unreliable narrator.) This second sentence is a marvel—a calibrated sort of muddle that tells us more than many a long paragraph could about the psychic disposition of our narrator and his underlying

premises about the world he will soon bid us enter. The first half of
that sentence models a forthrightness, a confidence, that is shock-
ingly undone by the qualification of the second half. Not only is
the narrator modifying his assertion, he is committing an act of linguistic near assault. For "an acquaintanceship" is not a simple corrective modification of "an extreme intimacy," it is a category
substitution that not only compromises him in our eyes as a teller
but also rather vividly foretells the deeper struggle of the book. In
saying "extreme intimacy," our man is briefly, and thoughtlessly, assenting to the pretentious usages of his class—the pretension
flagged for us by his restatement—whereas with the dash and the
hurried "or rather" he is, we sense, renewing his vows: to tell, as
honestly as he can, this saddest story. To stay at the diction level of
"extreme intimacy" would be to forsake exposing the truth. And,
of course, *The Good Soldier* derives much of its power and point
from the grating in the narrator's sensibility of appearances and
underlying realities, of pretensions and eruptive passions.

This split is taken up again, spun further into motif, in the next
sentence, where Ford specifies his players and then launches another of his contradictory constructs. "My wife and I knew Captain
and Mrs. Ashburnham as well as it was possible to know anybody,
and yet, in another sense, we knew nothing at all about them." The
effect of this parsing is to establish that the knowing of the first
kind is as nothing—doesn't deserve to be called "knowing"—
whereas the knowing of the second kind, connected to the sadness
of the opening sentence, is everything. The narrator does not
blame himself, however, but blames the English themselves, "of
whom, till today . . . I knew nothing whatever." Then we hear: "Six
months ago I had never been to England." And with this third
time marker—after "nine seasons" and "till today"—we have the
materials for a sketchy timeline, one that established the long history, the probable crisis of six months ago, and the narrator's
readiness, only today, to piece it all out. The diminishing increments contribute to a sense of underlying urgency, an urgency
we absorb together with the vertigo of the various definitional
corrections.

Which is all to say what? It is to say that the world of leisured privilege is summoned up—"nine seasons," "Nauheim," "good glove," and "Captain" are all dots that we connect—but that the narrative "I," grasped through his assertions and the self-canceling syntax of their presentation, creates in us a strong subliminal awareness of the conflict between surface and depth, appearance and reality, and that as a consequence we are denied the kind of entry that James's setup was meant to facilitate. Moreover, the logical construction of this opening, the movement (the reverse of James's) from specific (the Ashburnhams) to general ("the English heart"), makes us question the whole larger order on the basis of a single cited instance. We are only a few sentences into the novel, but already we have our cues. We will furnish a world modeled not on the integrated vista of country house and sunlit lawn. Rather, whatever place we create, whatever semblance of a physical world, a setting, it will not be underwritten or enhanced by the narrative sensibility, but will in fact be countermined by it. A few sentences, but somehow we know that the precedence given in other works to naturalistic illusion will be given instead to the forces that would unmask it.

It would not be hard to multiply examples, and if I had more time I would be especially interested in trying out a further line of interrogation; I will conclude by trying to summarize it here. Namely, as we move into the period of late modernity, a period characterized by cultural fragmentation, by the loss of central societal mythologies; into a culture whose fundamental operations are reconfigured by electronic communications and the proliferation of media images, the novelist experiences a particular crisis. Which is that his diction and syntax—his subliminals—can never figure anything more than a delimited supporting world and a partial set of assumptions. The deep correspondence embodied in James between grading sensibility and graded world—which world was taken to be the whole of the world—and that same world quivering from subterranean pressures in Ford, but still there to be invoked, and still standing for the larger sphere—is no longer possible. The subliminals of the contemporary novelist can now only serve the circumscribed order—or disorder—of the family system, or the reconstructed and reimagined historical account, or the quasi-nostalgic summoning of small-town or rural community. Or else—a very different business altogether—the subjective universe as screened through the confessional first-person narration. In other words, the world, as world, can no longer be served up as inscape—only very limited portions can—and this impossibility is the decisive limitation that the novelist must now and henceforth live with.

Docufiction

In 1917, Marcel Duchamp submitted to the world his *Readymade Fountain,* which, as any student of art history can tell you, was a porcelain urinal mounted on a pedestal. He took an object that was fairly dripping with prosaic—no, low—associations and subjected it to the cleansing context of the aesthetic. His act of framing made the point that the art was not in the thing, but in the *perception* of the thing. Mostly, though, he was tweaking the nose of the bourgeois museumgoer. So coolly skeptical a man would not have believed, surely, that he would revolutionize our way of looking at the world. The tyranny of daily life and daily perception is all but absolute. Everyone knows that. Art remains, at best, a sequestered order we escape to when we can.

Still, Duchamp's gesture has become a point of reference for all serious visual artists who have come along since. And insofar as their work manifests something of his conception, it continues to move through the bloodstream of the culture. Progress in the arts (if indeed it *is* progress and not just change) has always come about as the result of pressures and protests against the constraints of genre.

The novel, too, has been subjected in our age to one attempted renovation after another. Shaping subversions have ranged from stream-of-consciousness narration, which came to stay, to the collage cutup experiments carried out by William Burroughs, which may never be assimilated. Whatever their thrust, though, most of the moves were made with open reference to the reigning norm—they went against it.

Conceptually speaking, it may have been middlebrow novelist Truman Capote who carried out the most threatening assault—a coup d'état from within. In 1965, Capote began to publish installments of his eventual best-seller *In Cold Blood* in the pages of the

New Yorker. The material itself was straight tabloid stuff—an account of the savage slaughter of a Kansas farm family by two ex-convicts. What was different was that Capote set out his documentary sequences much as a novelist would have, staging scenes for dramatic tension, even going so far as to work up a structure of parallel narratives. But the real shocker came when the book was published: Capote had the temerity to bill *In Cold Blood* as a "non-fiction novel."

This may not seem very significant. Who cares, finally, what an infamous party-boy writer decides to call his book? Apparently, though, it was just the signal that a whole army of journalists had been awaiting. Overnight—almost literally, to hear Tom Wolfe tell it—the New Journalism was born. Wolfe, Jimmy Breslin, Gay Talese, Hunter Thompson, George Plimpton, Terry Southern, Joan Didion, and countless others began churning out a prose that felt entirely fresh. Nonfiction writers had fallen in love with the devices of fiction.

Magazine journalism has not been the same since. You cannot find a feature article in the popular press that does not make use of some, if not all, of the techniques that Wolfe enumerated in his canon-making anthology, *The New Journalism* (1973): scene-by-scene construction, realistic dialogue, third-person point of view ("presenting every scene to the reader through the eyes of a particular character"), and the precise recording of "significant" details. A formerly cut-and-dried mode has become a vital, exciting genre.

I am less sanguine, however, about the impact of Capote's framing maneuver on the so-called serious novel. What he instigated, Norman Mailer quickly turned to his own ends. *The Armies of the Night* (1968), Mailer's account of the 1967 march on the Pentagon (and his own prominent participation in it), was subtitled *History as a Novel, the Novel as History.* Then, a decade later, after a number of similar exercises in cross-dressing—*Of a Fire on the Moon* (1970) and *Marilyn* (1973) among them—he brought out his enormous "true-life novel," *The Executioner's Song* (1979), which detailed the criminal career of convicted murderer Gary Gilmore. More than simple nomenclature is at issue—the conflation of genres ultimately threatens the status of both fact and fiction.

Wolfe writes as follows of the docufiction procedure:

It consumes devices that happen to have originated with the novel and mixes them with every other device known to prose. All the while, quite beyond matters of technique, it enjoys an advantage so obvious, so built-in, one almost forgets what a power it has: the simple fact that the reader knows *all this actually happened*. The disclaimers have been erased. The screen is gone. The writer is one step closer to the absolute involvement of the reader that Henry James and James Joyce dreamed of and never achieved.

Wolfe has always enjoyed floating helium-filled assertions toward his readers, but his optimistic burbling here has an almost born-again vapidness about it. Facts are stranger and more involving than invented things, he says, so let's just report the facts and make great literature. Wolfe is essentially ignoring the whole history of Western art. Was it out of sheer blindness—an inability to see the forest for the trees—that man set out to render the world as *other* than what he saw? Hardly. Art (fiction included) came into being precisely because no accounting of the real facts, no matter how expertly done, could ever be enough. Long before Socrates, the perceptive understood that facts were facts, and that truth was what they *meant*. Meaning only begins when the contingent circumstances have been stripped away. And fiction moves in the realm of meaning—it is the afterlife of facts.

The "nonfiction novel" is an oxymoronic phrase and a moronic idea. The etymologist would ban language altogether before allowing it. The word *fiction* comes to us from the Latin: *fingere*, "to feign." A novel, meanwhile, is defined in the Oxford English Dictionary as "a fictitious prose narrative of considerable length." Neither Capote nor Mailer had any trouble with that last stricture—*The Executioner's Song* breaks the thousand-page barrier—but if we trust that words still mean things, then what these authors claim to be offering are nonfictional fictions, or unfeigned feignings.

Just where does the fiction come in? If the events really took place, then the feigning must consist in giving them narrative form, in the excerpting and arranging. But then virtually all written works, histories and biographies in particular, would have to be classed as so many different kinds of novel. What are histories or biographies but judicious orderings of selected bits of information?

The logical extension of this would be to say that *all* human information exchange is selective, and therefore fictional. Doubtless there is a grain of truth here, but it is not enough. Indeed, the moment at which everything becomes provisionally fictive is also the moment when we have to let go of the idea of fact. And without that idea, fiction itself becomes a meaningless concept. When you start thinking like this, you are in grave danger of becoming a deconstructionist. Deconstructionists deem all meaning indeterminate, all discourses suspect, and would like nothing better than to boil all separate disciplines and genres down into one primal soup.

My point is this: Real life has always outdone fiction in inventiveness, in twists of irony and sensationalistic flourishes. And the novelist has always known it. His ancient motto—*primum vivere, deinde scribere*—attests to his willingness to study and learn. In his terrible pride, however, he has invested his art with the prestige of higher truth. Something that *may* have happened but didn't is seen as having superior value, for by not being tethered to factual surface, the writer can attribute consciousness and volition to his creations. He is thereby free to explore the ways in which real-life circumstances might come to have human meaning.

The docu-novelist's claim that "all this actually happened" effectively replaces the imaginative creation of character and situation. Remove the claim and the reader has nothing to feed on. If *In Cold Blood* or *The Executioner's Song* had been *made up*, their artistic impact would have been negligible. By recording sequences of real events and saying "Look, they make a story," Capote and Mailer were not making art so much as they were celebrating an artistic perception. This, I think, is what their use of the word *novel* really signaled. We come back to Duchamp. If he had actually *created* a urinal, he would have been reviled for debasing the artistic function. By calling it readymade—which caused furor enough—he could be received as a conceptual revolutionary.

The showcasing of real-life events in a fictional frame does not, finally, enlarge the genre. Rather, it weakens both the event and the art. For art and life, fiction and fact, stand in an eternal face-off. "We have art," said Nietzsche, "that we may not perish of the truth." The truth he referred to was that of an unanchored, godless existence. But if we think of it differently—truth as deeper meaning—then we can twist his formulation to read: We have truth that we may not perish of the facts. To bring the raw materials of life directly into the sphere of art leaches off something of their obdurate otherness. Bring enough real life into art and you will have real life everywhere you look. Is this what we want? Oscar Wilde, that old artificer, knew what the game was about as early as 1891. He wrote the following in his dialogue *The Decay of Lying:*

> Art begins with abstract decoration with purely imaginative and pleasurable work dealing with what is unreal and non-existent. . . . Then life becomes fascinated with this new wonder and asks to be admitted into the charmed circle. Art takes life as part of her rough material, recreates it, and refashions it in fresh forms, is absolutely indifferent to fact, invents, imagines, dreams, and keeps between herself and reality the impenetrable barrier of beautiful style, of decorative or ideal treatment. The third stage is when Life gets the upper hand, and drives Art out into the wilderness. This is the true decadence, and it is from this that we are now suffering.

"Poetry" and "Politics"

The poetry-politics debate began when Plato booted the poet from his ideal Republic, maybe even sooner; it will go on so long as there is language. For the classicist-formalist temperament will never stop insisting that art is an *order* apart from the world, with laws of its own. And the opposition will forever maintain that *all* human endeavor, art included, is implicitly political. The poet Carolyn Forché has given concise summation of this latter, "romantic" position in her essay "El Salvador: An Aide-Mémoire" (in an anthology titled *Poetry and Politics,* edited by Richard Jones):

> All language . . . is political; vision is always ideologically charged; perceptions are shaped a priori by our assumptions and sensibility is formed by a consciousness at once social, historical and aesthetic. There is no such thing as nonpolitical poetry.

To say that there is "no such thing as nonpolitical poetry," however, is not quite the same as saying that all poetry is political. It is a question of emphasis. And the assertion that all language is political, much as I like the sound of it, is very nearly meaningless. The moment that you make all language political, you strip the designation of its particularizing power. It's like saying that all men are brothers—they're not; they're finally more *not* brothers than brothers. What's more, if all language is political, then some language will necessarily be *more* political, at which point the hierarchy that was thrown out the front door has come back in through the window.

Forché's good friend, the late Terrence Des Pres, hit upon this sad truth in his essay "Poetry and Politics," which was written for a symposium held at Northwestern University in 1984—a convocation grandly called "The Writer in Our World" (the proceedings

136

have been published as a book with that title). Des Pres begins his piece by rehearsing the terrifying facts about our present planetary situation: "If global violence is on the rise and, up ahead at no great distance, we see ourselves mocked and unnerved by the nuclear option . . . then I presume that we turn where we can for sustenance, and that some of us take poetry seriously in exactly this way—as a spiritual resource from which we gather fortitude and nourishment." So far, so good. I doubt whether anyone who values literature—or her own spiritual sanity—would disagree.

But then Des Pres makes a most interesting observation:

> To a degree, to a surprising degree, we turn *elsewhere,* not foremost or finally to poets of our own country, but to poets from abroad and mainly from cultures threatened by imperial takeover. We forgo the pleasures of native voice and endure the indignity of translation in order to come upon an authority seldom apparent among the 4,000 or so poets now publishing or the 50,000 poems-per-year that flood our literary magazines.

Speaking for myself, and for most of the people I know who read poetry seriously, he's right. We do not look to our poets, even the best of them, for clues about how to live in the face of Fear (capital *F:* the fear that makes all else in our well-appointed lives meaningless, that is, for our mad age, the alpha and omega of political reality). When the spirit feels the clutch of that fear, the hand reaches for Czeslaw Milosz, Osip Mandelstam, Paul Celan, Eugenio Montale, Anna Akhmatova, Zbigniew Herbert, Seamus Heaney, Joseph Brodsky.

Why? The reasons are, for the most part, obvious. Indeed, Milosz discussed precisely this poetic authenticity in his Norton Lectures a few years back (published in 1983 by Harvard University Press as *The Witness of Poetry*). Speaking about Polish poetry, but in effect poetry from all oppressed or embattled nations, Milosz proposed that mortal danger restores to the word the potency that heedless usage has stripped away; that under the tightening of the totalitarian screw, language becomes the spirit's last arena of freedom. American readers, I believe, look to this poetry because they sense, even through the veil of translation, that words have been mobilized for their noblest truth-telling ends, and that expression has been won through the ordeals of experience—all too often through extreme suffering.

No question, the difference between kinds of poetry—ours and theirs—is immense. Maybe George Steiner was right when he remarked that what is bad for a nation is good for literature. Still, however much we love literature, we are not about to start wishing hardship upon the citizenry of the free West.

Milosz was primarily interested in accounting for the various ways in which crisis renews poetry. Reading him we can learn some of the reasons why the poetry of the oppressed serves as a resource for the American reader. But it may be just as interesting to look at the situation from the other side. What is it about our culture that inhibits, or even *pro*hibits, the production of sustaining—let's say it: *political*—poetry?

I'm talking now about a *tradition* of political poetry. I will not dispute that we have any number of poets who write with deep political awareness—think of Philip Levine, Adrienne Rich, Allen Ginsberg, Denise Levertov, Forché herself—but somehow, their voices remain culturally marginal; they command authority only for the partisan coterie. Why should this be?

I can think of a number of possible explanations. The first is so obvious that it all but defies precise formulation. Namely, in terms of historical suffering—I mean invasion, bombardment, starvation, deportation, genocide, totalitarian oppression—America is a tyro. Our national experience, Vietnam included, has always been, for the majority of the population, one of action at a distance. We are recent; we lack generational sediment. What historical rhythm we have established does not include the shared memory of disaster, certainly not in this century. We have not been cursed with the calamities that, for better or worse, bind individuals across lines of caste, class, and family. We have known nothing like what the Poles experienced under the Nazi occupation, or the Russians under Stalin, or the Irish under the enduring British yoke. In America, the sufferings of individuals, whether of Vietnam veterans or the socially disinherited (now known as the underclass), have remained just that; and for that reason they have gone largely unrecognized. This is not because we lack the capacity for empathy. It's that we have no *collective* reference for grief, terror, and privation. Private wounds elicit no larger public resonance: The individual's history has nothing in common with the tribal history.

If we are, as a nation, without collective historical awareness, we are also without any possible means for remedying that. A collective sense of *anything* is impossible without a shared public forum, some means through which disparate voices can address, or confront, one another. How else can a people recognize itself as such? But America is just too big, its constituents too widely dispersed. The closest thing we have to a public forum is television. And this is a devastating irony, for television only simulates the sharing of experience. In reality, it alienates and privatizes, drives each of us deeper into a disconnected solitude. Television is monologue posing as dialogue; the participatory illusion ultimately works to atrophy rather than strengthen the human bond.

The media theorist John Maguire has captured the dilemma quite accurately. I quote from his correspondence:

> Dan Rather is in a public space. Everyone is watching him. I say something rude; it has no effect on him *or* on those watching and listening to him. The society is telling me that public space is Dan Rather's . . . and I am excluded. Integrating this message as I grow up, when in public I am tongue-tied, don't have opinions, would never heckle or snicker, and certainly never cheer or clap. Maybe I might roll my eyes if I silently disagreed with something . . . more than that would be overstepping my bounds. What right have I got to make my opinions public? I'm a watcher, not a sayer.
>
> Result: a society in which, when you walk on the street and say something in public, you get no echo, no feedback, no resonance. Those who can still act and speak freely have their skill and confidence undercut when the audience is so awfully, artificially and comfortably silent. Democracy declines, of course, when hardly anyone is willing to speak and when speech is no longer understood as possibly moral action.

The effects of this media creation, this false public space, on all discourse are insidious. Poetry, as the most linguistically concentrated of all arts, suffers especially. For poetry does not just combine the available words from the dictionary into persuasive patterns. No, it uses language; it draws its life from the rhythms and usages of the time—from the speech of the people. Poetry is built up, as Robert Frost long ago pointed out, upon an archive of available sentence sounds. These are the fundamental rhythmic patterns that underlie all of our spoken communication. In a culture where these are various and vigorous—Elizabethan England, for example—poetry is more apt to flourish; certainly it is more likely to engage a readership. The question, then, concerns the relation of the poet's idiom to what Ezra Pound called "the speech of the tribe." What *is* the speech of our tribe? The truth, I fear, is that in our day it is the ubiquitous, homogenized, nonregional prattle that we hear on television. It saturates the available airspace—you cannot avoid it if you try. And how, pray, are poets to draw from *that*? How are they to make a poetry that is as necessary and nourishing as bread, that can speak of real circumstance and of meaningful human response?

The words themselves have not changed—they look and sound much as they always have. The problem is that they *mean* less. Both speaker and listener are removed, abstracted from, the primary conditions in which language is rooted. Our lives are, in a very real sense, mediated. And the more we bathe in the light of the cathode-ray tube, the greater grows the gulf between the word and its referent reality. We can talk *about* things, but we find it extraordinarily difficult to *express* things. The same holds true for politics. We can discuss political matters—and we do so as perhaps never before—but our poetry cannot embody political vision. Such a vision must arise out of the direct, heartfelt recognition that our lot is joined with everyone else's. *That,* and not ideology, is the origin of a living political poetry. That is what our Eastern European brethren are able to provide.

Linguistic authenticity is the very quality that we revere in the work of a poet like Heaney. Although his lines are seldom political in any overt sense, they retain an implicit—I would even say organic—sense of communal connectedness. The language has specific gravity; it is adequate to the felt reality of life in a world of severe natural and social conditions; it is aware of ancestral bonds and local, tribal, responsibilities. Heaney convinces me that these implicit linguistic recognitions can often transmit a more vital political meaning than can more obviously topical kinds of address.

I will make a heretical contention: The most innocuous of Heaney's rural lyrics ultimately offers more political sustenance than the passionately "aware" lines of a poet like Forché. In saying this, I do not mean in any way to undermine the courage and enterprise of Ms. Forché. I simply want to show the extent to which the problem is one of linguistic culture and not poetics.

Here, first, is Heaney's poem "The Peninsula":

> When you have nothing more to say, just drive
> For a day all round the peninsula.
> The sky is tall as over a runway,
> The land without marks so you will not arrive
>
> But pass through, though always skirting landfall.
> At dusk, horizons drink down sea and hill,
> The ploughed field swallows the whitewashed gable
> And you're in the dark again. Now recall
>
> The glazed foreshore and silhouetted log,
> That rock where breakers shredded into rags,
> The leggy birds stilted on their own legs,
> Islands riding themselves out into the fog
>
> And drive back home, still with nothing to say
> Except that now you will uncode all landscapes
> By this: things founded clean on their own shapes,
> Water and ground in their extremity.

Now, the last passage of Forché's "Ourselves or Nothing," a poem dedicated to Des Pres:

> In the mass graves, a woman's hand
> caged in the ribs of her child,
> a single stone in Spain beneath olives,
> in Germany the silent windy fields,
> in the Soviet Union where the snow
> is scarred with wire, in Salvador
> where the blood will never soak

into the ground, everywhere and always
go after that which is lost.
There is a cyclone fence between
ourselves and the slaughter and behind it
we hover in a calm protected world like
netted fish, exactly like netted fish.
It is either the beginning or the end
of the world, and the choice is ourselves
or nothing.

I realize that it's not fair to compare a complete poem with an excerpt. My excuse is that I'm not so much interested in contrasting *poems* as I am in looking at two very different ways of using language.

The Forché passage is very much about global political reality, and it takes the large view. Spain, Germany, the Soviet Union, and El Salvador are all invoked, as are the emblematic images of mother and child, snow, barbed wire, blood and earth. The poem concludes with a strongly stated plea. Forché asks that we admit both complicity and ultimate responsibility. The final lines echo, perhaps intentionally, W. H. Auden's well-known ending to "September 1, 1939": "We must love one another or die."

So many pressing truths about our world have been stated—how is it that I remain as unaffected as I do? My first impulse is to fault myself, my own empathic failure. I am one of Forché's netted fish, hovering "in a calm protected world." I recognize the references, feel the accusatory bite of "mass graves" and blood that will "never soak into the ground." But the fact is, finally, that the language of the poem keeps me out. It is about politics; it does not express or embody the primary humanity that is the origin of all social contract. The phrases have been debased by newscasters. Passionate utterance has come perilously close to rhetoric. Her "silent windy fields" and snow "scarred with wire" engage nothing in me—the words have long since been leached of their referential reality.

In the late-night hour, haunted by anxieties and fears, I would much sooner turn for strength—not solace—to "The Peninsula." While the poem does not address the source of my unease in the way that Forché's does, and though it does not point out the necessary moral response, it manages in its quiet way to bring certain universal human priorities into alignment. "The Peninsula" is about the private struggle for equilibrium, about finding a true relation between an *out there* (in this case the natural world) and an *in here*. When we reach the penultimate line, with its lovely "things founded clean on their own shapes," we register the rare sensation of things converging with the words for things. This is a poem about the poet's mission. And that affirmation, the rightness of its expression, reaches me in a way that the injunction to choose "ourselves or nothing" does not. Heaney's poem reveals to me that we are connected across distances by language. It tears a hole in that netting that Forché has taken such pains to wrap me in. When I compare the two experiences, I feel inclined to reverse her pronouncement that "all language . . . is political," and to assert instead that all politics is language. Politics is, after all, that process whereby we transcend our self-enclosed condition; language is the tool that we have evolved for accomplishing this.

Running Out of Gas

There comes a moment—it is scored in the evolving grain of things—when the balance between a father and son draws up even, holds for an instant, and then begins its slow tipping in the new direction. I'm talking about power here. Not physical power, but proprietary, maybe psychological. That which, however defined, forms the archaic scaffolding of so many male encounters and exchanges.

The curious thing about this subtle but hugely consequential shift is how seldom it is negotiated. Usually it just comes about in the complex course of things. And when it does, the father tends to be the last to know. Denial is operative, sure, but often the son will feel compelled to carry on the pretense. He is loyal, wants to be decent; he is also mindful that one day, it will be his turn.

This whole business—what might be called the succession question—has been on my mind a good deal lately. Not because I'm thinking about my own father (though God knows I am), but because it suddenly no longer seems possible to ignore what is happening with our literary fathers.

How to say this? How to be tactful and properly grateful for everything they have given us—we have scarcely had time to reckon the gift yet—but also how to say what needs saying and preserve one's sense of honor as a reader and critic. I mean—*out with it!*—that our giants, our arts-bemedaled senior male novelists (and this will only deal with males) are not connecting. Not the way they did. Once they seemed to shape the very cultural ectoplasm with the force and daring of their presentations. Their books had, in any publishing season, the status of *events*. Now they don't. They have been writing manifestly second-rate novels in recent years and they are not—much—getting called onto the carpet for it.

I'm talking now about Philip Roth, John Updike, Norman Mailer and, to a degree, Saul Bellow, although one wouldn't need a shoehorn to get a few others onto the list. There have been other changes, granted. The publishing world has been ravaged by corporate greed and has, in recent years, suffered a deep crisis of confidence. But that can't account for the books. The latest novels—*American Pastoral, Toward the End of Time, The Gospel according to the Son,* and *The Actual*—are weak, makeshift, and gravely disappointing to all who believed that these novelists had a special line on the truth(s) of late modernity. Not one of the books can stand in the vicinity of their author's finest work.

Specific failing can, and ought to be, itemized, but not here. Oddly (or not, depending on how jaundiced is your view of the backstage machinations of the literary world), with the exception of Mr. Updike's newest, which has been K.O.'d right at the starting bell, the critical community has been kind to the grandees. All of us, I suppose, carry the burden of our gratitude for past performances. Maybe that's why Mr. Roth could walk his tedious scissors-and-paste job past most of the gatekeepers; why Mr. Mailer took only a few pokes; why no one quite dared suggest that Mr. Bellow's latest novella chewed serenely on not much cud.

But when this body of recent work is viewed alongside the writing of the younger brothers—Thomas Pynchon, Don DeLillo, Robert Stone, and John Edgar Wideman, to name several—the contrast is striking. These authors seem to be looking at the larger world, assessing the twin claims of politics and spirit. We feel in their books, certainly in *Mason & Dixon* and *Underworld,* some of the pressure of seriousness that we were once so sparked by in their elders. But these elders are no longer spinning the stuff of our times into lasting art. The once-thrilling researches into the self have proved exhaustible. No less important, they are not holding themselves to the literary standards they did so much to establish.

The generational perspective is, I realize, slightly misleading. Mr. Bellow (b. 1915) and Mr. Mailer (b. 1923) broke into print in the mid- and late-1940s, while Mr. Updike (b. 1932) and Mr. Roth (b. 1933) arrived in the late 1950s. They do share one big thing: They were all together on the great ride. They were there when fiction mattered, and fiction mattered, in part, because they were there. They drove, all four, like high-finned gas-guzzlers across the unfurling decades. They siphoned the postwar life boom right into their novels. Think of the exuberance, the forward pitch of early Mailer, the *spritz* of Bellow circa *The Adventures of Augie March* and *Herzog;* think of Mr. Roth's flaming portraits of renegade Jews and Mr. Updike's entitled suburban sinners.

On they rode—and for so long. Through the convulsions of the late '60s, shedding wives like inhibitions, trying to unscramble generational war and write the new codes of liberated sexuality. Indeed, much of their writing was about sex, eros standing as a kind of shorthand for unhampered living. There was very great wanting in all those early books. The writers were drawing their material up out of themselves by the bucketful. The novels were an elevated and electric sort of navel gazing, but that was what the period was about. We can't think back on that liberation period without thinking of them.

They continued—solid in the '70s, ensconced in the '80s. And still they fed on the reservoirs of self. Messrs. Updike, Roth, and Bellow all depended on proxy narrators, men of their own age and time period weathering social upheaval and experiencing the agony of the gender wars. Henderson, Herzog, Portnoy, Piet Hanema, Harry Angstrom . . . Only Mr. Mailer strayed a bit, turned to documentary, Egyptology and quasi-biographical impersonations. But what astonishing engines under those hoods! Consider that Mr. Bellow has been publishing books since 1944. Mr. Roth, the youngest of the bunch, has been at it for nearly forty years.

These writers have each had, in other words, at least two score years to be rendering the drama of their lives and times—first as precocious boy wonders, then as triumphant alpha males, makers of our postwar literature, and then—now—as senior eminences. They own a Nobel and more Pulitzers than you could fit into a henhouse. Is it any mystery that these novelists might along the way have begun to believe themselves the elect, the infallibles?

I'm talking about narcissism now, the male variety, with its attendant exalted belief that one is in some way coterminous with the world, steering it with will and desire. The pathology that, in one version at least, needs over and over to gain the admiring (as in *ad mirare:* "to reflect back") love of women, that struts pridefully forth holding sexuality—the penis—aloft as its talisman.

But the story does not end here with the male eternally rampant. Youth declines into maturity, maturity sinks toward dreaded old age. The lion paces a weary circle and lies down. No one would reasonably expect the artist to carry on in his former style. Opportunities for quiet recusal, for edging from the race, abound. But—Mr. Bellow excepted—these writers have kept on drilling out roughly a book a year—each, for as long as anyone can remember, holding the spotlight on himself by main force. Surely they are no longer striving to keep the wolf from the door. What gives?

We are back to the question of narcissism—to the monomaniacal absorption with self fostered at every turn by a media culture. Narcissism, it would appear, does not slacken with the years, it only grows. Only there is a problem. The very thing that made these artists avatars of the self-seeking liberation culture is now their unmaking. Not because we, as a culture, have ceased to focus on ourselves, but because they, as writers, have fallen victim to the law of diminishing returns. The self, however grandiose, is finite; the wells do dry up.

There's more. The narcissist is no more immune to time—to aging and death—than anyone else. As my wife, my therapist, formulates it for me, "Aging is a narcissistic injury." When the narcissist faces the loss of the self and its reflected glory, he reacts with rage. And indeed, checking in on some of the works of later years by our masters, we are overwhelmed by dissonant music from the downside of the artists: Mr. Bellow's Dean Corde in *The Dean's December* snarling at the underclass; the cataracting vituperations of Mickey Sabbath in *Sabbath's Theater*; Ben Turnbull in *Toward the End of Time* venting himself in every direction. We see anger at promises not kept, at prerogatives usurped, and deep bitterness about an America that has betrayed its youthful innocent promise. But also, with scorching vindictiveness at times—especially in Messrs. Updike and Roth—comes the lashing out at women. Women, the supposed adoring ones, whose job it was to keep the illusion of perpetual youth and power intact. Dare we tie this, as Mr. Updike seems to in his new book, to the failure in age of the sexual fix? Could the whole business really have been driven by the say-so of an upstanding phallus? A frightening thought.

Everything I've ventured here is rash and general, but I fear that if I split too many hairs, the big point will get qualified away. The fact is that for whatever host of reasons—cultural, personal/ psychological—our great seers are not seeing so well, nor crafting as intently as they once did. To be sure, literature is not a big-tent act anymore, not the way it was more than twenty years ago, but this is more reason, not less, for trying to honor the art. The struggle is to stem the tide, to create again a serious public through prodigious exertions of imagination and skill. And thinking now of Mr. DeLillo, Mr. Pynchon, and others, to turn the gaze of the reader back on the larger world.

What frustrates and saddens more than anything is the relinquishing of care. The books flow forth yearly, whether they need to or not. There is a sense of haste, of slackness, of the draft deemed sufficient; hanging over everything we sniff out the cordite whiff of arrogance. Is it that the times no longer propose faith in a recognizable posterity? Is the arrogance in fact despair? This is hard to answer. What is clear is that each of these recent books lacks that core impersonality, that transpersonal sense of necessity, that will to deeper meaning without which any effort must be judged ephemeral.

Ephemeral work ultimately holds the idea of art in contempt. Cynical, desperate, it furthers the erosion of the larger continuity. The challenge is there for the younger talents: to write in such a way, at such a level, that our much decorated masters get the idea and either bestir themselves or gracefully yield to the sons.

Second Thoughts

A few years ago I wrote a series of essays in which I proclaimed that the enterprise of fiction was in a state of serious crisis—a state that had a number of causes but that was most obviously connected to our sudden submergence under the fast-breaking wave of electronic technologies. I premised these saturnine essays on a fairly basic assumption, one to which I still subscribe, namely, that the health of the novel ultimately depends on its ability to mirror and explore the culture of the present, and that if novelists find themselves unequal to the task of taking our mutating circumstances as subject matter, the genre will forfeit its deeper authority. I cited the inordinate difficulty of presenting our mediated experience in dramatic ways and listed what I saw as some of the strategies writers used to evade the challenge at hand. These included writing about the narrowly domestic; using conveniently unmediated small-town settings; and turning to the past, either historical or familial. Needless to say, my views did not please everyone. More than one novelist took me to task, some for the narrowness of my premise, others for what they perceived as my scorn for the subsidiary options.

I still hold to my core notion—that if the novel cannot digest the stuff of the present it will, in time, doom itself to irrelevance and lose whatever prophetic vitality it may yet possess as its modernist inheritance. But as I have continued to think about the coming of the electronic millennium—and continued to read novels of all descriptions—I have come to see that I need to make certain adjustments to my theory. To put it most simply: I had not fully thought through all of the implications of the cultural changes that are upon us. I had not thought enough about how these changes impinge on our experience of time and history, and, in consequence, create a whole new category of need—one the novel is wonderfully suited to meet.

So, without changing my original premise, I would add a second: that the time of the novel, the phenomenological interior that necessarily reorganizes the reader's perceptions, may just be the ideal antidote for the time sickness that we are all, most of us unwittingly, beginning to experience. That the novel is not only a lens upon the present but also can serve to counteract some of the most pernicious tendencies of that present.

Postmodern time is, as we all know, fragmented, composed of competing simultaneities. Our daily operations pull us ineluctably away from the deep durational time experience that is, or was, our birthright. The novel, through language, through the complex decelerating system of syntax, pushes us against the momentum of distraction. It is restorative—and difficult. Indeed, it is often restorative precisely to the degree that it is difficult, especially as the difficulties of reading generally have as much to do with the reader's failures of attention as they do with the text on the page. One does not dive from CNN or *Masterpiece Theatre* into the deep brine of prose easily. All of the cognitive rhythms have to be slowed to andante.

I would argue, then, that the contemporary novelist who is not in any way addressing the changed reality of the present may yet be serving an important function. *For the reader,* that is—not necessarily for the genre itself. A crucial distinction. Through his deployment of the language, through giving expression to his vision, the writer may be creating a self-contained alternate order—a place where the ambitious reader can go to counter the centrifuge of late modernity, where he can, at least for a time, possess the aesthetic illusion of focus and sustain a single-minded immersion in circumstance no longer so generally available. That this is vicarious does not undermine its validity: It is a mode of surrogate living that most closely approximates what living felt like before technologies began to divide us from ourselves.

Any good novel, then (I won't quibble here about what constitutes "good"), can afford its reader a way of being—if not being *there,* in the other world, then being *here,* in this. It proposes a locus of reclamation, becomes a place inside the place we are situated, a charged time contained within the more diffuse time of daily living. And while this is not exactly a revolutionary function for the embattled genre, it will become increasingly important as the equation of existence grows complex beyond all calculation.

But this is general. The notion first came to me in far more specific terms, the product of one of those happy convergences that signals to me that I need to pay attention. One vector was my recent rereading of Richard Powers's novel *Prisoner's Dilemma* for a course I was teaching. The other was my near simultaneous encounter with Bradford Morrow's *Trinity Fields,* a novel I grabbed to read for pleasure during a family vacation. Here, I found, were two very different works that nonetheless shared something kindred at the core. *Prisoner's Dilemma* tells the story of Edward Hobson, a brilliant and idealistic man who succumbs to a strange illness and with the help of his wife and grown children creates a highly elastic web of denial around himself. Only the intensification of the illness itself can rupture the complicity of the family members. At this point, getting to the root of the problem means diagnosing the life of the man himself, a process that soon enough means taking an exacting look at the larger movements of history in his life. Private circumstance is seen to be ultimately inextricable from the envelope of societal circumstance. All things are, in the manner of Chaos science, linked. And in this case the trail leads finally back to Alamogordo, New Mexico, the desert site of the A-bomb test. Everything that has happened to Edward Hobson and his family can be seen as part of the concentric system of effects originated at ground zero.

Morrow's *Trinity Fields,* by contrast, tells the decades-long story of two friends. Brice McCarthy and Kip Calder are both sons of research physicists working at Los Alamos. Born on the same day in 1944, they come of age in the 1950s and then again through the turmoils of the sixties. Both are shaped in complex and destructive ways by their deepening awareness of what their fathers—and their government—were responsible for. And, as in *Prisoner's Dilemma,* the consequences of a specific historical moment (the Trinity blast figured in the title) are played out over an extended period in what becomes a searching inquiry into the mechanism of moral consciousness.

The two novels were present in my thoughts, were already nearing some sort of catalysis, when I chanced to read the opening chapter of Harold Bloom's *The Western Canon* and encountered this assertion:

> The historical novel seems to have been permanently devalued. Gore Vidal once said to me, with bitter eloquence, that his outspoken sexual orientation had denied him canonical status. What seems likelier is that Vidal's best fictions . . . are distinguished historical novels—*Lincoln, Burr,* and several more—and this subgenre is no longer available for canonization.

Here were the words to set off sparks in the contrarian's heart. Although I had, before, likewise relegated the historical novel to the cultural seconds bin—viewing it essentially as a detour around the subject-matter crisis—now, in the wake of my reading of Powers and Morrow, I thought I understood a new possibility for the novel. As a result, I have had to revise my somewhat dogmatic premise of what it is that a novel can, and ought to, do.

Formerly I insisted that the true life—the raison d'être—of the genre lay in its comprehension and dramatization of our historical moment, our present. The novel was to be a kind of petri dish in which the novelist would explore the ever-changing terms of "how it is." This was the sovereign artistic task. The emphasis was placed squarely on the *now,* and all other initiatives were necessarily secondary.

I was, I admit, too stringent. My analysis of the novelist's function did not fully accord with my analysis of the new reality, the electronic millennium. I mean: Our mediated lives, our frenzied rush to get on-line, to build a web of impulses around ourselves, have not only led to a loss of subjective deep time but have also severed us from any comprehensive narrative of history—our own, but that of preceding epochs as well. We have stepped into the postmodern swirl of dissociated images and decontextualized data. We are overwhelmed with impressions and bits and are ever more at a loss to integrate the jumble we harvest into any coherent picture. If this is so—and I write this in the days right after the Oklahoma City bomb blast, in the midst of the cataract of clips and chunks of horrifying data—then we are in dire need not only of works that reflect our present situation to us but also of works that process the things we may not have had the time or focus or will to deal with; works that serve as a kind of fertile unconscious out of which can be distilled the patterns and meanings we cannot live without. We need the novel, then, not only as a windshield through which to face what is in front of us but also as a rearview mirror that allows us to see where we have been. We need the form of the novel—the wrought artifact—because it makes available the kind of time essential for processing impressions and emotions. And we need specific works of historical imagination through which we can repossess what the exigencies of living in a high-speed information age are denying us. Seen in this way, the novel is a kind of slow-motion replay of materials that we have not been able to absorb properly. Unlike television sports, though, history comes into being only in retrospect. An event is not history—the etymological root of the word is *storia,* meaning "story" or "tale"—until it enters narrative. The narratives supplied to us by CNN and the daily press, premised on sensation and the kind of focus that magnifies and decontextualizes, are not vehicle enough. Nor can film, ideal though it is for visual simulation, offer the time immersion required. Nor can histories of the standard sort enlist the empathic imagination essential for true narrative engagement. It falls to the novel. And as we hasten away from centers and certainties, as the brave new world wraps us up in its oscillating energy field, the sense-making powers of the novel are one of our most valuable resources. If only we can buck the momentum of the present enough to recognize this, and then buck it further to act on our recognition.

This Year's Canon

Postmodernism: The designation carries the subtle curse of its own nomenclature. Logically sequent to modernism, it suddenly seems dated, exuding the "period" quality of Norman Bel Geddes's Art Deco, even as modernism feels neutrally permanent under the plexishield of received opinion. What gives? My guess is that postmodernism is a casualty of the very forces it sought to define, forces disruptive of stability and historical continuity. In the riotous cultural swarm of styles and references, it is not to be expected that any label will stick hard. Modernism, meanwhile, glares quietly from the shadows, like the varnished portrait of the family patriarch—who was, let us add, a bit of a rake in his younger years.

So what was—and flickeringly *is*—postmodernism? Hard as it is to define, we do believe that we know it when we see it. Postmodernism is the cultural style of globalism. Pluralistic, hybrid, suspicious—no, subversive—of comprehensive explanatory narratives, postmodernism adopts the stance of irony. It is mental, neural, cool, prefers sampling to soul, quotation to invention. It collapses the fiction of the historical time line and celebrates the contemporaneity of all styles—L.A., not new York, is its Mecca. Postmodernism enshrines the fragment, adores the gap and the synapse. Anti-authoritarian, it looks to enlist the watcher, the listener, the reader in the business of making meanings.

I could go on, but perhaps the interested reader is better referred to the discursive introduction to the new Norton anthology, *Postmodern American Fiction,* edited by Paula Geyh, Fred C. Leebron, and Andrew Levy. Or else to one of several opposing-term lists (themselves such postmodern entities) found in the casebook at the end of the volume. Culling almost at random from the theorist Ihab Hassan's comprehensive list, I offer:

MODERNISM	POSTMODERNISM
Form (conjunctive, closed)	Antiform (disjunctive, open)
Purpose	Play
Design	Chance
Hierarchy	Anarchy
Distance	Participation
Presence	Absence
Selection	Combination
Genital/Phallic	Polymorphous/Androgynous
Paranoia	Schizophrenia
Metaphysics	Irony
Determinacy	Indeterminacy
Transcendence	Immanence

Here is, so far as literary fiction is concerned, the first large-scale attempt to draw some boundary markers around this most protean cultural extrusion. Geyh and her colleagues do as good a job as is possible with what they surely recognize to be an implicitly paradoxical enterprise—suggesting a literary genealogy and a canon *of sorts* for a mode that essentially repudiates ideas of priority and centrality. They manage their task by sketching rather than inscribing links, and by holding open categories, conveying throughout that these are instances and examples, not definitive assertions. The volume thus subtly resists the canon-fixing mission of the other Norton anthologies and makes itself useful as a thoughtfully edited sampler.

The editors have divided the volume into various sections, the titles of which tell us a good deal about the complexion of literary postmodernism. After "Breaking the Frame," which features antecedent figures like Thomas Pynchon, Donald Barthelme, Ishmael Reed, and Grace Paley, we find "Fact Meets Fiction," celebrating the marriage of documentary and inventive impulses; "Revisiting History," which samples the rewriting of received historical perspectives by writers like Toni Morrison (in *Beloved*), Leslie Marmon Silko (in *Ceremony*), and David Foster Wallace (in "Lyndon"); "Revising Tradition," with works that seek to subvert formerly sacrosanct textual boundaries; and "Techno-culture," which ranges widely, from Don DeLillo (excerpts from *White Noise*)

to J. Yellowlees Douglas, to find writers who have allowed information technology to influence the content and presentation of
their writing. "A Casebook of Postmodern Theory" rounds out the
compendium, with a heady and heteroclite mix of documents,
everything from sections of Donna Haraway's "A Cyborg Manifesto" to Jean Baudrillard (from "The Precession of Simulacra") to
an extract from Fredric Jameson's "Postmodernism and Consumer Society."

Reading these last polemics and reflections, we realize how
readily postmodernism bears out the very diverse theories of aes-
theticians, philosophers, digital utopians, literary theorists, and
leftist thinkers, to name but a few interested parties. One might almost hazard that *anything* is now postmodern, so long as it does
not strive in obvious ways toward wholeness or formal order, and
provided that it rejects the meaning system that governed literary
art for so long. Of course the root question is irresistible: Were
these various pieces selected because they met a certain standard
of quality? If so (and how not?), then what are some of the criteria
invoked? Are there better and worse ways of being anarchic, participatory, combinatory, indeterminate, antiform, etc.? I suspect
that there are, but I would love to hear just how such valuations
are arrived at and justified.

The work of wunderkind David Foster Wallace gives us a way of
questioning the underlying ethos of literary "po-mo." Not only is
Wallace claimed by the editors as one of their own, but his short
story "Lyndon," plunked right in the center of the anthology,
looks to be its longest included work. But Wallace is also known as
the gadfly author of "E Unibus Plurum: Television and U.S. Fiction," an influential essay that ultimately tilts against the ironic
mode and ventures that the "next real literary 'rebels' in this
country might well emerge as some weird bunch of *anti*-rebels,
born oglers who dare somehow to back away from ironic watching, who have the childish gall actually to endorse and instantiate
single-entendre principles." In other words, the next desirable
step for writers might be to puncture the prophylactic of irony, to
find a way to present contemporary content in a straight-on manner, one free of the wised-up intonation we automatically adopt
whenever we inscribe quotation marks in the air with our fingers.

Seriousness is the issue. Riffling the pages of this chunky compilation, dipping in again and again just to make sure that I'm not twisting evidence for my own purposes, I verify a single rather overwhelming reaction: There is almost nothing between these covers that feels grown-up or—how to say it?—existentially useful. Almost every text here is shaped—I would say *warped*—by the ironist's inflection, or the "watch me" affectations of the would-be form breaker. Here is a fairly random sampling of some opening lines:

"Folks. This here is the story of the Loop Garoo Kid."
Ishmael Reed

"A woman, x, and a man, y, plan to meet at the prearranged co-ordinate, z, a fountain on the Place Anthony Mars in the south of France, on some late afternoon in summer at the end of the twentieth century."
Carol Maso

" 'We are doomed, Professor! The planet is rushing madly toward earth and no human power can stop it!' "
Robert Coover

"I've been commissioned by *Der Gummiknüppel* ('The German equivalent of *Martha Stewart Living* but with more nudity and grisly crime') to compose a poem for their ten-year anniversary issue."
Mark Leyner

" 'My name is Lyndon Baines Johnson. I own the fucking floor you stand on, boy.' "
David Foster Wallace

"The Deliverator belongs to an elite order, a hallowed sub-category."
Neal Stephenson

I could go on, but the point is made. Of course there are exceptions, but I'm not interested in hard percentages, only in the impressionistic assertion that there is much eccentric posing here. Much eye-catching prose, to be sure, but one would have to be of charitable heart to call more than a few selections in the book suitable reading for a thoughtful adult. I realize that it is not the point of postmodern literature to be E. M. Forster, Thomas Mann, F. Scott Fitzgerald, Willa Cather, Eudora Welty, what have you. But coached by years of reading the moderns to certain expectations, the shortfall of meaning is striking—I cannot see around it, quite.

Postmodernism carried out a revolution of sorts, an undermining of the sincerity of address that had underlain most art—even comic art—from the time of origins. The banishing of sincerity— carried out as an attack on hierarchy and the presumptions of high art—felt a little bit like the longed for overthrow of parental rule. There was permission, the sweet suspension of stricture—no more Sunday school!—and a sense of lightness that could only be good. But the pleasures of such liberation do not finally cancel out our vestigial need for purposeful connection. And now, faced wherever we turn with the effluvia of consumer culture and the undifferentiated rhetoric of media presentation, many of us experience a longing for some definition and contour: for substance. But substance—and here is the sad lesson of postmodernism—requires context. Requires, that is, an assumption of complex and ongoing history. Do away with context and you have only the perpetual-motion machine of fashion; you have manner, a postmodern shine that feels new, like a bright plastic toy just out of the box—until the charge of novelty is abruptly spent and our credulity feels cruelly mocked. Alongside this lightness, this ephemerality and disenchantment, modernism still looks vital.

Am I suggesting we go back? Of course not. But I am suggesting that postmodern style—its pluralities and easy ironies—no longer feels productive or even particularly liberating. The way forward— and *forward* is a modernist assumption—will require rediscovering certain understandings we may have believed we had outgrown or otherwise dispensed with. We will be walking backward into the future, and it will take some time getting used to.

III

When Lightning Strikes

It was 1952. I was 44, and I thought I was done. I was living alone in a biggish house in Edmonds, Washington. I had been reading—and re-reading—not Yeats, but Raleigh and Sir John Davies. I had been teaching the five-beat line for weeks—I knew quite a bit about it, but write it myself?—no: so I felt myself a fraud.

Suddenly, in the early evening, the poem "The Dance" started, and finished itself in a very short time—say thirty minutes, maybe in the greater part of an hour, it was all done. I felt, I knew, I had hit it. I walked around, and I wept; and I knelt down—I always do after I've written what I know is a good piece. But at the same time I had, as God is my witness, the actual sense of a Presence—as if Yeats himself were in that room. The experience was in a way terrifying, for it lasted at least half an hour. That house, I repeat, was charged with a psychic presence: the very walls seemed to shimmer. I wept for joy.

Theodore Roethke

He [the poet] is going to all that trouble, not in order to communicate with anyone, but to gain relief from acute discomfort. And when the words are arranged in the right way . . . he may experience a moment of exhaustion, of appeasement, of absolution, and of something very near annihilation which is in itself indescribable.

T. S. Eliot

. . . there is a certain domineering note, or tune, that is going through one's mind. It's a very strange thing. I say tune; I can just as well say noise. In either case, whatever it is, it's not just exactly a tune, a musical hum. For this hum has a certain psychological overlay. It's an extremely grey area . . . It's a certain frequency, so to speak, in which you operate and which, at times, you change.

Joseph Brodsky

For all of the differences in the kinds of poetry that are written, and for all the temperamental diversity among its practitioners, there is one point on which nearly everyone agrees: A poem cannot be thought or willed onto the page. Paul Valéry posed the question in *The Art of Poetry:* "Is it impossible, given time, care, skill, and desire, to proceed in an orderly way to arrive at poetry?" The answer from the chorus of poets is: Yes, impossible.

This does not mean that poetry can be produced without these elements, just that they do not suffice. In combination they may yield a readable verse, a neat line, some artifact of the kind that proliferates as never before in magazines and collections—but they will not yield poetry. Whatever else we may say about it, poetry has its origin in the unknown. At least some small part of any true poem must come to the poet as a gift, an unpremeditated spark from outside the circle of volition. This may be a word, a line, a scrap of rhythm. Slight it may be, but like the extended finger in Michelangelo's great fresco, it brings to life what would otherwise remain inert.

If poetry could be produced through a simple collaboration of skill and good wishes, we would long since have been inundated with the stuff. Or would we? Possibly much of the prestige that has always attracted people to the vocation derives from its mysteriousness, from the fact that, like love, it cannot be planned, controlled, or legislated. If one could make a poem the way one makes a rug or a table, would so many people burn in their secret selves to be poets? It's unlikely. They burn to be poets (or artists of some stamp) because they sense that creativity represents an inward power.

All poetry originates in a gift, but the circumstance, magnitude, and intensity of the experience will vary from poet to poet and from case to case. We may think of Rilke pacing the battlements of the Schloss Duino, quivering like a lightning rod when the first lines of the *Elegies* were dictated, as if from the turbulent sky overhead. But we must not forget the Rilke of the earlier "thing poems," working with the patience of an Old World artisan at the task of seeing. Creative inspiration is rarely scripted by David Lean—the mad-eyed Zhivago scribbling in front of a dripping taper is a figment of popular fancy. We would be more likely to encounter a demure creature sitting by an electric desk lamp or, these days, tinkering with the words arrayed on an illuminated screen. But this does not diminish the mystery, which still must exist, whatever the packaging. The difference between Rilke's ecstasy at Duino and another poet's thrill at the unexpected arrival of a line is quantitative, not qualitative.

Before we investigate the process of poetic creativity, we must clearly separate its two aspects. However merged they may at times feel to the poet, the volitional, conscious activity is very different from that which eludes the will. The Irish poet Seamus Heaney has given one sort of explication:

> Frost put it this way: "A poem begins as a lump in the throat, a homesickness, a lovesickness. It finds the thought and the thought finds the words." As far as I'm concerned, technique is more vitally connected with that first activity where the "lump in the throat" finds "the thought" than with "the thought" finding "the words." The first epiphany involves the divining, vatic, oracular function; the second, the making, crafting function.

Heaney's distinction is also acknowledged in the Greek and Latin etymologies of the word *poet*. In Athens, poet meant "maker"; the Romans called him *vates:* "oracle."

The world of the ancients, though geographically smaller than ours, was not only felt to be vaster, but was everywhere shadowed and deepened by a sense of the terrestrial unknown. World conceptions were neither as materialist nor as functionalist as those we proclaim. The ancients believed, among other things, that the Muse was the source of poetry. Homer's "Sing, goddess" and "Tell me, Muse" were literal petitions, not formulaic niceties. Inspiration was the taking-into-oneself of an outer-dwelling spirit—the word roots clearly show this—which the poet could try to assist through an act of "in-vocation" or calling in. If the poet was blessed with any talent, it was for being a medium, a hospitable receptor. As Plato tells us in the *Ion:*

> The poet is a light and winged and holy thing, and there is no invention in him until he has been inspired and is out of his senses, and the mind is no longer in him: when he is not in this state, he is powerless and unable to utter his oracles.

Once again we encounter the idea of the oracle. At first glance, these words do not square with the Greek designation of poet as maker, but the contradiction is only terminological. The implication of Plato's description is that the poet does not invent out of himself, but that he constructs with building materials obtained elsewhere.

Some variant in the belief in the Muse, in inspiration from without, survived for centuries, outlasting the pagan belief in a pantheon of gods, and coexisting with the consolidated Christian faith. Indeed, even in our century at least two esteemed poets—Robert Graves and John Berryman—pledged their fealty to the Muse; both insisted that their pledge was not metaphoric. We smile. But is this really so different from other poets claiming God as their source, or the spirits of the departed speaking through a Ouija board, or the so-called genius of the language itself? The creative current can be so unexpected and foreign, so different in feel from the lulling sway of the quotidian, that the poet naturally—and maybe modestly—hesitates to locate its source inside himself.

(Speculating along these lines, the psychologist Julian Jaynes has suggested that the early poets actually *did* hear a voice from within, but that the voice did not originate in an exterior spirit realm—it was caused by powerful emanations from the right side of the brain. Jaynes argues in *The Origin of Consciousness in the Breakdown of the Bicameral Mind* that our insistent cultivation of the analytic-deductive left brain has resulted in the gradual atrophy of the partner hemisphere. Neurological research may yet enlighten us as to the real identity of the Muse.)

It is impossible to trace the changing conceptions of poetic creativity with any linear or sequential neatness. Poets have always lived at an angle—to their milieu, to its prevalent beliefs, even to their fellow poets. Only the line of idiosyncrasy is constant. Nevertheless, we can generalize that by the late eighteenth century, at least in Europe, the poets' own conception had altered somewhat. There was a significant inward displacement of the creative focus. From Samuel Taylor Coleridge, Percy Bysshe Shelley, and William Wordsworth we hear little about the Muse and a great deal about the Imagination.

The Romantics believed that a faculty of untold resource and power had been implanted in each human being. Those in whom this Imagination was especially volatile became creators. Those who could not create could at least respond to its call in the works of others. This Imagination was not, in the last analysis, any less obscure or mysterious than the personal Muse, nor could it be summoned to action any more reliably. As Shelley wrote in a celebrated passage of his *A Defence of Poetry:*

> Poetry is not like reasoning, a power to be exerted according to the determination of the will. A man cannot say, "I will compose poetry." The greatest poet even cannot say it; for the mind in creation is as a fading coal which some invisible influence, like an inconstant wind, awakens to transitory brightness; this power arises from within, like the color which fades and changes as it is developed, and the conscious portions of our nature are unprophetic either of its approach or its departure.

How similar, finally, are Shelley's words to Plato's; the difference lies entirely in Shelley's phrase "this power arises from within." (Shelley in fact translated the *Ion*.)

We tend to think of history as a progression, and to assume that the latest explanation is always the most comprehensive and correct. And with the advent in our century of the psychological sciences, we think about poetic creativity in new terms. Instead of thinking of the imagination as the sovereign organ of creation, we call upon the id or unconscious, and in so doing we make tacit reference to a complex and sophisticated model of psychic functioning. Undeniably this represents a kind of advance, a step toward the demystification of the unknown; but we must be careful to remind ourselves that this new conception is not yet an explanation. If we look closely at poetic process we will see that the appeal to the unconscious reduces the enigma of creativity only slightly. True, the focus is again shifted. Instead of Shelley's "inconstant wind" and "invisible influence," we speak of energies generated by an individual psyche, energies that have specific determinants in the emotional history of that psyche. But can we say, really, what an emotion is, or according to what pattern or influence these energies organize themselves? To say that poetry has its roots in the unconscious does not end the search—it starts it.

The unconscious is not a spatial entity—it is not some inner California transected by seismic faults and manifesting strange behavior. Although we do get a static image from the old three-part division—ego, id, and superego—Sigmund Freud and his followers have all insisted that the psyche is a dynamic whole, a force field that can be no more located than could the pagan or Christian soul.

The unconscious represents a significant part of this force field. It enlists our instincts and drives—to that extent it can be called biological, but its changing contours enclose a bewildering system of nonbiological functions. In no way can it be considered simply as a battery or storage facility for primal energies. Indeed, part of the problem we face is in determining how broadly or narrowly we wish to construe its operations.

In the broadest, most inclusive sense, the unconscious comprises everything that we are not conscious of at a given moment: At any time, therefore, it embraces virtually all of our psychic contents. Obviously this is not a serviceable definition. We need some scheme that will account for more and less available materials. I may not be thinking about yesterday's meeting, but my impressions or memories are more readily brought to consciousness than are images from the family vacation of fifteen years ago (though I may, with patience and concentration, be able to reconstitute much of that event). What's more, it seems that we are not equipped to store our whole experience for ready—that is, *willed*—recall. There are certain sensations and details from that vacation that no effort can recover. Yet, for all that, they are not necessarily lost forever. I may have what is now called a Proustian experience, an unexpected triggering of associations, whereby some part of that forgotten past is suddenly restored to me. Evidently we preserve things in logically ordered *and* associative patterns, but these might not even intersect.

This description is still simplistic. Clearly we also have contents that are not merely stray or elusive, but that have been blocked from consciousness. According to Freud, our Oedipal trauma actually *creates* an unconscious; it brings into being a protective complex of repressive energies. Our murderous feelings, and our horror at having those feelings, are blocked from awareness and made unavailable. They do not disappear.

Once the repressive dynamic has been instituted, any excessive feeling or undesirable memory may be similarly suppressed. But these materials are, in a sense, the most "real" and most vital parts of ourselves, and though they are blocked, they are hardly inactive. No, they intrude constantly upon our well-governed lives: in dreams, fantasies, memory pangs, slips of the tongue. Miraculously enough, some members of our tribe are endowed with the ability to grasp and shape these real sensations—visually, musically, in body motions, in words. We recognize the shapes as beauty—they elicit powerful harmonic responses from us—and we honor the shaper as an artist, as one who can express what remains inchoate in us.

How does the poet gain access to this hidden life? What determines the unconscious extrusions that find their way into poetry? In what manner are they given form? Does the poet exert any control over his creative activity, or is he as passive as Plato's "winged and holy thing"?

Freud believed that the psyche was a closed system, that every psychic event had a cause, and that, as in every closed system, the governing principle was one of dynamic equilibrium. Accumulated pressures needed to be dislodged and redistributed. When this did not happen, the system started to break down: Neurosis and psychosis might ensue. Freud believed, though, that the unconscious was linguistically permeated, and that a talking cure was possible. Through speech—words—one could locate the problem, and through recognition and expression it could often be resolved.

Keeping in mind Freud's model, let us recall Randall Jarrell's maxim: "A good poet is someone who manages, in a lifetime of standing out in thunderstorms, to be struck by lightning five or six times." The metaphor is a memorable inversion, for of course the lightning is internal, as are the storms. What we really get is the image of the unconscious as a thermal system that periodically builds up a massive energy charge that it then releases. Jarrell's numerical

specificity—that the good poet is struck *five* or *six* times—suggests
either that there are few such discharges in a poet's life, or that not
every discharge can be successfully turned to account. And, indeed,
he is curiously on the mark, at least with respect to "good" poets.
How much *do* we preserve from any but the very greatest? Is it ever
more than just a handful of lyrics? As for the greats, we can only
guess what determined the frequency of storms for them. Were
they really better poets, or were they just very good poets far more
often? What would we think of Shakespeare if we had only five or
six sonnets to go by?

Jarrell's aphorism once again underscores the poet's passivity
before the sources of his art. It also brings us, by a circuitous route,
to Marcel Proust's ideas about memory. Strongly influenced by the
philosophy of Henri Bergson, Proust articulated—and, in his masterpiece, demonstrated—the distinction between "voluntary" and
"involuntary" memory. Whatever could be recovered consciously,
through volition, belonged in the first category. That which defied
the reason and the will—which possessed, as it were, a will of its
own—composed the second. For Proust, only the *mémoire involon-
taire* could generate the real materials of art, those sensations that
are intact within us and that have not been bleached by the conscious mind. However, it was no use attempting any kind of salvage
operation; those sensations would yield themselves only in epiph-
anic moments. Such a moment came for Proust when he dipped
his madeleine in the teacup; the taste restored to him the hitherto
lost feeling of a whole epoch of his childhood. It led, ultimately, to
his monumental re-creation of lost time. His celebration of the
epiphany (James Joyce was another such celebrant) is remarkably
similar to what we find in the testimonies of poets—only the scale
is different. What a poet might experience as a line, Proust experienced as an encompassing architectural vision.

If the mainspring of poetic creativity cannot be activated by will
or desire, and if we speak of the unconscious (or the involuntary
memory) as exercising something like independent volition, how
then do we begin to explain its dynamic? Do we imagine that the
unconscious is in some way actually composing poetry, that it
sends the poet a clue so that its product may be brought into the
light? Certainly many poets, like Proust, speak as if their activity

were not so much creation as the discovery of something already shaped and intact. And when a poet does suddenly take down a complete line—with the intuitive certainty that it is correct—where is this line coming from? In what way does the unconscious have language?

Whatever we venture at this point will be tentative. The unconscious is a pullulating field of material and energy that is, by definition, not available to the conscious self. There is forgotten material, repressed material, and there is the agency of repression, of which we are likewise unaware. We could not say that there is any linguistic shape to the unconscious, or that language is in any way *stored* or *held* in its field. But it does seem that there is a high degree of permeability, almost as if words and sounds made up, in their totality, an equivalent field. This may be because we process such a large part of our experience through language. Our words, whatever their origin, are not neutral counters. We charge them with our deepest emotions and our most intimate associations. The unconscious may not *have* language, but language, in a sense, is imbued with much of our unconscious. Freud recognized this permeability and founded his psychoanalysis on it. We may not be able to say precisely how language and psyche interact, but there is little doubt that they share a most intricate connection.

I would like to approach the question of poetic creativity backward, that is, from the point of view of the reader engaging a finished product. When we read a poem deeply, attentively, when we experience its language and rhythms, we find that we lose sight of the words themselves. Their surface, their sign appearance, falls away, and we are left with specific emotions and sensations (often images). Our reading has, in effect, carried us past language. The poem functions, finally, to bind these emotions and sensations into some kind of figure, to produce out of the variety of means a nonlinguistic harmonic resonance. When we look back at the black marks on the page, it is with a certain detached astonishment. How could *they* have combined to make such a feeling in us?

Could we not imagine a similar process working in the other direction? Just as the poem carried us past words and toward a specific organization of psychic sensation, might it not be that a

similarly specific sensation in the psyche of the poet attracted and
organized just those words and rhythms? Does an invariable and
determined configuration of psychic material precede composition? Are the "gifts" experienced by the poet just the first protru-
sions of something that demands to be excavated in its entirety?

These are crucial and far-reaching questions. And others follow
in their wake. We have to ask, for instance, whether the realized
poem, the "great" poem, could have been written differently. Very
differently, that is. Everyone, of course, can think of cases of great
poets altering or excising their lines. But were these changes not
likewise dictated by the pressure of an established inner configuration? Was this shape not the template for the final "right"
decision? Really this is a resurrection of the ancient free will/
determinism debate. Is creativity—the very emblem of free will—
determined? What would free will in creativity be? When a poet
brings two sounds, or two words, together, is he inventing the combination, or is he merely recognizing a rightness of valence, a
rightness already prescribed by a determined internal pressure? Is
there any ultimate freedom of choosing that is not a betrayal or
evasion of the exact dictates of impulse?

The Russian poetess Marina Tsvetaeva wrote:

> I obey something which sounds constantly within me but not
> uniformly, sometimes indicating, sometimes commanding.
> When it indicates, I argue; when it commands, I obey.
>
> The thing that commands is a primal, invariable, unfailing
> and irreplaceable line, *essence appearing as a line of verse.* . . . The
> thing that indicates is an aural path to the poem: I hear a
> melody, but not words. The words I have to find.
>
> More to the left—more to the right, higher—lower, faster—
> slower, extend—break off: these are the exact indications of my
> ear, or of something *to* my ear. All my writing is only listening.

Her countryman and contemporary Osip Mandelstam put it
with even more concision:

> The poem is alive through an inner image, that resounding
> mold of form, which anticipates the written poem. Not a single
> word has appeared, but the poem already resounds. What re-

sounds is the inner image; what touches it is the poet's aural sense.

To judge from these accounts, the unconscious psyche has something very definite to transmit, and the poem is not finished until that something has registered its "invariable" verbal print. We might think of it as a process of exorcism working through phonic and rhythmic equivalents. The word is more apt than it may at first seem. Nadezhda Mandelstam, the poet's wife, has left us a vivid account of Mandelstam's attempts to "brush off" and "escape from" the insistent and irritating hum that would start in his ears when a poem was ready to be written.

Such a view of poetic creativity has implications that fly in the face of much that is currently proposed by poststructuralist and reader-response schools of interpretation. Both advance their claims based on an assumption of linguistic indeterminacy. Deconstructionists such as Jacques Derrida view writing as a system of differences: Every text, indeed every word, secures its provisional status in relation to every absent possibility. Signifiers signify in every direction; determinate meaning is nonexistent; the reader does not so much read as *rewrite* the text. And Roland Barthes, thinking along similar lines, defined a "healthy" sign as one that declares its arbitrariness and refuses emblematic fixity. Moreover, reader-response critics insist that authorial intentions are unknowable and irrelevant—what matters is the ways in which a work is scripted by its recipient. As Terry Eagleton has written (in *Literary Theory*): "There is no clear division for poststructuralism between 'criticism' and 'creation': both modes are subsumed into 'writing' as such."

But if we regard creative composition as a response by an artist to an explicit and determining psychic pressure, and if a poet has, in fact, assembled phonic and rhythmic equivalents in accordance with an invariable inner directive, then the poststructuralist position collapses—for if it doesn't, literature must. Both views subvert the primacy of the conscious and intending authorial ego, but where the poststructuralists take this as sanctioning the erasure of the author, I would argue that it must force our attention onto the

unconscious. The poem has, in fact, the most determinate reality;
its arrangements are anything but arbitrary. Our task as readers is
to appropriate the text with the assumption that there is a specific
meaning. Whether or not we can ever verify this—and the author
may not be the best judge—is beside the point.

In responding in this way to a poem/text, we are, in a sense,
buttressing certain age-old assumptions: that language is adequate
for expressing even the subtlest human meanings, and that literature secures its social value precisely because it is the best means
of conveying and preserving the complex life of sensibility. The
nonlinguistic sensations that a poem (or any other work of literature) finally organizes in a reader, and the prelinguistic sensations
or forces that instigate the poem, may or may not be similar. We
have no way of proving the case either way. But the belief that they
are kindred is the main impetus for the activities of both parties.

It is one thing to think of the unconscious spewing forth language, quite another to think of a poet listening for finished lines,
lines that in many cases are already metrically patterned. Are there
different kinds of pressure, different paths of release? Why is
everyone not a poet? Are poets made or born? Every question is
like a plant putting out its radial stalks.

It would seem that certain individuals demonstrate from an
early age a special susceptibility to language, to words and their
sounds, just as others might to music, or numbers and combinations, or colors. Genetic inheritance may be influential, as may be
chance. It is the attraction, often described as love, that is recalled.
Here, for example, is Dylan Thomas:

> I wanted to write poetry in the beginning because I had fallen in
> love with words. . . . What the words stood for, symbolized, or
> meant, was of very secondary importance; what mattered was
> the sound of them as I heard them for the first time on the lips
> of the remote and incomprehensible grownups who seemed,
> for some reason, to be living in my world.

Seamus Heaney has expressed himself similarly:

> I called myself *incertus,* uncertain, a shy soul fretting, and all
> that. I was in love with words themselves, had no sense of a

poem as a whole structure, and no experience of how the successful achievement of a poem could be a stepping stone in your
life. . . . Maybe it began very early, when my mother used to re-
cite lists of affixes and suffixes, and Latin roots with their English meanings. . . . Maybe it began with the exotic listing on the
wireless dial: Stuttgart, Leipzig, Olso, Hilversum . . .

The obvious surmise is that such a feeling will lead the young
inamorato to books, that exposure will lead in turn to imitation,
imitation to the absorption of craft, and so on. The sense of a vocation is usually there long before the poet has anything compelling
to say. It is there as a desire, a willingness to stand in thunderstorms.

Writers are perhaps permeated by language to a greater degree,
or depth, than others—they have invested their being more fully
in it. But they have also absorbed the conventions of their craft. If
a gift line comes out in an iambic pentameter, it is probably not because the psyche naturally arranges its material in formal rhythmic
sequence (though some have argued that it does, that forms and
meters evolved because of their particular structural affinity to inner experience). More likely it is because the structural possibilities have been taken in along with the language and exist as
combinatory options at that threshold where impulse galvanizes
language. In terms of this learning and absorbing, the poet makes
himself, but the love that guides it is given, not made. Try as we
might to explain this love—as Muse, Imagination, psyche, or
neural firing—its mystery abides. The ancient belief that the poet
was the chosen instrument of the gods may not, when put into
modern dress, be so absurd.

On a Stanza by John Keats

Season of mists and mellow fruitfulness,
    Close bosom-friend of the maturing sun;
Conspiring with him how to load and bless
    With fruit the vines that round the thatch-eves run;
To bend with apples the moss'd cottage-trees,
    And fill all fruit with ripeness to the core;
        To swell the gourd, and plump the hazel shells
    With a sweet kernel; to set budding more,
And still more, later flowers for the bees,
Until they think warm days will never cease,
        For Summer has o'er-brimm'd their clammy cells.
from "To Autumn"

Somehow a stubble plain look warm—in the same way that some
pictures look warm—this struck me so much in my Sunday's
walk that I composed upon it.
Keats, letter to J. H. Reynolds

"Distance is the soul of beauty," wrote Simone Weil. Although it is
by no means the only gnomic aphorism on the subject (Dostoevsky: "Beauty will save the world." André Breton: "Beauty will be
convulsive or it will not be at all." Keats: "Beauty is truth, truth
beauty"), it remains for me the most tantalizing. The first time I
encountered it, I felt instinctively that it was true; that is, it gave
shape to a feeling that had long been inchoate in me. At the same
time, however, I could not unravel it into any kind of explanation.
The formulation seemed to retain a distance of its own, a subtle
paradox at the core. For I find that whatever strikes me as beautiful manifests not distance but nearness, a quality of transparent
immediacy; I feel that I am confronting something that I have always known. How can that "nearness" be squared with "distance"?

So long as I persisted in regarding Weil's words in the abstract, I remained baffled. It was only recently, when I tried to discover for myself why a certain poem was beautiful, that I began to understand. What Weil was addressing was the paradox at the heart of the aesthetic encounter. When we are stirred by beauty in a particular work of art, what we experience is the inward abolition of distance. It is only when we try to put our finger on the source of the sensation, when we try to *explain* the beauty, that the horizons are reversed. At that moment the near becomes the far, much as it does when we try to fathom our own reflection in the mirror: The more intently we look, the stranger becomes the object of our scrutiny.

I set myself what seemed at first a simple task: to say why Keats's "To Autumn" was beautiful. The poem has always been one of my personal touchstones. Whenever I feel the occupational contamination of "words, words, words . . ." I look to its three stanzas for the rightness that restores faith. Nor am I alone. Generations of readers have singled out this last ode for special praise. I have seen it cited many times as the most perfect poem in the language. A more suitable test case for beauty, it seems, would be hard to find.

Before starting in on my own, I took a quick tour through the writings of certain estimable critics and scholars. I wanted to get a taste for the kinds of approaches that had been adopted in the past, and also to make sure that I did not belabor anything that was old hat. In a few sittings I learned more than a mortal should know about Keats's strategies of "stationing," his deployment of harvest imagery, his secularism, his debt to Milton and Shakespeare, and so on. I found much that was fussy, and just as much that was fascinating. But in all of the pages I read, I found nothing that helped me to understand why the immediate encounter with the words on the page is so thrilling, why the melody of the thing lives on in the mind, or how it is that the sensations are carried from line to line with an almost supernatural rightness. The beauty of the poem was in every case assumed; no one tried to account for it. I had to wonder: Is beauty that has been made out of words impervious to other words? Or is there an etiquette that I remain ignorant of—that one does not bring up certain matters? I left the library with a heady feeling of exploratory license.

Osip Mandelstam once wrote: "Where there is amenability to para-
phrase, there the sheets have never been rumpled, there poetry, so
to speak, has never spent the night." I let these words guide my first
steps. For anyone can see at a glance that "To Autumn" resists summary. It rests on no clearly delineated narrative and carries no cap-
sule message. And while there *is* sense in the poem, it is not the
primary source of our response. But neither is that response, as
with some poems, a matter of startling, unexpected imagery or
metaphoric enlargement/reversal. We do not see the world as we
have never seen it before. Rather, we are presented with an array of
familiar, if heightened, sensations. Clearly, then, the magic must
have to do with the interactions of sense and verbal music, with the
rhythmic orchestrations and the intensifications that result.

I am convinced that the beauty of the ode is to be sought with
the fine crosshairs of sound and sense, that it inheres in the
subtlest details and is sustained from breath to breath—that generalizations will serve for nothing. We experience such a rapid succession of perfectly managed sensory magnifications that we are,
in a strange way, brought face to face with the evolutionary mystery
of language. The absolute rightness of the sound combinations
forces us to a powerful unconscious recognition: Sound is the primal clay out of which all meaning has been sculpted.

I intend here to give a fanatically (and phonetically) close reading of the first stanza of "To Autumn." To work through any more
than a stanza with as highly ground a lens would be tiresome to the
reader and to some extent redundant. Certain readers may object
to the procedure, claiming that the effects I find are too fantastic,
that I am amplifying phonic detail out of all proportion, and that
my findings are not part of the intended experience of the poem.
Let me defend myself (briefly) in advance.

First of all, I believe that when we read a poem we absorb and
process a great deal more than we are consciously aware of, and
that it is precisely those cues that we pick up at the threshold—that
we hear and feel but do not overtly take note of—that combine to
give us the aesthetic surge. A passage strikes us as a perfect expression, but we cannot quite say why. Indeed, I wonder if this
might not account for some of the mystery of beauty: that we confront an order or pattern that is opaque to the conscious monitors

but perfectly transparent to the preconscious, or unconscious. Maybe Weil's "distance" is really referring to a gap between parts of the psyche. In which case, perhaps the feeling of beauty depends on a tension—or charge—born of an opposition within one's own psyche.

My second defense is so rudimentary that it could easily be overlooked. That is, given Keats's poetic endowment—the evidence of which is, of course, the poetry itself—what we might perceive as a hairsplitting discrimination was perfectly conspicuous to him. Let's not forget that we read poetry in the odd hour, as amateurs; Keats pressed his lines into place with the full intensity of his being. When a poet is composing, the value of every sound is magnified a thousandfold. His radar is attuned to frequencies that we are not even aware of. (Yeats characterized this rapt state beautifully: "Like a long-legged fly upon the stream / His mind moves upon silence.") I would argue, therefore, that not only (A) if you find it, it's probably there, but also (B) however much you find, there is sure to be more. Poetry will not disclose its secrets so long as we impose a ceiling on its resonance and reference. The poet does not use language as we do when we write a letter or a report. It is present to him when he composes as a totality of possibilities—the slightest pressure at any point sends waves through the entire system. To limit the associational field is to hobble the response.

> Season of mists and mellow fruitfulness,
>   Close bosom-friend of the maturing sun;
> Conspiring with him how to load and bless
>   With fruit the vines that round the thatch-eves run;

The governing sensation of the full stanza, which is most tellingly enacted in its last four lines, is of active ripening—of nature swelling all living things with her ichor—and overflow. Keats's description is as straightforward as could be, and the lines are crowded with nouns and active, richly suggestive verbs. The presentation proceeds from the unbounded vista of the invocation through a series of increasingly particular close-ups, to culminate in the minute cells of the honeycombs. We do not have to dig past the surface to get at the delights of the sound—they are there to be scooped right off the page. And just as we can enjoy the play of colors in one of Claude Monet's haystacks—with no deeper understanding of his struggle to balance off the objective interactions of light and matter on the retina with the limitations of intermittent perception—so we may respond to the sonorities and the abundance of carefully arranged detail while remaining oblivious, at least consciously, of the underlying intricacies.

Literature is full of picturesque renderings of the natural world. But with "To Autumn" we are well beyond the picturesque. In these lines the words do not merely designate or connote—they take on a gestural life so explicit that they temporarily displace the world to which they refer. They do so by replacing it with a self-sufficient language world, where things are not only named and arranged, but into which are incorporated deep suggestions about the working of physical process. The mystery of it—that language should be capable of so much—defies explanation and analysis. At best, we can note some of the more conspicuous instances of this functioning.

"Season of mists . . ." Mists, as we know from our science primers, result from the condensation and evaporation of ground moisture, the very same moisture that is taken up by the capillary roots of trees and plants and that eventually fleshes out the cells of the fruits. The sun, which from our Ptolemaic perspective rises up as if out of the earth itself, creates the mist by hastening evaporation and subsequently "burns" it away. This process, recalled for us in the poem by the nouns "mist" and "sun," is fully enacted on a phonetic level. Here we get our first evidence of the ode's deeper linguistic rightness.

Observe, first, what the mouth must do to vocalize the line: "Season of mists and mel-low fruit-ful-ness." The lips widen and stretch to make the initial *ee* sound in "Season," contract the same position to pronounce "mists," and contract it yet again, just slightly, to form the syllable "mel-." If we think of these contractions as representing diminishing circumferences—as, say, cross sections of a funnel—then with the small *o* of "-low" and the *oo* of "fruit-" (which cannot be made without a pouting protrusion of the lips and an even smaller aperture) we have come to the narrowed apex. This would not necessarily be significant in itself, but when we consider the unstated physical process—the moisture being siphoned out of the soil and into the fruit through the myriad fine roots, the push against gravity—then these lip movements become instrumental.

But this is not all. There is also a simultaneous *lingual* event. For in order to enunciate cleanly the words "mel-low fruit-ful-ness," the tip of the tongue must sketch out the shape of a fruit. Try the sounds slowly and expressively. Notice how the tongue ticks off points along a circumference. Isn't there a distant impression of rondure? The event is further complicated, and its resonance deepened, by the fact that the sounds we are making signify so directly: "mel" (the Latin root for "honey"), "fruit," and "ful(l)ness." We have spoken only one line, but we have already abetted the ripening process and have tasted the contours of a small, sweet fruit.

One of the first things we notice about the opening lines of the stanza are the many sibilants. These function in several ways. First, their purposeful positioning virtually forces us to create what might be called an associational field. We screen them differently than we would in other contexts. When we hear on the newscast, for example, that there are "early morning mists in low-lying areas," we do not feel free to conjure with the sounds; we know that they are being used in a strictly denotational mode. The situation is obviously different when it is Keats writing: "Season of mists and mellow fruitfulness." And there is more involved than just placement and rhythmic emphasis. We assume an intentional pressure: The sounds were mobilized because they were the best possible equivalents for the desired sensation.

The proximity of the *s* sounds in the first three words—there are four—encourages us to associate the sibilance with mist. This is not that unnatural, in any event: The *s* holds latent suggestions of moisture (if only because rain makes a hissing sound), which a context like this would immediately activate. But there is also a very subtle and effective sensory crossing that takes place once we know the poem. For just as the sense of the first two lines allows us to make a link between the *s* sounds and the mists, so in the fourth and fifth lines the battery of *t*'s ("thatch-eves" and "cottage-trees") invites us to connect the *t* sound with the hard opacity of the actual trees. Pictographically, of course, the shape of the letters en-

courages such a leap—the sinuosity of the *s* corresponding with
the undulant movement of the vapors, and the *t* resembling a
branched tree. Once this association has been subliminally registered, we can find in the word "mists" both a phonic and a visual
representation of cloudy exhalations swirling about the branches
of an orchard tree. And once we make such an association, needless to say, we are drawn into the poem in a profound way.

> Close bosom-friend of the maturing sun;
> Conspiring

The deliberate profusion of sibilants also creates an unmistak-
able hiss in the opening lines. This gathers momentum through
the first two lines and is not released until we encounter the perfectly situated participle "conspiring." The word works on us both
etymologically and through the sound itself. To "conspire" means,
literally, to breathe together. We get a sense of complicity, of mutual exhalation, of dampness of exhalation (mist represents nothing so much as breath vapor), and, as I will discuss later, sexual
activity. At the same time, the word discharges completely the hiss
that has gathered in the preceding lines. The vertical thrust of
"spire"—which suggests with a single stroke that the sun has
moved up in the sky—compresses an otherwise gradual event: The
mist is burned off in the space of a syllable. We might observe, too,
that "close," "bosom," and "conspiring" all keep the solar emblem
o near the mist-suggesting *s*—with the pitched *i* of "spire" that connection is sundered.

A series of slight syllables follows the break: "-ing," "with," "him,"
"how," and "to." We can almost imagine that Keats is drawing out a
slender vine or branch, tapering it to slightness before attaching
the round and dense-feeling "load." The line is a beautiful illustra-
tion of the relative gravity of word sounds. The weighted—but dis-
tinctly lighter—sound of the monosyllable "bless," positioned as it
is after "load," figures in the ear the supple movement of a laden
vine and gives us the aural equivalent of a diminishing bob.

> load and bless
> With fruit the vines that round the thatch-eves run;

The enjambment of "bless / With" further accentuates the down and up motion, and the appreciably lighter *oo* of "fruit" continues the upward arc, even as the placement of the noun in a passive construction finally connects it to the vine. The syntactical inversion of the rest of the line echoes the preceding "load and bless / With fruit." Both phrases require an extension of the breath and thereby render more palpable our sense of elongated curling vines.

This fourth line is pivotal. With "vines" and "thatch-eves," we cross for the first time from the all-inclusive apostrophe of autumn into a particular kind of landscape. Helen Vendler has worked out the full topography of the poem in *The Odes of John Keats*—I can add nothing to her discoveries. But I would underscore the importance of the transition. Just as the stanza narrows down from a vast environment to the "cells" of the honeycombs, so too does it move us from a diffuse seasonal mistiness into a realm of highly tactile particulars: "thatch-eves," "moss'd cottage-trees," and "hazel shells":

> To bend with apples the moss'd cottage-trees,
>   And fill all fruit with ripeness to the core;
>   To swell the gourd, and plump the hazel shells
>   With a sweet kernel;

The central lines of the stanza are dominated by sensuous detail. I have already proposed that the clustered *t*'s call to mind the actual density of an orchard. The impression is further solidified by the incidence of strong stresses at the end of the line: "*moss'd cottage-trees.*" And the numerous vowel and consonant doublings add to the effect—*pp, ss, tt, ee,* and *ll* twice in a mere eleven words—as if nature's prodigality extended to the alphabet itself. Nor is their impact strictly visual. An alerted ear—and what ear can fail to be quickened by a poem like this?—finds the subliminal stutter in words like "apples" and "cottage." Again, it is the associational field that imparts significance to these normally incidental combinations.

> And fill all fruit with ripeness to the core;

Here, at last, the iambic pentameter resolves. And with wonderful effect. The harmonic regularity of nature is at last disclosed. The very filling of the fruit conforms to the eternal paradigm. The line both denotes and enacts measure. Nor is it accidental, I think, that the first evenly cadenced line should sit at the very center of the stanza, at its "core," as it were. For as I observed at the outset, the dominant action in these eleven lines is one of gradual over-flow. This line, then, as the midpoint, marks the perfect peak of ripeness. The liquid has filled its container to the limit; the next five lines will send it brimming over.

> To swell the gourd, and plump the hazel shells
> With a sweet kernel;

If *s*'s can be said to invoke mists, and *t*'s trees, then what are we to make of the loading of *l*'s in these central lines—"fill," "all," "swell," "plump," "hazel," and "shells"? Pronouncing the sixth and seventh lines with exaggerated care, we quickly discover how in-tricately mingled are the *l*'s and the other consonants, especially the *r*'s. It is the consonantal weave that keeps the tongue dancing without rest along the roof of the mouth, an activity that, when wedded to the sense, gives us the suggestion of a great many fruits burgeoning simultaneously. Especially effective is the placement of the exquisitely plosive "plump"—we feel as though things are bursting on every side of us.

It is worth noting here, too, the subtle reversal that Keats has de-vised. Where "fill all fruit with ripeness to the core" describes an inward movement, as though ripening were a process beginning at the surface and continuing toward the center, the remaining ac-tions of the stanza are all outward: swelling, plumping, and o'er-brimming. Again, this underscores the importance of the sixth line. We can view it, if we choose, as the node of a chiasmus (X) fig-ure, Lines 1–5 *in*-still the fruit with moisture; lines 7–11 move out from the center and culminate in a *dis*-tilling activity.

One curious element in the middle part of this stanza is Keats's repetition of the word "fruit." This is in addition to his use of "fruit-fulness" in the first line. In both instances, the general term is fol-lowed by cited particulars, either "apples" or "the gourd" and "the hazel shells." The oscillation between the general and the specific (the whole ode, it seems, proposes a landscape that is neither en-tirely typified nor altogether singular) allows the universality of cyclic return to play against concretely sensuous detail. The repetition of "fruit" prevents us from immersing ourselves in an unequivocally particular setting. What's more, the word sends us back to the original denominations and commands of Genesis ("Let the earth bring forth grass, the herb yielding seed, and the fruit tree yielding fruit after his kind . . ."; "Be fruitful, and multiply . . ."; and so on). I would not like to stress this connection too strongly, however, for the order apostrophized in "To Autumn" is secular, not Edenic. The biblical echo points back to timeless harmonies, but it does not invite us to consider "Man's first disobedience."

Before turning to the final lines of the stanza, we might remark one more interesting subtlety. Keats has, in the sixth line, disassembled the signal word "fruitfulness," scattering its components: "And *fill* all *fruit* with ripe*ness* . . ." We pick this up subliminally, unaware that part of our pleasure in the line comes from this all-but-imperceptible echo. The weft is tightened; the evenly cadenced core of the stanza touches us with what feels like perfect inevitability.

> to set budding more,
> And still more, later flowers for the bees,
> Until they think warm days will never cease,
> For Summer has o'er-brimm'd their clammy cells.

The most remarkable event in the stanza as a whole is Keats's flawlessly executed enactment of the physical sensation of overflow. The cluster of strong accents—"And *still more, la*ter"—instigates a rising tension. The near regularity of the penultimate line cannot quite appease the ear. It inspires, instead, a precarious suggestion of arrest; we feel the tense convexity with which liquid holds shape just before spilling over. And then comes the midline impact of "o'er-brimm'd," a word that both describes and encodes the action. The three unaccented syllables preceding "-brim-" ensure that the emphasis will fall on the instant at which convexity yields.

A number of critics have connected the feeling of surfeit generated by the stanza with Keats's decision to adopt an eleven-line (instead of ten-line) stanza. The added quantity has obvious effects on the reader, and Keats has made the most of these. By giving the penultimate line acceleration and rising pitch—"cease" pitches forward like the crest of a wave—he has made it all but impossible for us to take our natural pause. We are driven on to complete the stanza, to extend our exhalation past the normal limit. We feel the expenditure with our whole pneumatic apparatus, even as we murmur the three sets of doubled *m*'s—"Summer," "o'er-brimm'd," and "clammy"—mimicking the languorous vibration of satiated bees.

The sexual suggestion of these last lines cannot be passed over. If we listen to the whole stanza and follow its rhythmic progression, we cannot but register the climactic moment that comes with "cease" (who was it who called the orgasm "a little death"?), and the echoing contraction of "-brimm'd." Although Keats may not have orchestrated his lines with such an end in mind—consciously, at least—a reader has to be wearing earplugs to be unaware of it. Nor is it just a question of rhythmic emphasis. The honey hoarded by the bees (never named, but conjured up early on by the "mel-" of "mellow") is substantially akin to the "honey of generation" in Yeats's "Among School Children." For that matter, doesn't the entire stanza combine its images of swelling fruits and rising liquids under the aspect of its opening conceit—that the "conspiring" earth and sun are the intimate begetters of all that lives (in which case "Close bosom-friend" is something more than platonic in its suggestion)? Nor should we forget that the thrice-named "fruit" is itself seed. Not just fecundity, but procreative fervor underlies the imagery and sensation of this stanza.

As I said at the outset, I'm not going to work my way dutifully through the complete ode. My purpose is not to advocate any new interpretation. Neither am I under the illusion that this stitch-by-stitch approach will tell us anything about the "meaning" of the work. As far as I'm concerned, there is in this case no meaning extrinsic to the obvious sense of the words on the page. I do hope, however, that the close reading of a single stanza will emphasize that its aesthetic effect—our perception of beauty, if you will—derives largely from a complex series of sound and sense interactions, many of which are apt to elude us as we read. And that, further, our experience of beauty may well have something to do with the gap, or *distance*, between what we are aware of perceiving and what we pick up subliminally.

Two questions remain. First, let us suppose that we have uncovered a great many of these inconspicuous interactions. Have we then, by eliminating much of the distance between conscious and unconscious perception, somehow slackened the mainspring of beauty? Can we, in other words, pick a poem apart so completely that understanding supplants astonishment? I would say not, for the simple reason that our psyches are not structured in such a way that we can both read in a participatory manner and at the same time reflect on the ways in which that involvement has been achieved. The very workings that we uncover through an operation of willed dissociation—like the ones that I have just pointed out—function, when we read, to keep us fixed inside the language circuit. And if we do, through one of those unaccountable psychic switches, find ourselves staring at the cause of a particular poetic effect, our response might very well be enhanced. For what we recognize at such a moment is the preternatural fitness of language for the transmission of subtleties of perception.

The second question is complex and cannot be fully dealt with here. Namely, to what extent was the poet aware of, and responsible for, the felicities that I have been extracting from his work? Or, to put it another way, can we legitimately locate effects that the poet was not in some way aware of and intending? As I said earlier, we must always keep in mind that the poet's aural endowment is probably greater than ours—though *how much* greater is impossible to gauge. How we answer the question of intention, however, will depend on what we believe about the process of poetic composition. If we believe that it is consciously governed, willed, dependent on the taking of infinite pains—a nonsensical view, in my opinion—then the poet's own awareness matters greatly. If he did not intend *x*, then *x* does not exist.

As soon as we allow the unconscious a role in creativity, on the other hand, the reader is given a great deal of license. For then it is not a case of the poet's inventing lines, but rather of his finding sounds and rhythms in accordance with the promptings of the deeper psyche. The poet does not rest with a line until he has released a specific inner pressure. Or, to put it another way, the pressure looks to the language for its release. It magnetizes and attracts certain elements from the phonic spectrum and sets them into combinations. The poet presides over this process—in a sense he is *its* instrument—working toward that feeling of "rightness" that is his ultimate standard. Needless to say, he very often might not know why he brings two sounds together. When we turn up the most uncanny effects in his lines, therefore, we have every reason to believe that his deeper "Muse" put them there, even if *he* did not.

Rainer Maria Rilke

Boris Pasternak chose to begin his memoir, *Safe Conduct,* with a curious description of an incident:

> One hot summer's morning in the year 1900 an express left Moscow's Kursk Station. Just before it started, someone in a black Tyrolean cape appeared outside the window. A tall woman was with him. Probably she was his mother or an elder sister. They talked with my father about something familiar to all three of them and which evoked the same warm response. But the woman exchanged occasional phrases in Russian with my mother, while the stranger spoke only German. And although I knew the language perfectly well, I had never heard it spoken like that. For that reason, between the two rings of the departure bell, that foreigner on the crowded platform seemed like a silhouette among solids, a fiction in the thick of reality.

The obliquity, sustained for several pages, is pure Pasternak. When we have all but forgotten the episode, he names the shadowy stranger: Rainer Maria Rilke. The older woman, whom Pasternak does not identify, had to have been Rilke's friend and former mistress Lou Andreas-Salomé. The precocious onlooker was ten years old at the time of the encounter.

When Pasternak does finally name the poet, he reveals the true nature of his enterprise: to write an autobiography that would recover not what happened but what *mattered.* He begins with his first—and only—glimpse of Rilke because Rilke had come to embody his ideal of poetic perfection. Pasternak was not alone in his veneration. When he died in 1926, Rilke was recognized as the undisputed giant of European poetry. Marina Tsvetaeva called him "poetry itself."

Sixty years later, Rilke's stature remains undiminished. Indeed, his oeuvre has engendered so much activity among translators of late that it almost seems he is still out there, producing. Poems hitherto unknown in English turn up in almost every new collection, and collections appear quicker than one can read them. More remarkable, however, is the fact that this surge in publication and popularity (the books do sell!) flies in the face of prevailing literary trends. In literature as elsewhere, this is the era of quotidian caution, while Rilke is the prophet of the terrors and ecstasies of soul making.

Are we, then, in the throes of another highbrow fad? Or are readers finding a genuine spiritual guidance that is unavailable elsewhere? Or is it simply a matter of poetic excellence reaping its due recognition? Yes to all three questions. But that explains little. For no single Rilke exists in all that welter of books. The trajectory of the poet's career passed through a number of sharply defined, at times even antithetical, phases. From the extreme Romanticism of the early work (*The Book of Hours, Stories of God*) to the long-fought-for "objective" vision in the *New Poems* of 1907; from the call for inward transformation in the *Duino Elegies* to the elegant lightness of the last poems written in French—Rilke made a unique art at every turn of his life. One does not just *read* the man, one joins up with him at one point or another on his pilgrimage. Before we can assess the boom, we must assess the career.

In 1900, when Pasternak saw him, Rilke was twenty-five years old, poised at the brink of poetic maturity. Although he may have looked like a "silhouette among solids," he was of this world enough to be a canny self-promoter. He had been sending his youthful poems, stories, and plays to editors and publishers all over Germany and central Europe. (The popular image of Rilke as a creature of pure spirit, aloof from the hustle of the marketplace, derives more from his later years. Then, thanks to the devotion of his publisher, Anton Kippenberg, and the generosity of a number of wealthy friends, he was free to cultivate his Muse as he saw fit.) Recent biographies by Wolfgang Leppmann and Donald Prater show just how much of his energy Rilke consecrated to flattering, wheedling, and beseeching the influential.

Rilke's traveling companion, Lou Andreas-Salomé, was, by 1900, looking for ways to put distance between herself and her young admirer. She had a reputation as an outspoken freethinker, but she was also a married woman old enough to be Rilke's mother (she had broken Friedrich Nietzsche's heart some fifteen years before). By the time of this trip to Russia, their second, the poet had been demoted from lover to friend; Lou would soon resort to geographical distance.

Rilke didn't seem to mind this first change of status. What mattered most to him, judging from the lifelong pattern of his relationships, was the proximity of a sympathetic female presence. He would almost never be without some gifted, emotional woman within earshot. He had his Odilies, Sidonies, Loulous, and Magdas . . . A certain kind of woman found the poet irresistible. It was only when the beloved showed signs of wanting something more permanent that he invoked his amatory credo: Love me, love my solitude. Or, as he put it in his First Duino Elegy: "Isn't it time that we lovingly / freed ourselves from the beloved and, quivering, endured . . . (?)" How much of this ambivalence had to do with his mother—a hysterical, doting woman, who liked to outfit her young son in dresses—is for the psychologists to decide.

When the Russian journey ended, Lou imposed a separation. Rilke traveled by himself to the artists' colony at Worpswede near Bremen and fell in love with a young sculptress named Clara Westhoff. Their precipitous marriage was a mistake. The bald chronology tells it all: 1901, Rilke and Clara are married; that same year, the birth of a daughter, Ruth; 1902, Rilke moves to Paris, alone. The charade was carried on for years—Rilke would establish quarters; he would send for his family. It never happened. But as late as 1906, he was still writing to Clara that the touching of their solitudes was the highest possible affirmation of their love. As John Berryman put it in his third *Dream Song*, "Rilke was a *jerk.*"

But jerk or no, Rilke did become a sublime poet. And it was in Paris, Walter Benjamin's "Capital of the Nineteenth Century," that the sublimity first manifested itself. Perhaps "manifested itself" misleads in emphasis—the lyrics and prose writings of Rilke's Paris period resulted from the strictest discipline. The young poet finally abandoned his rhetorical spiritualism for an art rooted in sensory vividness. The two bright stars by which he steered his course were Auguste Rodin and, some time later, Paul Cézanne.

Rilke learned as much from their punishing ethic of daily work as
he did from their aesthetic example.

Clara was useful in at least one respect—she gave Rilke an
introduction to Rodin. Upon his arrival in Paris, Rilke went immediately to the master's studio in Meudon. Before long, he was
visiting regularly. He followed Rodin, watched him work, and began to assemble notes for a study. Rodin's work habits—the sculp-
tor never stopped—astonished Rilke. If only the poet could work
like that! Then, with great speed and resolve, Rilke found a way.
He would direct his gaze outward; he would forge his objective impressions into a more sculpted kind of lyric. Scarcely three months
after his arrival in Paris, Rilke had written "The Panther," the signature poem of his new style.

To grasp what a volte-face was involved, we need only glance at
Rilke's earlier style. The prose of his *Stories of God* (1900) and the
poems of the first part of *The Book of Hours*, written immediately after his return from Russia, show the poet struggling with spiritual
ultimates. Strongly influenced by Nietzsche, as well as glimpses of
the Russian peasant culture, Rilke was evolving his idea of God as
an entity yet to be created. As he wrote in *The Prayers*, a lengthy
cyclic poem of the period:

> We are building Thee, with tremulous hands,
> And we pile atom upon atom.
> But who can complete Thee
> Cathedral Thou?

Compare this with the rigorously framed perception of animal
otherness in the justly celebrated panther poem:

> His gaze has from the passing back and forth of bars
> become so tired, that it holds nothing more.
> It seems to him there are a thousand bars
> and behind a thousand bars no world.
>
> The supple pace of powerful soft strides,
> turning in the very smallest circle,
> is like a dance of strength around a center
> in which a mighty will stands numbed.
>
> From time to time the curtain of the pupils
> silently parts—. Then an image enters,

goes through the taut stillness of the limbs,
and is extinguished in the heart.
trans. Edward Snow

Soon would follow masterpieces like "Orpheus. Euridice. Hermes."
and "Tombs of the Heterae."

Rilke searched during this crucially formative period not so
much for a poetry of objective description as for a way of displac-
ing focus from the observer to the thing observed. The poem was
to be a bridge thrown from an *in here* to an independently existing
out there; the poet strove to purge his perception of subjectivity.
This is, of course, an impossible project; language cannot attain
anything like the neutrality of color or clay. But in the effort, Rilke
learned an aesthetic rigor that would henceforth temper his tendency toward Romantic effusiveness. (The tendency was indulged
freely in his correspondence, however, which he used as a proving
ground for images, impressions, and turns of phrase.) The *New
Poems* have often been cited as a pioneering of the principle that
T. S. Eliot would later dub the "objective correlative."

Rodin was, as Rilke found out, a temperamental master. The
poet served for a time as his secretary and factotum. He was fired
during one of Rodin's rages. But Rilke's admiration for the artist
remained unswerving: He published two separate essays on the
man and his art. The first, dating from 1903, is an intoxicated
proclamation of Rodin's creative force. The 1907 essay, far more
subdued, acknowledges the enormous difficulties inherent in all
artistic endeavor. The poet had clearly learned a few hard lessons
in the intervening years.

Rilke's encounter with the genius of Cézanne came at the exhibition of the Salon d'Automne in 1907. If exposure to Rodin
changed his work, the paintings of Cézanne confirmed his decision and spurred him further along his chosen path. In a remarkable sequence of letters to Clara—now published as *Letters on
Cézanne*—Rilke set down the day-by-day impact of his visits to the
salon. His letter of October 13, 1907, shows more clearly than any
manifesto how much his sense of artistic mission had changed:

> If I were to come and visit you, I would surely also see the splen-
> dor of moor and heath, the hovering bright greens of meadows,

the birches, with new and different eyes; and though this transformation is something I've completely experienced and shared before, in part of the Book of Hours, nature was still then a general occasion for me, an evocation, an instrument in whose strings my hands found themselves again; I was not yet sitting before her; I allowed myself to be swept away by the soul that was emanating from her; she came over me with her vastness, her huge exaggerated presence, the way the gift of prophecy came over Saul; exactly like that. I walked about and saw, not nature but the visions she gave me. How little I would have been able to learn from Cézanne, from Van Gogh, then.

Later, in the same letter, he adds: "[Cézanne] knew how to swallow back his love for every apple and put it to rest in the painted apple forever"—his aesthetic ideal of the Paris years could not have been put more eloquently or concisely.

Those years—from 1902 until the outbreak of war in 1914—were by no means stationary. Almost every few months, Rilke would interrupt the ordeals of composition in order to travel. There were reading tours, guilty—and brief—visits to Clara and Ruth in Germany; then there were the more pleasurable trips to Capri, Venice, Egypt, Spain, and elsewhere, most of them subsidized by his patrons and friends. (Rilke's social successes were such that he never soiled his hands with anything worse than ink so long as he lived—quite an accomplishment for the son of a retired railroad official.) Every departure from Paris marked Rilke's desire to shake off oppressive solitude and the recurrent threat of artistic stagnation. Similarly, with every return he announced his resolve to recover the productive power of his first happy Paris season. He had a new project now: Shortly after his poetic breakthrough, Rilke had begun working on the prose experiment that would eventually be published as *The Notebooks of Malte Laurids Brigge.*

Malte was, for Rilke, an enormous effort of spirit. The book was nearly plotless, a sequence of meditations moving back and forth through the memory of its eponymous narrator. If the *New Poems* represented a distancing from the subjective claim, *Malte* was the poet's effort to impose sculptural shape on his deepest preoccupations. It is the closest thing we have to a portrait of the artist as a young man. Rilke drew many of the feverish, gritty descriptions of street life in the poorer quarters of Paris directly from his own journals. Where Malte diverges from his creator is in his memories of growing up in a haunted Danish manor—the solidly bourgeois poet (born in Prague) had to draw these chiaroscuro passages out of his own imagination.

In *Malte,* Rilke first extensively developed the theme that would be central to his *Duino Elegies* and *Sonnets to Orpheus:* that death is the hidden "other half" of life; that we carry it within ourselves like a seed that we must tend as it germinates and grows. Already Rilke was building his philosophy around a welcoming, rather than re-fusing, of the inevitable. His late lyrics are utterly singular in fus-ing death obsession with a spirit verging on the celebratory.

No less important is Malte's powerful retelling of the parable of the Prodigal Son, with which Rilke chose to end the book. In his version, the son leaves home in order to escape the stunting force of his family's love. He returns only after he has come to under-stand how earthly, mortal love perverts the intransitive love that is God's. The prodigal does his best to endure everyone's "vain" and misdirected affections. The book ends with these most enigmatic sentences: "He was now terribly difficult to love, and he felt that only One would be capable of it. But He was not yet willing." The words obviously embody Rilke's own conviction. For one who had single-mindedly turned his back on the flawed love of his fellow mortals, the phrase "not yet" must have conjured a terrifying hollowness.

Rilke nearly collapsed from exhaustion after finishing *Malte,* and for the next two years all production stopped. The poet began to wonder if he might not have depleted his powers once and for all. A period of restless traveling followed: Germany, Italy, Prague, Algiers, Cairo. Then, in October of 1911, he accepted the hospi-tality of Princess Marie von Thurn und Taxis-Hohenlohe, going to stay at her magnificent castle at Duino on the Adriatic Sea. The story of his first great inspiration is well known: how in January of 1912 he interrupted the writing of a business letter to walk on the castle ramparts, how he heard a voice call out of the wind the be-ginning of what became the First Elegy: "Wer, wenn ich schriee, hörte mich denn aus der Engel Ordnungen?" By the evening of the same day Rilke had written the whole of that elegy, and in the days immediately following he completed the Second; the Third and Sixth were written a year later. But the follow-through, the creative burst that would bring the cycle of ten to completion, would not come for a full decade.

Erich Heller has written, in an essay titled "Rilke in Paris," that "for the time being, for the ten years between Duino and Muzot [where the sequence was finished], Rilke did not quite understand what the voice that was in the storm demanded of him, the voice that then at last did speak to *him*." Heller's point is a good one. Rilke could not have been ready for the whole dictation. The *Duino Elegies*, along with the quickly written *Sonnets to Orpheus*, are the very apotheosis of inwardness. Their ultimate claim is that it is the destined human task to transform the materiality of the world into spirit ("We are the bees of the Invisible," wrote Rilke to his Polish translator). But in 1912, the poet was still very much occupied with the obdurate reality of the *out there*. He had not yet relinquished one vision of poetic salvation for its opposite. Indeed, it may be that Rilke's inability to write any poetry during the long war years had less to do with his sorrow at the geopolitical struggle than with the fact of a psychic contest between two very different ways of understanding experience.

On June 20, 1914, before the outbreak of the war, Rilke wrote as follows to his old friend Lou: "Lou, dear, here is a strange poem, written this morning, which I am sending you right away because I involuntarily called it 'Turning-point,' because it describes *the* turning point which no doubt must come if I am to stay alive." The poem, too long to quote here in its entirety, ends with these lines:

> For there is a boundary to looking.
> And the world that is looked at so deeply
> wants to flourish in love.
>
> Work of the eyes is done, now
> go and do heart-work
> on all the images imprisoned within you; for you
> overpowered them: but even now you don't know them.
> Learn, inner man, to look on your inner woman,
> the one attained from a thousand

natures, the merely attained but
not yet beloved form.
trans. Stephen Mitchell

On the surface, this looks like a complete reversal of Rilke's program. In truth, it is a most radical extension. "Work of the eyes is done," he writes. Only now, after the objective seeing of the world has been undertaken, can the next phase begin: transformation. Implied in the phrasing is a larger vision of interdependence. For the poet is not merely bringing the *out there* back into the crucible of his subjectivity. No, the world "wants" to flourish in love. As Rilke would later ask in the Ninth Elegy: "Earth, isn't this what you want: to arise within us, *invisible?*" Poet and world are no longer seen as separate; a single breath of spirit seems to move through all things.

As Rilke once held that mankind had to make God, so he affirms in "Turning-point" that all of creation needs man in order to realize its ultimate destiny as pure spirit. What G. W. F. Hegel began as philosophy—the idea of the self-realization of a World Spirit through history—Rilke sought to bring to completion in his poetry. And what is this vision, finally, but a secular eschatology? If the redemption of the world cannot be had through God, or Son, then the task falls to us. The similarities between Rilke's aims and Nietzsche's have often been remarked. There is, however, one crucial difference. Where Nietzsche adjured his superman to *will*, Rilke—as the cited passage suggests—called for pliancy and receptivity above all. His "inner woman," who here sounds very much like the Jungian anima, is a figure of maternal gestation, not conquest. The last lines of the Tenth Elegy, similarly, imply that final happiness is something *granted:*

> And we, who have always thought
> of happiness as *rising*, would feel
> the emotion that almost overwhelms us
> whenever a happy thing *falls.*

Eight years would elapse between "Turning-point" and the completion of the *Elegies.* It was to be a creatively barren time for Rilke.

Although he greeted the outbreak of war with jubilation—he actually began a series of hymns to the god of battles—he quickly perceived his own foolishness; he thereupon succumbed to an inertia that lasted until long after the war ended.

Reading about this period reminds us of the difficulty—even futility—of the biographer's job, especially when his subject's activity was almost entirely internal, as Rilke's was. And when there are not even writings, nothing but the artful posturings of the letters, all purchase disappears. It is as if the poet, in the prime of maturity, had simply stopped living for a decade. Prater and Leppmann have both scratched the ground for revealing details, but neither has turned up much besides the expected string of amours. We get the clear impression that Rilke remained almost immune to the surrounding catastrophe. Apart from a brief interval in uniform— influential friends quickly got him released from duty—the poet spent most of the war years living in stylish security in Munich. In both of these biographies, he recedes from view, and he never fully reappears in either.

We can blame the confusion of war, the paucity of information, any number of things—but isn't it possible that the outer man *did* more or less disappear? After all, the creative explosion of 1922— when Rilke wrote five elegies and the complete cycle of fifty-five *Sonnets to Orpheus* in a two-week period—did not come from nowhere. The preceding years would have seen a great hoarding of inner resources. If you compute the sums, not much remains for living.

Except as it is revealed in his art, Rilke's inwardness stayed hidden. Before the mystery of the creative artist, said Sigmund Freud, psychoanalysis must lay down its arms. The same applies to biography. For all that they have uncovered about the circumstances, places, and people in Rilke's life (Prater is painstaking to a fault; Leppmann moves swiftly, but tends to glibness), neither biographer has begun to answer the central question. How did the selfish, snobbish, and decidedly unsympathetic man portrayed in their pages come to produce such an utterly singular body of work? Even a modicum of theorizing would be welcome.

In 1919, after years of doubt and depression, Rilke left Germany for Switzerland. There he eventually secured for himself the isolated château at Muzot—it would be his last, his only, real home. Those were the walls that he stroked "like a big animal" on February 9, 1922, when the second immense inspiration came to him. On February 11, he could write to Marie Taxis:

> Only just now, Saturday, the *eleventh* at six in the evening, did I finish! —Everything in only a few days, it was an indescribable storm, a hurricane in my spirit (like *before* at *Duino*), everything that is fiber and tissue within me was strained to the breaking point. There could be no thought of eating, God knows who nourished me.
> But now it's done. Done. Done.
> Amen.

In the next nine days, Rilke wrote twenty-nine more sonnets—only then was he really done.

One convulsive shudder had produced two very different kinds of masterpieces. Where the *Duino Elegies* are declarative, their long lines bearing a freight of images, expostulations, and ideas, the *Sonnets to Orpheus* hover with wingbeat delicacy at the very edge of the expressible. The *Elegies* argue the transformation of the world; the *Sonnets*, through the mediating persona of Orpheus, come closer to enacting it. With the very first lines—"A tree ascended there. Oh pure transcendence! / Oh Orpheus sings! Oh tall tree in the ear!"—Rilke announces the highest possible claim for poetry and song: the conversion of all that exists into sound.

It is impossible, of course, to do any more than hint at the visionary force of either work. But neither am I convinced that their central mysteries can even *be* elucidated or paraphrased. For Rilke's insistence was on language and song as experience, as events in the ear. There are no shortcuts. Readers, even practiced readers, are likely to be rebuffed again and again. Those who have no German face an additional obstacle. No translation, however skillful, can reproduce the sound values of the original. And the sound values, especially in the purely lyrical *Sonnets,* are fully half the experience. Compare the texture of the German of the first two lines from the well-known Sonnet 13 (second cycle):

> Sei allen Abschied voran, als wäre er hinter
> dir, wie der Winter, der eben geht.

with Stephen Mitchell's semantically faithful rendering:

> Be ahead of all parting, as though it already were
> behind you, like the winter that has just gone by.

The meaning has been carried with some elegance, but the dense weave of vowels, consonants, and rhymes—"als wäre er hinter / dir, wie der Winter"—has been sacrificed. The problems every translator faces are here exacerbated, for sound itself is an intrinsic part of Rilke's theme.

When the *Elegies* and *Sonnets* were at last finished, Rilke enjoyed an enduring sense of accomplishment: He spoke of having fulfilled his poetic mission. He did continue to write poetry, but no longer in German. He felt that he had taken his mother tongue to the limit and could do no more with it. In his last years, then, Rilke wrote more than four hundred lyrics in French, most of them in thematic sequences. In their near-transparent lightness, they are cousins of the *Sonnets*. But every so often, as in this section from *The Roses*, one can also hear echoes of the Rilke of the *New Poems*. This evocation of the rose has quite a lot in common with the description of the pacing panther:

> All that spinning on your stem
> to end yourself, round rose,
> doesn't that make you dizzy?
> But drenched by your impetus,
>
> in your bud you just ignore
> yourself. It's a world that whirls
> around so its calm center dares
> the round repose of the round rose.
> *trans. A. Poulin Jr.*

Rilke died on December 29, 1926, not from the prick of a rose-bush thorn, as the legend would have it, but from a rare and painful form of leukemia. He did prick his finger while gathering roses for a visitor, and the resulting infection may have hastened the eruption of his final illness, but the myth only simplifies and trivializes a long struggle and denies the poet what he most insisted on: that he be allowed to die his own death. He was buried at the cemetery in Raron, Switzerland; chiseled on his stone is this most beautiful epitaph:

> Rose, pure Contradiction, Delight
> to be No-one's Sleep under so many
> Lids.
> *trans. Rika Lesser*

By the time he died, Rilke had achieved world renown. The celebration of his birthday in December 1925 brought greetings and Festschrift honors from every side. Among the salutations was one from the painter Leonid Pasternak, whom Rilke had met in 1899 during his first visit to Russia. Replying to Pasternak's letter, Rilke added a few words of praise for the poetry of his son, Boris. The compliment was passed along, not without effect. "It's as if my shirt were split down the front by the expansion of my heart," an ecstatic Boris wrote to his sister. He promptly wrote a reply to his idol:

> The magical coincidence that I should come to your notice was a staggering event to me. . . . I was alone in a room; none of my family were here when I read the lines about this. . . . I rushed to the window. It was snowing, people were walking outside. I could take nothing in, I was crying.

In the same letter, Pasternak urged upon Rilke the kindred genius of his friend Tsvetaeva—would Rilke permit her to write to him? Soon letters were passing from poet to poet; only Rilke's final illness brought the three-way volley to an end.

I don't know that a more passionate document exists than the recently published *Letters, Summer 1926*. Personal confessions and poetic celebrations are charged with eroticism; emotions run high. Rilke: "Yes and yes and yes, Marina, all yeses to what you want and are, together as large as YES to life itself . . . : but contained in the latter there are, after all, all those ten thousand noes, the unforeseeable ones." Tsvetaeva: "Rainer, just always say yes to all that I want—it won't turn out so badly, after all. Rainer, if I say to you that I am your Russia, I'm only saying (one more time) that I care for you."

Letters are, of course, letters. And since we shouldn't even really be reading them, we make certain allowances. But even with

allowances, the whole business cloys. Is this the soil of temperament required for the nourishing of a vital lyricism? Or is this
more like the hypertrophy—rhetorical emotion consuming itself—
that must prove fatal to any romanticism? Who *was* this Rilke (this
Tsvetaeva, this Pasternak)?

Our removal in time makes this question very hard to answer,
and reference to the historical epoch does not clarify matters any.
After all, by 1926, T. S. Eliot had published *The Waste Land*, Ernest
Hemingway had written the tough prose of *In Our Time*, and W. H.
Auden was already putting together the impudently discordant
poems that would make his reputation. The Rilke-Pasternak-
Tsvetaeva letters represent, if anything, the last phosphorescence
of the nineteenth century. The large-scale abrasions of modernity
make these outcries of feeling and sensibility sound hysterical and
outmoded—more remote from us than anything in the Roman
elegists, or even Sappho.

The idiom of Rilke's work is, fortunately, a good deal more
austere and demanding than the idiom of his correspondence.
And if we can't say precisely who he was as a man, we can at least
try to make some sense of his legacy. Who is Rilke for us today?
What cultural forces—or needs—underlie the flourishing Rilke
industry?

Rilke is not, let us note, one of those suddenly discovered
"greats." Editions of his work have been available in English since
the late 1930s. And he has always had a following. Not just among
poets and literati, either. Romantics of every stripe found the
singing-master of their soul in the difficult, breathless cadences
set out by M. D. Herter Norton and J. B. Leishman, his two most
prolific early translators. Generations of English and American
readers came to know the *Duino Elegies* through the peculiar Ger-
manized English of the Leishman-Stephen Spender version:

> Every Angel is terrible. Still, though, alas!
> I invoke you, almost deadly birds of the soul,
> knowing what you are. Oh, where are the days of Tobias,
> when one of the shining-most stood on the simple threshold,
> a little disguised for the journey, no longer appalling,

(a youth to the youth as he curiously peered outside).
Let the archangel perilous now, from behind the stars,
step but a step down hitherwards: high up-beating,
our heart would out-beat us. Who are you?
from the Second Elegy

The sense is no more problematic than in any translation of the *Elegies,* but there is no suggestion that the work belongs to the genus of the modern.

The Rilke boom that we are witnessing is very much bound up with the retranslating of the oeuvre. A. Poulin Jr., Stephen Mitchell, and Edward Snow—to name the three most energetic workers—have brought a good part of the output over into a swifter, simpler, more Americanized idiom. They have sought to release Rilke from the trappings of the awkward and archaic and to give him a place in the modernist pantheon. Rilke's current popularity has everything to do with his new readability.

The 1977 publication of A. Poulin Jr.'s versions of the *Duino Elegies* and *Sonnets to Orpheus* may have been the first herald of change. Look at Poulin's rendering of the very same lines:

> Every angel's terrifying. Almost deadly birds
> of my soul, I know what you are, but, oh,
> I still sing to you! What happened to the days of Tobias
> when one of you stood in the simple doorway, partly
> disguised for the trip, radiant, no longer appalling;
> (a young man to the young man as he looked out amazed).
> If the archangel, the dangerous one behind the stars,
> took just one step down toward us today: the quicker
> pounding of our heart would kill us. Who are you?

A "journey" has become a "trip," "hitherwards" is now "today"—indeed, the gravity of the older version has been eliminated. In its place, a hopped-up ("Every angel's terrifying") phraseology, a freer narrative line. As Robert Lowell wrote: "It's hard to imagine the *Elegies* first written in English. Rilke has sealed them in German, which is part of their essential mystery and foreignness. . . . Now, because of Mr. Poulin's translation, I experience the *Elegies* almost as English." Lowell, of course, was anything but a purist when it came to issues of translation. His own *Imitations* (he takes on several of Rilke's lyrics) were blasted by scholars and translators alike for their brazen deletions and alterations.

Poulin, too, was drubbed by a number of critics. But the taboo had been breached. His translations made it much easier for those who would follow. Of these, Mitchell has been the most prolific and consistently skillful. He has single-handedly reprocessed the *Letters to a Young Poet, The Notebooks of Malte Laurids Brigge,* both the *Sonnets* and the *Elegies,* as well as a number of the lyrics. Mitchell's idiom strikes a compromise between the kind of stripped and speeded voice that Poulin found, and the more ceremonious and awkward diction of some of the earlier translators. His rendition of the stanza in question runs as follows:

> Every angel is terrifying. And yet, alas,
> I invoke you, almost deadly birds of the soul,
> knowing about you. Where are the days of Tobias,
> when one of you, veiling his radiance, stood at the front door,
> slightly disguised for the journey, no longer appalling;
> (a young man like the one who curiously peeked through the
>   window).
> But if the archangel now, perilous, from behind the stars
> took even one step down toward us: our own heart, beating
> higher and higher, would beat us to death. Who *are* you?

Mitchell keeps the stateliness of the Leishman-Spender translation, but he combs out its worst knots. "Still, though, alas!" "shining-most," and "hitherwards" have all been eliminated. But "I invoke you" has won out over Poulin's colloquial "I know what you are." Mitchell is generally canny in his choices. He tries to position himself midway between poet and reader, effecting at every turn a solution that both gratifies the poet's expressiveness and the reader's desire to understand. Erich Heller, one of the better explicators of Rilke, has written of Mitchell's renderings: ". . . the *Duino Elegies* succeed almost always in converting the energies of thought into telling images. . . . A list of these happy transformations of the abstract into concrete pictures would fill pages. In accompanying this most impressive 'imaging' in English, Stephen Mitchell proves his mastery of the art of translation."

Whatever cavils native German speakers might have about word choice or idiom (I have heard it said that *any* translation of Rilke's German into English is doomed to be a travesty), the fact is that the poet is now available in a reasonably plain English. But availability is one thing, popularity another. It would seem that more and more readers are looking to Rilke because they think—or already know—that he has something they want, or need. Why Rilke?

I can think of several possible reasons. The most obvious is that in our ironic, materialistic period, Rilke's poetry represents a distillation of the most endangered values. Rilke stands for inwardness, spiritual quest, the primacy of feeling over intellection (the same things that Hermann Hesse represented for young idealists in the sixties). To read Rilke—whether you understand him or not—is to cast a vote against the status quo.

In one sense, obviously, this is true of nearly all poetry and reading of poetry. But Rilke is something of a special case, because his work offers a complete secular cosmology. It is a system (a most elusive and vague one, true), a way, an answer. The poet announces a grand, and ultimately beneficent, spiritual order behind this world of appearances. What's more, his system is being set before us precisely at a time when other systems, other ways, seem to be losing their appeal.

In an essay about the Emerson "revival," Richard Poirier made an observation that pertains most closely to the reception of Rilke as well. One factor adduced by Poirier "has been the exhaustion of T. S. Eliot's version of modernism, and of the Christianizing New Criticism that went with it." Simply, if you take God out of the picture, you leave a habit and a hunger that are not easily appeased. Rilke's poetry provides all of the drama of intense spiritual struggle and offers some promise of solution. Moreover, this solution does not seem to depend on a transcendent or immanent deity; it requires, instead, an assent to death, a liberation of yearning. How enticing, how secular, and how inchoate are these lines from the Ninth Elegy:

But because *truly* being here is so much; because everything here apparently needs us, this fleeting world, which in some strange way keeps calling to us. Us, the most fleeting of all.

Once for each thing. Just once; no more. And we too,
just once. And never again. But to have been
this once, completely, even if only once:
to have been at one with the earth, seems beyond undoing.
trans. Stephen Mitchell

Condense this and you get, essentially: Life, in spite of death, matters; that things perish makes them all the more precious. Ancient wisdom, but we never tire of it. As Paul de Man has written (in *Allegories of Reading*): "Rilke's work dares to affirm and to promise, as few others do, a form of existential salvation that would take place in and by means of poetry." But de Man makes a point of greater suggestive power when he writes of the reader using Rilke "as a reflector for his own inner image." This allows us to explain, perhaps, how Rilke can be at once so vague and difficult and so popular. Lines like the ones I just quoted are, in effect, like the burnished surface of a mirror. One can read into them at any depth one chooses. Like the verses of the *I Ching* or the *Tao Te Ching*, they offer no impediment to interpretation. Like the Eastern texts, too, Rilke's *Elegies* and *Sonnets* have behind them the authority of a world comprehended. One reads harder, projects more vividly, because one has invested the text with a scriptural potency—it seems to know the reader better than it will ever *be known*.

I do not want to make it sound as though the work has no determinate value of its own. It does. But that value may have more to do with giving shape and expression to perpetually obscure psychic processes, and less with supplying answers to our deepest questions. Rilke was one of the great explorers and colonizers of the inner realm. No poet in our age—and possibly no poet ever—has gone so far in representing both the violent rushes and subtle tropisms of the interior life. Rilke invented an idiom of his own for emotional and spiritual events. Moreover, this idiom, unlike the language of psychoanalysis, is neither taxonomic or explanatory. It incorporates movement and desire—it *expresses*. And through its particular imagistic richness and intensity—those "concrete pictures" Heller identified—it directs the reader steadily toward a recognition of his spiritual needs. Again, de Man: "Many have read him as if he addressed the most secluded parts of their selves, revealing depths they hardly suspected or allowing them to share in ordeals he helped them to understand and to overcome." Like Fyodor Dostoevsky, Rilke splays the curtain of the everyday to disclose the primary truth of our condition: that we have all been, as the existentialist philosophers would say, "thrown into being." Like Dostoevsky, too, he continually reminds us that our vaunted material progress has not brought us one step closer to explaining that fact. Whether we think of Rilke as a prophet or a spiritual rhetorician, we cannot deny that he is a barometer for the atmospheres of essential desire.

Robert Lowell

> It seems there's been something curiously twisted and against
> the grain about the world poets of our generation have had to
> live in.
>
> *Robert Lowell to John Berryman, March 1959*

The concept of the generation is a curious one, if you think about
it. Strictly speaking, there's no such thing—except, of course, in
the family context. People are born, and die, continuously. But
just beneath that continuum we seem to register mysterious mag-
netic fields of sensibility. I have in mind something more than just
shared experience—the sharing is of perception and feeling. But
what determines this, and how do people recognize it in one another? Almost invariably we end up invoking that ectoplasmic construct known as *Zeitgeist,* or "the spirit of the times."

If the generation business is confusing in the cultural present,
it gets a good deal clearer in retrospect. Consider the case of a
group of midcentury American poets: Elizabeth Bishop, Randall
Jarrell, Delmore Schwartz, John Berryman, Theodore Roethke,
and Robert Lowell. Not so long ago they were still among us,
practicing their diversified craft. I meet people all the time who
knew or studied with Lowell, Berryman, Bishop . . . But now
these poets are gone and the sifting and sorting of contours have
begun.

In recent years we've seen the publication of James Atlas's bi-
ography of Schwartz, Eileen Simpson's memoir of her marriage to
Berryman, *Poets in Their Youth,* Ian Hamilton's *Robert Lowell,* John
Haffenden's life of Berryman, and sizable collections of Schwartz's
and Jarrell's correspondence. The biographer and critic Jeffrey
Meyers has just come out with *Manic Power: Robert Lowell and His
Circle,* the first full-fledged group biography. Out of the welter of

documentation we are witnessing the emergence of a historical entity known as the Lowell Generation.

I expect that the lives and reputations of these poets will be reckoned every bit as strenuously as those of T. S. Eliot, Ezra Pound, Robert Frost, and Wallace Stevens have been. This is not to say that they are all of the same stature—only Lowell and Bishop sustained greatness in their work—but they have captured the eye of posterity with the lurid drama of their lives. Look at the biographical headlines. Lowell, Jarrell, Berryman, Schwartz, and Roethke all suffered the devastations of mental illness. Except for Jarrell, they were all alcoholics. Berryman and Jarrell and, later, Lowell's protégées Sylvia Plath and Anne Sexton committed suicide. The affairs and wrecked marriages are beyond enumeration. They achieved their art at the expense of great destruction. And much of the art was *about* that expense. As Lowell put it—rather mildly—in "Dolphin":

> I have sat and listened to too many
> words of the collaborating muse,
> and plotted perhaps too freely with my life,
> not avoiding injury to others,
> not avoiding injury to myself—
> to ask compassion . . . this book, half fiction,
> an eelnet made by man for the eel fighting—
>
> my eyes have seen what my hand did.

It will be objected that these were extreme cases, that such intense disorders were not common among the stable, hardworking majority, that the relatively serene careers of other poets of that generation—Richard Wilbur, Richard Eberhart, Stanley Kunitz— give the lie to mania. True enough. But there is *something* in all this madness and tragedy, some extent to which it tells the story of a specific epoch in American cultural life.

These poets were the last outriders of a spent ideology— Romanticism. This is where their heroic aura comes from. It's no coincidence that the lines popularly regarded as their collective epitaph (Lowell adapted them for his poem "To Delmore Schwartz"; Eileen Simpson mined them for her title) belong to Wordsworth:

We Poets in our youth begin in gladness,
But thereof come in the end despondence and madness.

The auto-da-fé that they made of their lives illuminates a great
deal about the place of poetry in American life, both in their time
and ours.

What drove these individuals? Personal circumstances were, to
be sure, at the root. "Each of these poets," writes Meyers (referring
to Lowell, Berryman, Jarrell, and Roethke), "had an unhappy
childhood. They suffered from unmanly or absent fathers and
from strong, seductive mothers." And later: "The poets' serious
problems with their parents led to tempestuous marriages, which
were characterized by infidelity, alcoholism, violence and mental
breakdowns." Their literary ambition was part of the drive for
psychic compensation—they would redeem their flawed pasts
through art. Not surprisingly, some of them were the first to break
with the constraints of impersonality and to pioneer what we now
call confessional poetry. But fame, which they all considered the
secular equivalent of absolution, was never enough. Even when
they had it, they made life hellish for themselves.

Unhappy childhoods, though, can't explain the whole tortured
phenomenon. Poets since the days of Homer have grown up in
blighted families. Doubtless there are thousands writing today
whose need for artistic redemption is every bit as great as that felt
by Berryman, Jarrell, or Roethke. No generation is exempt from
the miseries that are our human lot. How is it, then, that we have
seen nothing that can rival the public and private catastrophes
wrought by this group? *What happened?* To understand them, we
obviously have to look past psychobiography.

Meyers's book, for all the promise of its title, is not very useful
in this respect. Although he has laid out the well-known case histories of his players with some care, he does not examine the conditions that shaped the larger milieu. This is a shame, especially as
his opening chapter, "The Dynamics of Destruction," introduces
this tantalizing suggestion:

The poets' careers began in the 1940's and coincided with the
emergence of the United States as the most powerful country in

the world. They believed they were the truthtellers, bearers of culture, sacrificial victims driven mad by a need to escape from an increasingly crass and ugly society. As their audience diminished and their significance decreased, the poets felt they must transcend this hostile society through a finer and more intense conception of reality.

I can see why Meyers is loath to press the connection further. Nothing could be more difficult to assess than the impact of global politics and the attendant social transformations on the practice of a small group of poets. But this inchoate play of forces may well have been the prime catalyst for their mad excess.

If the Romanticism of the late eighteenth and early nineteenth centuries was in large part a response to the encroachment of industrialization and utilitarian ideologies (read Shelley's *A Defence of Poetry*), then couldn't this midcentury explosion of tormented lyricism have been a reaction of the same kind—against the postwar centralization and bureaucratization of power? Where the French and American revolutions sparked the hope of change, so, too, did the confident prosperity that followed our emergence from the war.

I referred to these poets earlier as the last outriders of Romanticism. What I meant was that there was a period in the late forties and early fifties—before the balance tilted decisively away from them—when it was possible for poets to sustain a Romantic faith. They could believe for a time that intellect and imagination had a shaping role to play in American life.

Maybe every poet—every artist—feels this kind of optimism at the outset of his or her career. What was different about this group was that it was able to nurture the dream for a prolonged period. Our society did not congeal into monolithic imperialism overnight. There was an interval—from the end of the war to Eisenhower's landslide defeat of Adlai Stevenson in 1952—during which the future seemed open. The poets gave vent to their great ambition. Only when that future failed them did their work wither into tormented confession (the last discharge of Romantic protest); only then did their lives start to slide into chaos.

Politics, of course, was only part of the story. There were other factors at work, too. We can't forget, for one thing, that these poets

came of age under the tutelage of the New Critics. Their masters—
John Crowe Ransom, Allen Tate, Cleanth Brooks, Robert Penn
Warren—were not only poets themselves (Brooks excepted), but
were the prominent teacher-critics who had put the rigorous study
of poetry at the very center of the liberal arts curriculum in the
American university. The energies first released by Eliot and the
modernists had not yet dissipated. A poet could still believe that
his endeavor placed him at the very hub of the culture. And indeed, for these young poets nothing—but *nothing*—mattered so
much as their trade. As Lowell wrote in his obituary for Jarrell,
"Woe to the acquaintance who liked the wrong writer, the wrong
poem by the right writer, or the wrong lines in the right poem!"
You will not find devotion like this among poets writing now.

Again, *what happened?* Meyers cites "an increasingly crass and
ugly society," diminishing audience, and decreasing significance.
Who is to say what congeries of forces brought all this about?
Material prosperity combined with internationalist politics combined with reactionary anticommunism combined with industrial
and bureaucratic standardization combined with the electoral
debacle—the "egghead" Stevenson was crushed by "Ike." Lowell
caught the mood in "Inauguration Day: January 1953":

> Ice, ice. Our wheels no longer move.
> Look, the fixed stars, all just alike
> as lack-land atoms, split apart,
> and the Republic summons Ike,
> the mausoleum in her heart.

That mausoleum was where the bright hopes of the Lowell circle
were finally interred.

Saul Bellow conveys a vivid sense of these atmospheric changes
in his novel *Humboldt's Gift*. When we first meet the eponymous
Von Humboldt Fleisher (the character was modeled directly on
Bellow's longtime friend Delmore Schwartz), he is flush with ego-
maniacal passion. America, he believes, is the poet's mission. Its
vast material reality is there to be melted down in the crucible of
the imagination, to be transformed into art such as the world has
never seen. But Humboldt mistakes his early success—he reached
a poet's equivalent of stardom in the thirties and forties—for a nod

of confirmation from the larger world. He soon finds out the truth. When his later books are not so well received, when his bids for academic power are repeatedly frustrated, he suffers mental collapse. Although his failures did not directly cause his illness, it's clear that they created a favorable climate for it.

Humboldt dies of a heart attack in a seedy New York hotel. When he sees the obituary, Charlie Citrine, Bellow's narrator, responds with anguished indignation:

> The *Times* was much stirred by Humboldt's death and gave him a double-column spread. The photograph was large. For after all Humboldt did what poets in crass America are supposed to do. He chased ruin and death even harder than he had chased women. He blew his talent and his health and he reached home, the grave, in a dusty slide. He plowed himself under. Okay. So did Edgar Allan Poe, picked out of the Baltimore gutter. And Hart Crane over the side of a ship. And Jarrell falling in front of a car. And poor John Berryman jumping from a bridge. For some reason this awfulness is peculiarly appreciated by business and technological America. The country is proud of its dead poets. It takes terrific satisfaction in the poets' testimony that the USA is too tough, too big, too much, too rugged, that American reality is overpowering. . . . So poets are loved, but loved because they just can't make it here. They exist to light up the enormity of the awful tangle and justify the cynicism of those who say, "If *I* were not such a corrupt, unfeeling bastard, creep, thief, and vulture, I couldn't get through this either. Look at these good and tender and soft men, the *best* of us. They succumbed, poor loonies."

Bellow has hit on something here. In a psychically obscure—but very real—way, Humboldt/Schwartz, Jarrell, Berryman, and the others were brought to the edge of their precipice—and over—by the proudly brutal apathy of their culture. They caught sight of a nobler fate for themselves, and then every chance of attaining it was taken away. The fact that they had glimpsed the alternative was what set them up for tragedy.

It is now a full decade since Lowell, the last surviving member of Meyers's core group, died. Things in the poetry world feel very different now. We don't see nearly so much torment and self-destruction—and for the sake of the potential victims and their families, we should be glad. More and more, poetry is becoming a safe, grant-and-university-sponsored kind of thing. I'd say that the change—the "calm"—has a great deal to do with societal changes and with the disappearance of certain hopes and expectations. Things have come to such a pass in Olliemanic-Silicon Valley-Star Wars-Wall Street-*cynical* America that no one even considers that poetry—or art of any kind—might make a difference. As history reveals, the Romantic vision comes alive only when some chance of transformation is felt to exist. The French Revolution lit up the poets once; our emergence from World War II sent up a much smaller spark. Still, there was a moment when the balance seemed to teeter—before it tipped for good.

Seamus Heaney

I first heard Seamus Heaney read his poems in the mid-1970s, in a large assembly hall at the University of Michigan. It was late afternoon, and the event was poorly attended. A handful of students and poetry types were scattered about in the hangar-size space; the microphone chirped and whined. The poet was not yet "known," and probably no one would have blamed him if he had just booked it out the back exit. But of course he didn't. Instead, he stepped out and performed what is by now the familiar Heaney miracle: He filled the inhospitable space with what W. H. Auden once called "the furniture of home." With a few self-deprecating introductory feints he shucked off the dread formality that haunts all readings and took possession of the room.

The young Heaney had, I remember, a remarkable face. The cheekbones were high and flat, and the effect, with the narrowed eyes and long jaw, was Easter Islandish—as though one of the great heads had been reimagined onto a likely set of shoulders. His voice as he read was a low purr from the back of the throat, just short of a full-out brogue. And the poems? They were so rough and loamy—so *real*—that I felt I could put on a pair of rubber boots and go walking around in them. I was not alone in my response. By the hour's end Heaney had pulled his listeners out of their slouching repose and the scatter had become compact. There was the feeling that something of great importance had just transpired.

Heaney's career has since advanced like an accelerated-motion study of a well-tended tree, the main trunk growing thicker (as has his own), the radial shoots levering out and branching with unconstrained inevitability. Indeed, this career is one of very few about which there is no sense of accident and luck. Every move appears necessary, not just in hindsight but as it is happening. The reader—listener—has the curious sensation of being in contact not with just a poet or a poem but with a complete poetic destiny. I am convinced that some collective intuition of this has helped foster Heaney's public success. People sense the real thing long before they fully understand or appreciate it. Although Heaney, it must be said, more than any other major poet of our time, has been understood and appreciated.

From the first to the most recent, the poems are based in strong sensation and built with durable—and accessible—sounds and rhythms. In his way of making larger resonances from the materials of nature, Heaney resembles Robert Frost. His work shows the same two-handed grasp of the primary; in a world bent on severing its rural umbilicus, he would yet have us connected to a rougher, more vivid set of conditions.

The poet has now culled his own work to produce *Selected Poems 1966-1987*. It is a beautiful book to hold and heft, and one is all but compelled to start with the first poem and read through to the end—a procedure that most such compendiums discourage. With Heaney's selection, moreover, comes a double reward: One has the pleasure of the poems themselves and the gratification of partaking in a very palpable process of growth and change. That partaking is a reminder, to anyone who needs it, of the vitality of the link between the life and the expression. If you were to run a saw through the bole of this book, it would be clear that the artistic growth has been consistent, the evidence a target shape of concentric rings. The dynamic itself is one of departure and return; the irresistible vector of exploration at some point always curves back into the consolidating circle.

The earliest Heaney poems embody the immediate circumstances of his rural upbringing in Ireland's County Derry. In "Follower," for instance, from *Death of a Naturalist* (1966), he wrote of his father's work with the plow, at the same time intimating his own unfitness for the generational yoke. The language modulates from clear-eyed description—

> An expert. He would set the wing
> And fit the bright steel-pointed sock.
> The sod rolled over without breaking.

—to an emotional recognition tendered with no trace of sentimentality:

> I wanted to grow up and plough,
> To close one eye, stiffen my arm.
> All I ever did was follow
> In his broad shadow round the farm.
>
> I was a nuisance, tripping, falling,
> Yapping always. But today
> It is my father who keeps stumbling
> Behind me, and will not go away.

Subsequent work, from the books *Door into the Dark* (1969), *Wintering Out* (1972), and *North* (1975), shows Heaney quite naturally striking out for less immediately personal subjects and larger themes. The poems of this period reflect his deeply Romantic beliefs about language—that words at their etymological source (and in the poet's psyche) are all but literally an incarnation of place and thing—as well as his obsession with the sedimentary process of history. In "Gifts of Rain" he maps the confluence of place and word:

> The tawny guttural water
> spells itself: Moyola
> is its own score and consort,
>
> bedding the locale
> in the utterance,
> reed music, an old chanter
>
> breathing its mists
> through vowels and history.

Lines in the later "Bone Dreams" depart from a found bit of bone to brood over the mysteries of ancestry. His thread back into the dark is his discovery of the kenning "bone-house" for "body":

> In the coffered
> riches of grammar
> and declensions
> I found *bān-hūs,*
>
> its fire, benches,
> wattle and rafters,

> where the soul
> fluttered a while
>
> in the roofspace.
> There was a small crock
> for the brain,
> and a cauldron
>
> of generation
> swung at the centre:
> love-den, blood-holt,
> dream-bower.

The poems in these early books, particularly in *North,* return repeatedly to the images of centuries-old corpses retrieved intact
from the preserving muck of bogs. What is interesting is that
Heaney, for all his fixation on forging bonds to the ancestral past,
also appears gripped by the physical otherness of these human artifacts. The precision of his language, as in these lines from "The
Grauballe Man," is as much a marking out of distance as it is an attempt at capturing the seen:

> His hips are the ridge
> and purse of a mussel,
> his spine an eel arrested
> under a glisten of mud.

Similar ambivalence attends Heaney's efforts to bring himself
to face the enormously loaded subject of Irish sectarian strife. It is
obvious that he feels he ought to, and just as obvious that his heart
lies elsewhere. In "Exposure," the last poem from *North* included
in this volume, the poet ponders his place as poet and citizen.
What will appear in later work as a more astringent self-scourging
is tinctured here by a certain pride of attainment:

> I am neither internee nor informer;
> An inner émigré grown long-haired
> And thoughtful; a wood-kerne
>
> Escaped from the massacre
> Taking protective colouring
> From bole and bark, feeling
> Every wind that blows . . .

What Heaney is referring to, more explicitly, is his decision to move with his family from the embattled north to a cottage in Wicklow, in the south. The move was a controversial one, and the poet did not escape the recriminations of his fellows, but the yield was the beautiful poems that make up the book *Field Work* (1979). Here, without surrendering the self-questioning that gave shadow to the more public life, Heaney made the first full circuit back to self and the immediacies of place and circumstance. If his first book was a young man's declaration, then this was the testament of a man in the full flush of maturity. The poems are tender, erotic, and alive through the least iamb with the flux of the natural world.

At the heart of *Field Work* is the sequence of "Glanmore Sonnets," and it shows the poet at the very top of his form. Heaney's natural descriptions are unrivaled in their power of intimation. The language, exquisitely precise, also manages a larger symphonic effect—it brims over its word-by-word designations to summon the emotion behind the memory. Here is the fifth sonnet:

> Soft corrugations in the boortree's trunk,
> Its green young shoots, its rods like freckled solder:
> It was our bower as children, a greenish, dank
> And snapping memory as I get older.
> And elderberry I have learned to call it.
> I love its blooms like saucers brimmed with meal,
> Its berries a swart caviar of shot,
> I buoyant spawn, a light bruised out of purple.
> Elderberry? It is shires dreaming wine.
> Boortree is bower tree, where I played 'touching tongues'
> And felt another's texture quick on mine.
> So, etymologist of roots and graftings,
> I fall back to my tree-house and would crouch
> Where small buds shoot and flourish in the hush.

To my mind, this is the essential Heaney, writing what might be called the music of the self in time. No poet is more adept at tracking the subtle and charged incursions of memory, or fixing the spell of the once-seen and once-known in language. The brocade of sounds is as dense as anything in Keats. And what a delight in making there is! Notice how the straight iambic line "I love its

blooms like saucers brimmed with meal" paves the way for the clustered stresses of "swart caviar of shot"—one feels the weight of the
berries directly in the center of the palms. But note also the foxy
play of tenses in the penultimate line. The verbs refuse to resolve;
the self remains suspended between the then and the now, and
the memory sustains its unsettling vividness.

Many another poet would have considered *Field Work* the attainment of a career and contented himself thereafter with repris-
ing its successes. But true to the imperatives of his development,
Heaney pushed on, out from the rural contemplation that came
to him with such right readiness and into a phase of moral self-
interrogation. All of the old questions about the writer's place and
duty were renewed. His next major work—aside from the free rendering of the old Irish story cycle in *Sweeney Astray* (1983)—was a
self-consciously Dantean pilgrimage poem, *Station Island* (1984).
Here, in long narrative sections, Heaney portrayed himself as un-
dertaking a penitential retreat, encountering in the process diverse figures—apparitions—from his personal and cultural past. At
the core, as ever, was the struggle between the claims of political
engagement and those of contemplative detachment. Confronted
by the shade of a relation who had been murdered for his politics,
Heaney's persona can only mutter:

'Forgive the way I have lived indifferent—
forgive my timid circumspect involvement . . .'

Several sections later, however, he gives close heed to the coun-
sel of the greatest of Ireland's literary men, James Joyce:

'Your obligation
is not discharged by any common rite.
What you do you must do on your own. . . .

And don't be so earnest,

so ready for the sackcloth and the ashes.
Let go, let fly, forget.
You've listened long enough. Now strike your note.'

Station Island is Heaney's most necessary but artistically least sat-
isfying book. The poet clearly needs to weigh his desires and mo-

tives thoroughly before he can move forward, but the structure he has chosen—of pilgrimage and encounter—forces on him the incessant haggling with narrative devices; the work creaks from its arrivals, departures, and set-piece declamations. The result is hardly to be scorned—long passages move with a muscular flex and ripple—but the simple fact is that this is not what Heaney does best.

That work did, however, break open the sluice gates again. With the poems in his collection, *The Haw Lantern* (1987), Heaney has begun again the return to his source places. The book may not be his most powerful—it is not as shaped to theme or obsession as some of the earlier books—but it does contain, in a sonnet sequence called "Clearances," the most beautiful poems Heaney has ever written. The occasion is the death of his mother. As the momentum of the sonnet form makes it a desecration to excerpt, here is the whole of the third in the sequence:

> When all the others were away at Mass
> I was all hers as we peeled potatoes.
> They broke the silence, let fall one by one
> Like solder weeping off the soldering iron:
> Cold comforts set between us, things to share
> Gleaming in a bucket of clean water.
> And again let fall. Little pleasant splashes
> From each other's work would bring us to our senses.
>
> So while the parish priest at her bedside
> Went hammer and tongs at the prayers for the dying
> And some were responding and some crying
> I remembered her head bent towards my head,
> Her breath in mine, our fluent dipping knives—
> Never closer the whole rest of our lives.

Reaching the end of the poem, I feel as though some obstacle in my own life has been removed. And I see, suddenly, the real source of Heaney's great appeal. Beyond the poems, their images and recognitions, is a tremendous love for the world—the beauty and power of the language are but its outward signature.

Atmospheres of Identity: Elizabeth Bishop

The writing of a master always makes us reflect, again, on the mystery of writing—how it happens, what it *is*. For a master reminds us with her every sentence that while prose can be, in some cases, improved, there are no directions or guides for "rightness," that quality that strikes us as an embodiment beyond all analysis, as a form of being that has surpassed its orchestration of moving parts. Here we include—but do not confine ourselves to—verbal texture, rhythmic movement and modulation, diction, the selection and placement of detail, the presentation of situation and the decision about digression versus elision that is renewed at every pen stroke.

The best prose, masterly prose, is a window onto the self of the writer—not the self enslaved by the contingencies of the moment, but the self more essential: the self that looks out artlessly from the photographs of the child, or that feels like a thing gathered and hoarded behind the concertedly thoughtful poses of the adult. How is it that one self writes one way and another completely differently? The sentences of different writers move—even breathe—differently. Nouns have different weight depending on what sort of medium they are suspended in. A certain sensibility will always insert the qualifying phrase, the discriminating twist, as if to say that with enough pressure, enough care, the words can map the least iridescence on the shifting scales of the world. Another will approach to pounce, or grip by main force, then suddenly round on himself, breathing in essences and exhaling them as a kind of cloud formation.

I think of George Orwell or William Hazlitt or Edward Hoagland or M. F. K. Fisher or any number of other writers whose worlds I happily inhabit and who are entirely exclusive of one another. How completely, I wonder, does a given reflection or episode take its character from the mode of narration? And how much of what we regard as narration is just a more or less oblique transposition to the page of the mysterious formations of the self? In other words, is there really any world to be encountered in a writer's prose, or do we go to that prose to feel how the complex projections—manifestations—of the author's sensibility merge with or ricochet off our reading selves? Could these engagements with books really be the occasion for the subtlest linguistic intimacies, with subject matter merely serving as a legitimizing pretext? And what if it were so?

I have had these inklings and questions in mind recently because I have been reading the prose of Elizabeth Bishop. Reading it to discover what it says, yes, but also in order to study the deeper manifestations of the *how* of the saying. I first opened *The Collected Prose* because I wanted her particular impressions of things—her childhood, Brazil, and so on—but I soon found myself more occupied with the atmospheres of identity that seem to hover everywhere around the matters presented. Something about Bishop's writing made me feel as if I were in contact with the self behind the sentences, almost as if the reverie induced by my reading were not merely adjacent to but contiguous with her own language impulses.

Bishop, it should be said, is a great poet, alive across a generous spectrum; as a prose writer she is brilliant, but only in the narrowest way. In her various memoir essays and stories she brings forward, over and over, the soul of the child she was—either directly, in writing about childhood memories, or indirectly, by filtering some other subject (travel in Brazil, her friendship with Marianne Moore) through the scrim of an innocent's sensibility. This, as will be seen, is operative even on—*especially* on—a syntactical level.

I will not report here on the stuff of Bishop's prose, except to affirm that much of it retails impressions from her girlhood years, especially the period when she lived with her grandparents in a village in Nova Scotia. The other pieces—her witty memoir of working at a correspondence school for would-be writers, her introduction to the diary of Helena Morley, and so on—finished as they are, lack the special intensity that derives from her efforts to write her way back into the earlier epochs of her life.

Interestingly—and tellingly—a selective tissue-sample approach to the writing does not do violence to some larger integrity, not much anyway. Bishop's prose does not, as does the prose of so many other writers, ride on accretion. Her unique ability, which is directly bound up with her limitations in the genre, is to render the world as if seen through the eyes of a preternaturally watchful child. There is a powerful—and fruitful—tension on the page between the highly receptive senses and the countering force, the fear, that would keep the world at a manageable distance.

Here is a passage from her autobiographical essay, "The Country Mouse":

> Grandpa once asked me to get his eyeglasses from his bedroom, which I had never been in. It was mostly white and gold, surprisingly feminine for him. The carpet was gold-colored, the bed was fanciful, brass and white, and the furniture was gold and white too. There was a high chest of drawers, a white bedspread, muslin curtains, a set of black leatherbound books near the bed, photographs of Grandma and my aunts and uncles at various ages, and two large black bottles (of whiskey, I realized years later). There were also medicine bottles and the "machines." There were two of them in black boxes, with electrical batteries attached to things like stethoscopes—some sort of vibrator or massager perhaps. What he did with them I could not imagine. The boxes were open and looked dangerous. I reached gingerly over one to get his eyeglasses, and saw myself in the long mirror: my ugly serge dress, my too long hair, my gloomy and frightened expression.

I offer this paragraph in order to make a few observations. First, that it, like most of the other paragraphs in the essay, is excerptible. We don't require background information: The prose does not refer backward, nor does it ride on the surge of anticipation. A portion of the world is registered, described, almost as if a camera eye had lopped off one full portion of the past and would soon be taking the next.

But this is no mere surface oddity. The writing embodies the perceptual movement, and this verges—here and elsewhere—on dissociation. We feel almost no sense of cumulation or causal connectedness. Rather: one thing, another, another. The Humean world, the child's world. Intense, not yet grounded in the explanation-making impulse.

Reading, we are affected by the calm tone—uninflected, utterly unemphatic—as well as by the simplicity of the expression. Colors are white, gold, and black. The chest of drawers is merely "high," the black bottles "large." Nor are the presumably mysterious machines regarded in any way that reflects a child's deeper curiosity; only the surfaces are grazed. Moreover, the sentence constructions are passive, the syntax parsimonious in its means ("The boxes were open . . ."; "There were also medicine bottles . . .").

But how could it not be so? The little girl is terrified—by life, by loss. She is living with her grandparents because her mother has been institutionalized—she is reflexively compelled to hold the looming particulars of the adult world at a distance, even if the natural movement of a child's sensibility would be to get in close, devouring each protruding bit of matter. How differently Vladimir Nabokov would have written it! But then he, as a child, was lord of the dacha. From Bishop's presentation we glean intuitively, without having to be nudged, that these are the observations of a child who is stepping hesitantly into a foreign space; she will not linger to investigate because she is deeply cowed. Her only actual brush with the surface of things comes late, when she reaches "gingerly" to get the eyeglasses.

Bishop's technique here is in some ways similar to that used by Ernest Hemingway in his fiction, though his adaptation of primer constructions was more stylized. Hemingway deployed his repetitions and pruned back observations to suggest the badly damaged nerves and depleted responsiveness of his characters. Bishop, by contrast, transmits an almost arrested innocence—a self struggling to stave off further news of the adult world. The black bottles are not, just then, understood to contain whiskey, though Bishop sees fit to tell us that she realized this later; the possible purposes of the machines remain unplumbed.

It is natural, of course, that a writer seeking to re-create the childhood scape from the inside would use the stylistic devices at her disposal. But what we discover as we read on is that Bishop has, perhaps unconsciously, adapted these very same options for her other purposes as well, in the process producing a prose that could be called "faux naive": not primitive—Bishop is too enamored of the natural surface for that, but syntactically restricted in a way that keeps the surface simpler than her mastery of diverse means might otherwise allow.

In 1967, Bishop wrote an essay, "A Trip to Vigia," in which she narrated a visit she had undertaken with a shy Brazilian poet to a town some hundred kilometers distant from where she was then living. Here we see a different sort of convergence of matter and method. This is a travelogue, and what is a travelogue but a sequential showcasing of the world as it offers itself to the senses? The best ones—and Bishop's is delightful in every way—give evidence that new sights and experiences have broken the crust of habit. The renewal of perceptual clarity is seen, invariably, as a return to a state of prior innocence.

Here is Bishop entering a small backcountry store during a stop:

> The store had been raided, sacked. Oh, that was its normal state. It was quite large, no color inside or cloud-color perhaps, with holes in the floors, holes in the walls, holes in the roof. A barrel of kerosene stood in a dark stain. There were a coil of blue cotton rope, a few mattock heads, and a bundle of yellow-white handles, fresh cut from hard *ipé* wood. Lined up on the shelves were many, many bottles of *cachaça*, all alike: Esperança, Hope, Hope, Hope. There was a counter where you could drink, if you wanted. A bunch of red-striped wicks hung beside a bunch of rusty frying pans. A glass case offered brown toffees leaking through their papers, and old, old, old sweet buns. Some very large ants were making hay there while the sun shone. Our eyes negotiated the advertisements for Orange Crush and Guarana on the cloud-colored walls, and we had seen everything. That was all.

As with the earlier passage, we get a sense of the eye moving deliberately from thing to thing, only here—and perhaps this is an indication of maturity, or greater self-confidence in the presented "I"—discriminations supplant what were formerly approximations. The handles are "yellow-white," and the toffees are seen "leaking through their papers." The eye lingers now, engages more with the grain of things. But the enumeration also feels—as it can in Bishop's numinously charged poetry as well—like a way of holding other aspects, or awarenesses, at bay.

This description also violates many of the standard precepts for lively writing—almost, we feel, deliberately. "It was quite large . . ."; "A barrel of kerosene stood . . ."; "There were a coil . . ." And on and on. Yet the perceptions themselves—the barrel standing in the stain, the odd invocation of "cloud-color"—flex against the bonds of the rudimentary sentence structure. We finish the paragraph with the feeling that we have been and have seen, even if the impression itself is humble and in some primary way gravity-bound.

A prose style *is* a metaphysics, and the fact that we do not just now pay much attention to writers' styles only means that we are letting our relation to things—the things that are the case—get muddled. In Bishop's work—and this is one of the reasons she is so prized by readers—there is no such confusion. We come away from whatever we read, poetry or prose, with a sense that the world has been seen steadily, indeed with the kind of heightened (or restricted) focus that we feel we may possess in our finest moments. The writing confers an impression of control, of elusive materials caught into place; of specific things known because observed with great care.

But by the same token we rarely feel that the "I" of these pieces ever acts on the world, or in any way even ruffles the surface of things. This sensibility would never presume; its reticence is Prufrockian. To act, to interfere, to get caught up in any sort of business with other people—this would be almost hubristic. It would presuppose a volitional self, and Bishop's is not. Recall her famous poem "In the Waiting Room," wherein she reports her experience—she is almost seven—of realizing "you are an *I*, / you are an *Elizabeth*, / you are one of *them*." Reading her prose I often think that it was all she could do to hold that precious awareness intact through her life, that there was scarcely enough surplus to use for living. Bishop's great achievement was to turn what would be in a less grounded person a serious psychological deficit into the cornerstone of her art. In her work self-effacement is somehow transmuted into what feels like an extraordinary humility before life—not just things and beings, but the underlying, or in-dwelling, force that makes them possible. "I'm just looking," she seems to be saying, but as we look with her we feel the world recharging itself for us.

The final piece in the book, "In the Village"—called a story, but by Bishop's own admission a scarcely modified work of autobiography—is the narrative of life in a Nova Scotian village as seen through the eyes of a little girl. It is, more particularly, the account of a mother's return from a stay in an institution—before the collapse that would return her there for good. "Unaccustomed to having her back," writes Bishop, "the child stood now in the doorway, watching." The mother is being fitted for a dress; she wants to come out of mourning for her husband. But suddenly the dress seems all wrong and she screams. The daughter is transfixed; in her imagination the scream hangs over that village "forever, a slight stain in those pure blue skies." And if we look, following the risky path of the explanatory conceit, for some way of understanding that limpid, detached, slightly stunned quality in Bishop's writing—where it comes from—we might linger meditatively on the image of that little girl standing in that doorway, observing as the dressmaker "was crawling around and around on her knees eating pins as Nebuchadnezzar had crawled eating grass."

The Leaning Umbrella:
A Reflection on Flaubert

Although I'm probably as jealous as the next writer of the awards and honors bestowed on my fellows, I have never really coveted anyone else's style or subject—there are limits. Recently, however, I came across an advertisement for a book titled *The Perpetual Orgy: Flaubert and "Madame Bovary"* (1986) by the Peruvian novelist Mario Vargas Llosa. It was billed as the record of Vargas Llosa's lifelong passion for the novel and its eponymous heroine, a work of celebratory investigation. It was as if I had been in love all these years without knowing it—my realization came with the announcement of betrothal. At that moment, I felt that I had never wanted anything more than to write that book.

I read *The Perpetual Orgy* in a single gulp. I simultaneously hoped that Vargas Llosa would say everything I'd felt and thought about *Madame Bovary,* and that it would miss the mark completely. It turned out to be a case of both and neither. The book was brimming with insights and exclamations; Vargas Llosa pointed out a hundred things that I had never noticed. On the other hand, he neglected to explore some of the facets of *Bovary* that have haunted me most: how Flaubert revealed Emma's destiny as the interaction of character and circumstance—she *willed* her end—or how much the crystalline perfection of the novel's design was rooted in hatred. Observations that Vargas Llosa made in lowercase, I would have capitalized, while certain of his other points seemed marginal to me. Still, it was an admirable labor of love, and Vargas Llosa deserves the gratitude of Flaubert lovers everywhere. These few added reflections are just my way of soothing a galvanized nerve.

Madame Bovary is more than just a supremely crafted novel or a harrowing narrative of a fate unfolding. It is, if I may adopt the fashionable phraseology, fiction in its purest state of fictionality.

Unlike certain contemporary texts, however, which remind the reader of their status through the various kinds of authorial sub-version (I'm thinking of self-consuming artifacts like Italo Calvino's *If on a Winter's Night a Traveler* and John Fowles's *The French Lieutenant's Woman*), Flaubert achieves this effect through the sheer perfection of design. Every scene, every sentence, every *word* has been set into place with tweezer precision; there is not a superfluous syllable in the book. The author's ideal was the creation of a self-sustaining fictional world, one that would be functional down to the smallest cogwheel. To achieve this, he absented himself entirely: at no point can we say, "This is Flaubert speaking." ("The artist," he wrote in a famous letter, "must be in his work like God . . . everywhere felt, but never seen.") *Madame Bovary* manifests a complete relational integrity. Its elaborate invented world exerts on the reader the full pressure of necessity; the least of its actions is at once a cause and an effect. Naturalistic illusionism—and fictionality—can be taken no further. After Flaubert, the novel as form could only decline, or change.

Any number of novels, I find, can compel participatory involvement. If the characters and the situation are in the least bit interesting, I have no trouble suspending disbelief and immersing myself. Disbelief seems to *crave* suspension. Too often, however, this illusion of being inside another world has more to do with the reader's desire than with the author's skill. I don't know how many novels I've gone back to, only to find that the mainspring has broken—the language will not come alive again. I realize at those times that I have authored much of my own reading experience.

Madame Bovary is different in this way. No matter how often I return to it, no matter how well or poorly I am disposed toward Emma (I have been taken in by her, I have pitied her, I have reviled her), Flaubert's serene-seeming world is waiting to receive me. I do not have to break my way in with exertions of the imagination. The terrain, the town, the rooms—everything is there, undiminished in its palpability. I feel, then, as if I have been off traveling, that I am returning to a place and a way of life that the intervening years have left intact. This is not to say, of course, that Flaubert has left nothing to the reader's imagination. On the contrary: Because the ground has been laid out for us so meticulously, we are that much more free to conjure the fine points for ourselves.

Flaubert's agonies of composition are legendary. In letter after letter, he chronicled his ordeal—the days spent grooming the cadence of a single sentence, the long, depressed *marinades* on the couch in his study. To Louise Colet he wrote:

> What a beastly thing prose is! It's never finished; there is always something to do over. A good prose sentence must be like a good line of verse, *unchangeable,* as rhythmic, as sonorous. That at least is my ambition (there is one thing I'm certain of: there's no one who has ever had in mind a more perfect type of prose than I have; but as for the execution, what weaknesses, good Lord, what weaknesses!).

Passages like this have contributed to the popular impression that Flaubert was primarily a stylist, that form and presentation had precedence over content. Preposterous! What Flaubert was after in his struggle for a stylistic absolute was a total elimination of the form-content distinction. He believed, like few writers before or since, in the fundamental correspondence between words and the world; every sensation and material detail had its linguistic equivalent. The triumph of style would be implicitly the triumph of content as well.

But Flaubert's obsession went far beyond the painstaking construction of sentences. Structure, too, was a matter of absolutes. The right disposition of description and incident could create in the reader the illusion of an autonomous reality. The composition of *Madame Bovary* took as long as it did—five years of concentrated daily work—not just because the sentences took that long to write, but because the design was of such intricacy. The least movement of a walk-on character, the dilations and contractions of the time frame, the subtle associative echoes between scenes—*everything* had to be plotted out in advance. Flaubert hovered over his planning sheets like a demented watchmaker. No matter how intently one scrutinizes the text, it's impossible to see through the artifice of its construction.

I have read the book six times now (I've never gone back to anything else more than once). The first time—it was, I remember, the summer after my sophomore year in college—I was bent on improving myself. I was delighted to discover that a so-called classic could be so involving. The gusts of Emma's suffering had me spinning like a weathervane. As the end drew near, I begged her creator to intercede on her behalf. When she finally died, I was crushed. But I felt that I knew once and for all about the implacability of fate. My immersion had been emotional: I had picked up nothing of the subplots or the satiric interludes.

Since then, I have reread *Madame Bovary* for pleasure as well as for teaching purposes. Each time I have been startled by the changes I've found. It's almost as if the master himself had been there during my absence, adding, subtracting, altering the way the sunlight strikes the slate roofs, bringing minor characters forward into greater prominence. The world is deeply familiar, as I said, but I see so many things in it differently. Emma's visit to the ball at La Vaubyessard, for example: In my memory the festivities go on and on. My last rereading convinced me that my text had somehow been abridged. And Emma's love affair with Rodolphe: I've added a volume of hesitations and coy exchanges to the scene leading up to her surrender.

My first impulse, quite naturally, was to attribute all inconsistencies to the fallibility of my own memory. But no—the longer I live with the novel, the more certain I am that Flaubert intended this experience for his reader. The whole narrative has been structured to expand in retrospect. Through the considered arrangement of resonating details, through the strategic use of time compressions (Vargas Llosa illuminates these expertly), and, most of all, through the associative play of Emma's own memory, Flaubert secures a self-augmenting afterlife for his episodes. My confusion about the ball illustrates this perfectly. The scene itself was not long. But Flaubert let Emma recall one detail after another in her subsequent reveries. What's more, he had arranged it that she should find, and keep, the vicomte's cigar case; the object acquires for her an almost Proustian density of association. It is inevitable that the scene, in recollection, rises up like one of those intricate ships that fill their bottles at a tug of the string.

Reading through *Madame Bovary* with students has only confirmed my sense of its inexhaustibility. We have ranged back and forth, combing the narrative like a team of detectives. The premise behind the activity is very simple: that Flaubert inserted nothing gratuitously, that every detail has a function that can be traced and explicated. What's interesting is that for all our patient plucking of strands, not one student has vented the familiar complaint— that the process is "nitpicky" or irrelevant. More often, I have felt their awe. It is a revelation to most that prose can hold so much, and that microscopic inspection can produce such a yield. I hate to tell them that Flaubert is a special case, that most novels dissolve like cigar ash under similar scrutiny.

Vargas Llosa's keen excitement sent me back for still another plunge. I don't know whether it was my own state of mind, or whether his observations had influenced me, but this time I was intrigued above all by the novel's spatial depth, its material solidity. Objects seemed held in the grip of gravity, and the air surrounding them was not mere absence—its transparence conveyed a sense of cubic volume. Flaubert, I realized, was possessed of an extraordinary optical sophistication. He staged every perspective and vantage to enhance the reader's illusion of three-dimensionality.

The principle behind this is not unlike that of the stereoscope, where the eye superimposes two differently angled images to create a simulation of spatial depth. Knowing that the reader converts verbal description into discrete mental pictures, Flaubert assembled his narrative in such a way that almost every image would call up the memory of a counterpart. Early on, for instance, as some of the Yonville residents gather at the inn to await the arrival of the new doctor, Flaubert lets it drop that Monsieur le curé is waiting to see whether the Hirondelle might not also be carrying the umbrella that he had left behind at the convent in Ernemont. Caught up in the bustle of the Bovary's arrival, we put the detail completely out of our thoughts. But then, pages later, as the new arrivals are leaving the inn to go to their home, we get this: ". . . the stable boy, lantern in hand, was waiting to light Monsieur and Madame Bovary home. There were wisps of straw in his red hair, and his left leg was lame. He took Monsieur le curé's umbrella in his other hand, and the company set out."

A mere trifle. We forgot, and now we remember. But with this simple completion of the circuit, Flaubert makes us understand that the world did not disappear while the new Yonvillians ate and chattered by the fire. A leaning umbrella (I picture it so) forces us to fill in a world.

A single instance would not, of course, suffice. Here is another. When she is standing in her attic, clutching Rodolphe's good-bye letter, Emma glances out and sees their neighbor Binet in the window opposite. He is bent over his lathe. Much later, when she is in the throes of desperation, rushing from place to place to beg for money, Madame Tuvache and Madame Caron climb to the latter's attic to spy. From their place they watch Emma open the door and step into Binet's workroom; he is, as ever, at his lathe. There are hundreds, maybe thousands, of similar cross-references in *Madame Bovary*, most of them visual. And every time that we are made to recall an image that we have pushed aside, the impression of an independently existing world is fortified.

I dwell on these aspects of the novel because they have most recently been in my thoughts. Even so, every observation I have made has supplanted innumerable others that I would have liked to have made. On the subject of Emma's boredom, for example, or on the question raised by Walker Percy in one of his essays: Why does it exhilarate us to read about another person's despair? Or, or . . . A perpetual orgy, I suppose, is one in which the participants are never sated.

A Gatsby for Today

Since it was first published, in 1925, *The Great Gatsby* has established itself as an American classic—more tellingly, as a classic that people actually read, and love. There are some good reasons for this. F. Scott Fitzgerald's novel is at once formally elegant and piercingly romantic in its expression—a compelling story, but one imbued with the features of legend. It goes off like a flashbulb, freezing a bold array of images on the retina; the fade is delicious, stirring. And then there is the beauty of the writing, the lyric thrill of the sentences. Here is Nick Carraway arriving for his first visit at the home of Daisy and Tom Buchanan:

> Their house was even more elaborate than I expected, a cheerful red-and-white Georgian Colonial mansion, overlooking the bay. The lawn started at the beach and ran toward the front door for a quarter of a mile, jumping over sun-dials and brick walls and burning gardens—finally when it reached the house drifting up the side in bright vines as though from the momentum of its run. The front was broken by a line of French windows, glowing now with reflected gold and wide open to the warm windy evening, and Tom Buchanan in riding clothes was standing with his legs apart on the front porch.

Kinetic and sportive at first, the description comes to rest in a stationary—heraldic—image of power. This is a prose that has learned a few tricks from the movie camera.

But economy and stylistic grace, even when coupled with a good page-turning story, are not enough to ensure that a work will rise above seasonal excellence to become a classic. To attain that status a novel—or a work in any genre—must perpetually renew its relevance for audiences. Some books must wait for changing cultural circumstances to give them point; they go in and out of print as the incalculable mood of the general readership dictates. Others, the true classics, survive the vagaries of the marketplace by tapping the stratum of the universal, embodying our essential dreams and conflicts.

Gatsby succeeds on these latter terms. If the novel is not universal in the Shakespearean or Dantean sense, it is nevertheless thoroughly and perfectly American, a pure distillation of our collective experience. But even as it endures as a classic, *Gatsby* is also able to manifest a particular immediacy at certain times. Just now, I would say, it has a special resonance. Indeed, it might well be a kind of breviary for the nineties, not only because it gives us portraits of our recent and current psychological climates, but also because it tells us something about who we are at a point when we very badly need to know.

There is, of course, the obvious relevance— *Gatsby* as a cautionary tale. The Jazz Age of Fitzgerald's 1920s corresponds in so many ways to our recent 1980s: the glitter and public strut of money, and the fiscal and moral leveraging that made it possible; the reckless rush away from the centers of gravity, and the sudden, terrible realization that gravity writes no exceptions—all this is in the book. The wild party and the hangover. We know it well: morning after in America. Like Nick at the outset of the story, we are waking up, slightly stunned, wondering what happened and what it means. Nick says, "When I came back from the East last autumn I felt that I wanted the world to be in uniform and at a sort of moral attention forever; I wanted no more riotous excursions with privileged glimpses into the human heart."

Gatsby unfolds over the course of a long summer and follows the logic of a dream. One of the marvels of the book is the way in which the narration changes. Although Nick has alerted us in the first few pages to the crashing outcome, we forget. We forget because Nick forgets. His narration becomes fresh and expectant, untainted by hindsight. He is a young man gone east to make his way; he has rented a bungalow next to a fabulous manor house tenanted by a singularly mysterious character.

We first catch sight of our eponymous "hero" when Nick returns home from his dinner with the Buchanans. Nick is out breathing the night air when he realizes that he is not alone: "fifty feet away a figure had emerged from the shadow of my neighbor's mansion and was standing with his hands in his pockets regarding the silver pepper of the stars." He is about to call to the stranger, but when he observes that the man is fixated by a faraway gleam of green light, he desists. And then the man who will be Gatsby is gone.

The first encounter, then, is with the fundamental mystery of Jay Gatsby. And for a time the mystery only grows. Nick starts seeing more of the Buchanans and begins to date Daisy's friend, the cool but companionable Jordan Baker. Then he goes to one of Gatsby's legendary parties, which are, he eventually learns, nothing more than shimmering nets thrown out in the hopes of snaring Gatsby's long-lost love, Daisy. We see Gatsby as Nick sees him, magnified and dazzling in the strobe lights of rumor. They say he is a German spy, a nephew of Kaiser Wilhelm, a killer. A killer . . . against such opulence, the speculation about the dark deeds is but a further exaltation of the image. The collective instinct is unerring: Such a magnificent flower can only be sprung from an evil soil.

Gatsby is never more thrilling, more fantastic, than in those early, champagne-lit conjectures. Soon enough Nick will meet his neighbor and be drawn into his machinations. And though he will remain to the last an unknown quantity, Gatsby will slowly wither from episode to episode. After the mist of legend blows off, he becomes merely mysterious—a financier with peculiar connections, none more peculiar than his "gonnegtion" to Meyer Wolfsheim, the man who allegedly fixed the 1919 World Series. Then, when his quixotic obsession with Daisy is revealed, his mysteriousness is replaced by an aura of tragic pathos—Gatsby in love is as foolishly human as any of us.

Yet it is this love, the scale of it, that confers on Gatsby whatever grandeur he finally possesses. Without it he is the Wizard of Oz—a behind-the-scenes operator with extensive ties to bootleggers and dubious financiers. When his dream of love is destroyed, he is nothing but his extravagant props—he is ready for George Wilson's bullet. In the end only his old father, Nick, and a few stragglers attend the funeral. And it is one of these stragglers, "the owl-eyed man," who gets the last word that day: "The poor son-of-a-bitch."

On the surface, then, Fitzgerald has written a parable on the perennial American theme of outsized dreams and their bitter ruin. "I coulda been a contender," Brando says in *On the Waterfront*. In the last scene of *Death of a Salesman*, Charley sums things up for Biff: "Nobody dast blame this man. A salesman is got to dream, boy. It comes with the territory." And on and on. We do not have to work very hard to connect Fitzgerald's vision with the narrative of public life in our era—our Wall Street pirates, our stumping politicians looking for the light in the distance as they kick up the dust around their own suspect doings. Self-making is a bloody business. And Nick's awakening—"I wanted the world to be . . . at a sort of moral attention forever"—is ours.

But this parable of rise and fall, of magnificent mansions bought by dirty dealings, is not what determines *Gatsby*'s greatness or its ultimate relevance. That is only part of the picture. Indeed, running behind or beneath the obvious legend is a secondary narrative, a narrative that is less about paying the piper than it is about dreaming, about the power of our expectations and our longings. And it is the vibration that is set up when this presses against the ostensible plot that makes *Gatsby* so galvanizing—and so American. To put it simply, the novel argues with itself, and does so just as we do in our own souls. It purports to speak of incidents and moral consequences, but underneath it is communicating something much more ambiguous and suggestive.

First the sober opening:

> In my younger and more vulnerable years my father gave me some advice that I've been turning over in my mind ever since.
> "Whenever you feel like criticizing any one," he told me, "just remember that all the people in this world haven't had the advantages you've had."

Our narrator is going to give us a lesson, tell us a story about wising up—about coming to mature terms with human frailty. He is back from the East and Gatsby has fallen. But already by the fourth paragraph we sense that Nick is at odds with himself. Directly after his claim that he wants "no more riotous excursions with privileged glimpses into the human heart," he introduces the name of Gatsby—Gatsby, who "represented everything for which I have an unaffected scorn," but in whom Nick had found "an extraordinary gift for hope, a romantic readiness such as I have never found in any other person and which it is not likely I shall ever find again."

This ambivalence is never really resolved. There is the tale, and there is the teller. And time and again we are given clues that the teller, our collective mouthpiece, that stand-up decent fellow from the Midwest, does not quite believe the tale—certainly not the lesson it would impart. The language repeatedly gives him away. Shrewd and cynical as he can be when characterizing the Buchanans or Jordan, he cannot get the note of reverence out of his voice when he writes of Gatsby and his gaudy displays. Here he notes the preparations for another of Gatsby's parties: "On buffet tables, garnished with glistening hors-d'oeuvre, spiced baked hams crowded against salads of harlequin designs and pastry pigs and turkeys bewitched to a dark gold." The prose—*glistening, harlequin, bewitched, dark gold*—is enraptured.

And the bacchanal itself? Again the tone and the rhythm inform on the observer:

> Laughter is easier minute by minute, spilled with prodigality, tipped out at a cheerful word. The groups change more swiftly, swell with new arrivals, dissolve and form in the same breath; already there are wanderers, confident girls who weave here and there among the stouter and more stable, become for a sharp, joyous moment the center of a group, and then, excited with triumph, glide on through the sea-change of faces and voices and color under the constantly changing light.
>
> Suddenly one of these gypsies, in trembling opal, seizes a cocktail out of the air, dumps it down for courage and, moving her hands like Frisco, dances out alone on the canvas platform.

If Nick is a man remembering scenes of past extravagance—the fireworks before the fall—then he has clearly been seduced by the promise all over again; against this indrawn breath of excitement any sober rectitude must feel willed.

Even after Gatsby has fallen to earth, after the dark secrets have come out, the lessons been grudgingly learned, Nick sustains a wistful yearning that the sad facts cannot destroy. Back in the Midwest, having survived to tell the tale, he reflects:

> West Egg, especially, still figures in my more fantastic dreams. I
> see it as a night scene by El Greco: a hundred houses, at once
> conventional and grotesque, crouching under a sullen, over-
> hanging sky and a lustreless moon. In the foreground four
> solemn men in dress suits are walking along the sidewalk with a
> stretcher on which lies a drunken woman in a white evening
> dress. Her hand, which dangles over the side, sparkles cold with
> jewels. Gravely the men turn in at a house—the wrong house.
> But no one knows the woman's name, and no one cares.

It would be a despairing image, ought to be, except for the fascinated absorption of the narrating voice. Nick can't resist making
his dream a tour de force, imparting to its staging a strange beauty.

None of this is incidental. Every cadenza, every perfectly orchestrated description, is part of the design, guiding the reader to
the romantic surge of the book's final passages. These passages
would surely strike us as excessive and overblown were they not
most patiently prepared for. Step by step, mostly by way of the tone
and the subliminal suggestiveness of the language, we have been
made to recognize the true unconscious disposition of Nick's
American soul. The man who began with both feet on the ground
and his head screwed back on has unveiled the contrary side of his
character. And it is the progress of this unveiling, its sudden final
momentum, that imparts to *Gatsby* the magic of renewability.

The final passage is one of the best known in our literature, but
I cite from it again:

> Most of the big shore places were closed now and there were
> hardly any lights except the shadowy, moving glow of a ferryboat
> across the Sound. And as the moon rose higher the inessential
> houses began to melt away until gradually I became aware of the
> old island here that flowered once for Dutch sailors' eyes—a
> fresh, green breast of the new world. Its vanished trees, the trees
> that had made way for Gatsby's house, had once pandered in
> whispers to the last and greatest of human dreams; for a transi-
> tory enchanted moment man must have held his breath in the
> presence of this continent, compelled into an aesthetic con-
> templation he neither understood nor desired, face to face for

the last time in history with something commensurate to his capacity for wonder.

And:

> Gatsby believed in the green light, the orgiastic future that year by year recedes before us. It eluded us then, but that's no matter—tomorrow we will run faster, stretch out our arms farther. . . . And one fine morning—
> So we beat on, boats against the current, borne back ceaselessly into the past.

This might well be the most lyrical patch of prose in our literature. Taken by itself it sounds florid, overwrought. There is only the last sentence, implacable beneath the lulling sway of its syllables, to mitigate the visionary excess. But encountering it as we do on the far side of Gatsby's exploded paradise, we are stirred at the deepest level. In a stroke Fitzgerald has forged the link between Gatsby's belief in love—the fabulous self-making enterprise it fostered—and the originating dream of the first European settlers. The mystery of this corrupt but also pathetic and forgivable man is seen as an attribute of something larger. As Nick says of Gatsby:

> He had come a long way to this blue lawn, and his dream must have seemed so close that he could hardly fail to grasp it. He did not know that it was already behind him, somewhere back in that vast obscurity beyond the city, where the dark fields of the republic rolled on under the night.

Nick has here restored to him the greatness of his desire. It is a desire that partakes of everything we feel when we consider our own fate, private and collective, under the larger dispensation, what the philosophers once called "the aspect of eternity." Insofar as we feel the inchoate promise of ourselves and our historical presence, we are joined to him.

"So we beat on . . ." The boats are not defeated by the current—nothing so simple. They are "borne back ceaselessly into the past." And what is that past but the vision of those Dutch sailors, the imagining of a new history before which all other initiatives pale? If *The Great Gatsby* is indeed a cautionary tale, then it is really cautioning us against selling ourselves short, against turning in fear or disappointment from the lyrical call of our nature. Gatsby was not a fool for dreaming, only for not knowing how dreams intersect with realities.

Similarly, if *Gatsby* is a book for us today, it is not so in the obvious moralizing way. We are not asked to repudiate our more excessive selves. Rather, we are to recover in altered form something of the power of that intoxication, that amorous bent toward greater possibilities of feeling and action. Our basic excessiveness is not about greed or display, nor is it a frantic escape from the roll-call confinements of dailiness. It is a surviving trace of the awe that set everything into motion. And wounded and compromised as we may feel, there is a clue about renewal in that essential American image of dark fields rolling on under the night.

Jack Kerouac

I first read Jack Kerouac's *On the Road* when I was a junior in high school—a little more than twenty-one years ago. Someone had given my mother a copy of the book; I immediately "borrowed" it, consumed it, and started it circulating among my friends. Soon we were all obsessed—hitchhiking everywhere we could, trying to be like the characters in the novel.

Our every late-adolescent desire for movement, escape, *action*, was brought to a blaze. Not that much fanning of sparks was needed. After all, it was 1968. If it hadn't been Kerouac, it would soon have been someone else.

Although Kerouac had begun writing *On the Road* in 1948, and it had first been published in 1957, the book could not have felt more present tense. Kerouac had caught hold of a spirit we understood; he raised a call to arms. What for me had been just inchoate turmoil and longing had now been set down in words. I grew restless and excited when the book's narrator, Sal Paradise, announced:

> . . . the only people for me are the mad ones, the ones who are mad to live, mad to talk, mad to be saved, desirous of everything at the same time, the ones who never yawn or say a commonplace thing, but burn, burn, burn like fabulous yellow roman candles exploding like spiders across the stars and in the middle you see the blue centerlight pop and everybody goes "Awww!"

That was it right there: madness, excess, something nonstop and feverish to hold against the blandness of our suburban childhoods.

When I went off to college, I found that we had not been unique: everyone, it seemed, had been reading Kerouac. And Allen Ginsberg and Gregory Corso and William Burroughs and

Ken Kesey (and Tom Wolfe *on* Kesey). This was our noncurricular education. These were the spirits who conferred their benediction on us, on our efforts to live differently—more intensely—than our parents had.

What a shock it was to hear, late one fall afternoon in 1969, that Kerouac had died. At forty-seven. Of an abdominal hemorrhage. Our perennially young and vital adventure guide—AKA Sal Paradise—was gone. The friend who called with the news said that we had to go to the funeral. I agreed. We packed our knapsacks and left immediately, determined to hitch from Ann Arbor to Lowell, Massachusetts—wherever *that* was. We got as far as Boston; by then the funeral was over, and we were cold and jittery from lack of sleep. We told each other that it was the going, not the getting there, that mattered.

Other shocks followed. Obituaries reported that Kerouac had lived out his last years in an alcoholic stupor. The photos confirmed it—his once beautifully chiseled American face looked bloated and sad. We hadn't known. And then came the most distressing story of all. Our hero had told reporters some time before his death that he felt alienated from the "counterculture." He'd tagged himself—I remember wincing at this—"a bippie in the middle."

Later I learned of other myths, not only about Kerouac the man—his politics and attitudes—but also about the writer. The myth about the way he wrote *On the Road* is a case in point. The story—which the author did nothing to discourage—was that he had written the book in a record-breaking three-week burst; that he had lit himself up with Benzedrine and had typed his inspired recollections directly onto one continuous roll of teletype paper. Now, this is not pure invention. The final version *was* written quickly, with the help of pills, onto just such a roll (Kerouac dumped it proudly in front of his editor, Robert Giroux). But Kerouac was not taking dictation from the angels. He had been working on the book for close to eight years, wrestling it through innumerable drafts. Kerouac adopted his final compositional stratagem because he was after a quality of improvisatory immediacy. He wanted to break with the stolid straightforwardness of his first novel, *The Town and the City* (1950). He had picked up cues from the simplified notational prose of Burroughs's *Junkie* as well as from the breathless letter-writing style of his friend Neal Cassady. He announced his new prose in *On the Road*'s first lines:

> I first met Dean not long after my wife and I split up. I had just gotten over a serious illness that I won't bother to talk about, except that it had something to do with the miserably weary split-up and my feeling that everything was dead. With the coming of Dean Moriarty began the part of my life you could call my life on the road.

Kerouac's opening may owe a debt to the "Factualist" aesthetic that Burroughs was then advocating. But its beguiling promise of escape and renewal connects it with two great classics of American individualism. Listen first to the voice of Herman Melville's Ishmael:

> Whenever I find myself growing grim about the mouth; whenever it is a damp, drizzly November in my soul; whenever I find myself involuntarily pausing before coffin warehouses, and bringing up the rear of every funeral I meet . . . then, I account it high time to get to sea as soon as I can.

Now listen to the voice of Mark Twain's Huck, as he shakes free from the oppressive confinements of the Widow Douglas:

> Says I, "*me-yow! me-yow!*" as soft as I could, and then I put out the light and scrambled out of the window onto the shed. Then I slipped down to the ground and crawled in amongst the trees, and sure enough there was Tom Sawyer waiting for me.

But unlike *Moby-Dick* and *Huckleberry Finn*, *On the Road* is not mostly a work of imagination. Rather, it details, adhering quite strictly to circumstance and chronology, Kerouac's adventures during four separate cross-country jaunts undertaken between 1946 and 1950. He changed the names, of course, and highlighted or downplayed certain episodes, but the result—to judge by the biographies—is remarkably true to his own experience. Kerouac is Sal Paradise, the narrator; Cassady (later the star of Wolfe's non-fictional *The Electric Kool-Aid Acid Test*) is Dean Moriarty; Ginsberg is Carlo Marx; Burroughs is Old Bull Lee; and so on. (Part of the enduring cachet of *On the Road* has to do with the fact that so many of its main players became notorious counterculture icons.)

I decided that I would commemorate the passing of two decades by rereading *On the Road*. I knew, of course, that everything would be different. How could it not? In 1968 it had been a book whose title promised *discovery*. Now the cover blurb announced that I was about to read "the book that turned on a generation." Braced as I was, however, I still got a terrible jolt. There is simply no adequate protection against the ways we grow and change.

The novel, *qua* novel, is not really much at all. Kerouac's alternately matter-of-fact and ebullient prose tracks Sal Paradise through his far-flung travels. The pattern is simple: About once a year, Sal gets restless in his secure lodgings with his aunt (the *mémère* to whom Kerouac remained neurotically attached all his life) and launches forth from New Jersey to the beckoning West. Each time, he hooks up with Dean Moriarty, his "mad" mentor, the aging juvenile delinquent who represents (to him) velocity, kicks, and enlightenment. Others join up and disperse, moving about like molecules of a boiling liquid. The American highway system is the spice route of their dreams. "Somewhere along the line," says Sal as he first sets out, "I knew there'd be girls, visions, everything; somewhere along the line the pearl would be handed to me."

Kerouac is sequential, at times almost diaristic. On the first trip west—perhaps because it *is* the first—every movement is tabulated. We follow Sal from the bus rides that get him started, to the long, "careening" (a favorite Kerouac word) rides that come once he gets west of Chicago and puts out his thumb. But Sal's enthusiasm allows for a heady narrative pace:

> The greatest ride in my life was about to come up, a truck, with a flatboard at the back, with about six or seven boys sprawled out on it, and the drivers, two young blond farmers from Minnesota, were picking up every single soul they found on that road. . . .
> I wasn't on the flatboard before the truck roared off; I lurched, a rider grabbed me, and I sat down. Somebody passed a bottle of rotgut, the bottom of it. I took a big swig in the wild, lyrical, drizzling air of Nebraska. "Whooee, here we go!" yelled

a kid in a baseball cap, and they gunned up the truck to seventy and passed everybody on the road.

Wild and *lyrical* are two more favorite Kerouac words—they crop up in most of his more energized riffs, especially through the first half of the book. It's as if Sal can't kick the language up quite as high as he wants it—he makes these loosely deployed adjectives carry so much of the freight of the inexpressible. But once—for me at least—they did carry it. When I first read *On the Road*, no one needed to tell me how a night or a town or a train or a bum could be "lyrical"—they just were. Kerouac's scattershot words and phrases accorded perfectly with my jumbled-up feelings about life. Now, for whatever reason, I seem to crave more precision—a passage like that no longer delivers.

On Sal's first trip west, he wants to "dig" everything. And everything is there to be dug. When he gets to Denver, his first real layover, a gang of friends and friends of friends is waiting. There follow rampaging nights with the hard-partying Bettencourt sisters and the Rawlins clan: "We started off with a few extra-size beers. There was a player piano. Beyond the back door was a view of mountainsides in the moonlight. I let out a yahoo. The night was on."

New sights and the promise of good times are, of course, part of what lures Sal away from home again and again; but the real draw is Dean—the outlaw, the limit breaker. Sal wants to be near him as much as possible. Dean steals cars, he tears between the coasts in nonstop driving binges, he loves every "gal" in every diner along the way. He is Sal's "yellow roman candle," his life force; he is the catalyst that helps Sal break through his essential passivity.

Sal and Dean have one of those eternally boyish American friendships. Although women are desired, discussed, and dallied with, they are also always in the way—nagging, getting pregnant, threatening to stop the fun. Leslie Fiedler long ago identified the homoerotic nature of the bond (yes, Ishmael and Queequeg, Huck and Jim . . .) in *Love and Death in the American Novel*. And biographers of Kerouac now bear out that his friendship with Cassady did extend to some hesitant, experimental sex.

In any event, what weaves together the separate travel episodes is the unfolding history of a friendship—a history that begins with Sal's enchantment with the charismatically amoral Dean Moriarty and that ends with his pained disillusionment. In an early, blinded description, Sal writes: "And a kind of holy lightning I saw flashing from his excitement and his visions, which he described so torrentially that people in buses looked around to see the 'over-excited nut.'" But after he has been deserted and betrayed enough times, Sal finds his perceptions shifting. Dean's mad avidity is not so much heroic as desperate. He is fleeing his own inner void—the legacy of his rummy father, who abandoned him among the bars and poolhalls of Denver when he was a young boy.

By the end of the book, Sal's "thin-hipped" hero has become a figure of profound sadness. In the very last scene, when Sal is on his way to a concert, riding in the back of a hired Cadillac, he looks out at his friend: "Dean, ragged in a motheaten overcoat he brought specially for the freezing temperatures of the East, walked off alone." He then adds this valedictory cadenza: "nobody knows what's going to happen to anybody besides the forlorn rags of growing old, I think of Dean Moriarty, I even think of Old Dean Moriarty the father we never found, I think of Dean Moriarty."

It is probably a mistake to go back to the decisive books of one's youth. They are causes; the reader has long since become, in part, their effect. Clear vision is just not possible. I feel myself in a position somewhat like Sal's. It was not so much that Dean had changed from what he was—more that Sal had watched the vivid mantle of desires and dreams that he had created around Dean slowly dissipate. So, too, has the magic of *On the Road* dissipated for me.

Reading this book at sixteen, my friends and I wanted nothing so much as to be like Dean and Sal—close to the ground, connected, in motion, "paying our dues." We aspired to the "beat" ideal, with its double connotation of "worn-out" and "beatific." And when it led, as it inexorably did, to the hippie ethos of turning on, tuning in, and dropping out (how quaint it sounds!), many of us followed. But that next step was also a kind of last step—the premises of hippiedom were quickly consumed on the pyre of its excesses. Thus, once again, effects had come around to swallow their causes; henceforth, "beat" would also mean something like "protohippie."

All of this went through my mind as I reread *On the Road*. Indeed, at some point I realized that I was not so much reading a book as taking stock—of those times, of these times, of myself in both. For me, the hardest thing was to see past the jadedness and cynicism of the eighties—to remember even a little of what life felt like back then. I don't know that I was able to, finally. The notes were as scored, sure, and the sounds were the same. But I kept feeling as if I were listening to a party record the morning after the party. It sounded sad, nothing like the way it had sounded while I was dancing to it.

Destinies of Character

A few months ago, and purely for pleasure, I read Anne Tyler's latest novel, *Breathing Lessons*. It is as good an example as I can think of just now of a serious, naturalistic mainstream novel. The two main characters, Ira and Maggie Moran, a middle-aged married couple, are the solid supports for—and makers of—the book's simple plot. The novel begins as they are about to set forth by car to the funeral of the husband of one of Maggie's oldest friends. Their long day will be filled with incidents and encounters. First, they will meet up with a number of old friends at the funeral. Later, as they are driving back, Maggie will insist that they visit their former daughter-in-law—she has a scheme, which ultimately fails, for reuniting her son's family. The novel will end with Maggie and Ira back in their bedroom, preparing for sleep.

Outwardly it is not an enticing story line—certainly not as I have summarized it here. But every reader knows how irrelevant such summaries are. They characterize a novel about as usefully as an occupation defines a person. The presentation is everything, the registration of sensation and the weaving of a credible texture of psychic life. And, no less important, the creation around each principal character of a receptive space. This is hard to define. I'm thinking in terms of an opening or access, a means of getting close up to the life, but an access with certain set limits. For there must be an opacity as well, a degree of otherness that keeps the characters at a slight remove; we accompany them without *becoming* them. Some romances or thrillers may ask for a maximum investment of our fantasies. The more "serious" novel, however, has less to do with what we wish than with what we are; identifications are always partial.

Breathing Lessons opens as follows:

> Maggie and Ira Moran had to go to a funeral in Deer Lick, Pennsylvania. Maggie's girlhood friend had lost her husband. Deer Lick lay on a narrow country road some ninety miles north of Baltimore, and the funeral was scheduled for ten-thirty Saturday morning; so Ira figured they should start around eight. This made him grumpy.

At first, we do not so much suspend disbelief as give consent; we decide to let the natural momentum of our imaginings give life to the figments assembled on the page. When I first encounter a character, my response may be likened to the throwing of a switch. I not only confer potential identity, setting up a contour that I believe will soon start to be filled in, I also establish an axis of past, present, and future along which the life, or lives, will flourish. Maggie and Ira, whom I assume out of convention to be married, are equipped with a generic marital history (which will be modified as needed) and a future that may or may not find them still together. I read on, starting in now on the second paragraph:

> They planned to wake up at seven, but Maggie must have set the alarm wrong and so they overslept. They had to dress in a hurry and rush through breakfast, making do with faucet coffee and cold cereal. Then Ira headed off for the store on foot to leave a note for his customers, and Maggie walked to the body shop. She was wearing her best dress—blue and white sprigged, with cape sleeves—and crisp black pumps, on account of the funeral.

I am enlisted. I don't yet see Maggie, I'm not sure what sprigging is or what cape sleeves look like, but a person is stirring to life—and the obstacles of page and print begin to recede. Although at first I know little more than that Maggie drinks coffee and is old enough to have a friend who has lost a husband, I feel myself being taken up into the momentum of her day. That day is already tinctured by her character. Faucet coffee and cold cereal. I see a habitually late person, a bumbler, but one who also possesses an inelegant, improvisational readiness. I am inclined to like her—certainly I'm not threatened or warned away. And when I learn that she is wearing her *best* dress, that she is the kind of person who keeps a best dress, I feel touched. It's already clear to me

that while untold mischief may erupt from this woman, she bears
no evil. I adjust my reading sights accordingly.

But even less than two paragraphs into the novel, I am doing a
good deal more than concretizing a pair of personalities out of a
set of given signals. I am also already engaged in laying slight
translucent strands—webs of association and memory—athwart
the narrative. "Faucet coffee" conjures a flash of myself in a room
I once rented, fixing a cup of Maxim from the tap (a ghost of a
taste, a split-second snapshot of the blue metal cup I used to drink
from); simultaneously, or nearly so, I get an equally fleeting image
of Glenda Jackson in the movie *Sunday, Bloody Sunday:* Her character at one point also makes coffee at the sink.

I mention these instances because similar perceptual flickerings
accompany my reading with varying intensity from the first page
to the last. They do not merely happen alongside my reading—in
some important sense they *are* my reading. Or, to tilt the emphasis
slightly, they are *my* reading. Granted, I cited relatively trivial associations. At other times, though, perhaps when I am more caught
up in the emotional rush of a given scene, I may experience a
more extended wash of memory. No matter the scale, it is always
my life coming toward me—but obliquely, held inside a frame of
fictive reality. And snatching myself from an unexpected angle
gives me a vitalizing shock, the emotional equivalent of a double
take before a surprise mirror.

Precise physical visualization of characters is not all that important
to me when I read. A book is not a movie. I don't need to know
what Maggie's nose looks like or how she styles her hair—unless, of
course, her hairstyle tells me something about how she views herself, in which case it is information I'm avid for. Indeed, my outward picture of Maggie and Ira remains quite blurry throughout.
I see pleasant general faces, bodies with a normal stock of gestures
and tics. I notice, too, that Tyler has gone to no great lengths to in-
cise highly specific images in my mind. No, she has given me just
enough to support the illusion of their in-the-world-existence. The
rest is for me to fill in, should I choose to. (I do not.) This is not,
on Tyler's part, an abnegation of authorial responsibility. To the
contrary, she has allowed me to know Ira and Maggie better than

I know most "real" people, precisely because the distracting and limiting details of outwardness have been cut away. I get direct access to the voices of the inner life.

The opening sections always make for the hardest work. The reader has to exert considerable energy to get the world into place and to make out the basic character relationships. We do construct—the novel's world does not spring to life of its own accord. But soon enough this changes. Situations and settings have been pegged out; the characters are convincingly in motion. What's more, they have very quickly acquired their own store of time. Within pages we feel them to possess a past, even if it is only the past of those pages. And as the novel gathers momentum, this illusion deepens, adding ever-greater verisimilitude.

The characters' emergence into time works to activate our own time sense. We are suddenly aware of ourselves less as entities in a constantly shifting present, more as cumulative beings: We open up to our own histories. And this, in turn, makes us all the more susceptible to the kind of associative play that turns reading into self-exploration.

A third of the way into *Breathing Lessons*, Maggie, Ira, and the others who have come for the service return to the widow's house. She has a surprise planned. When everyone is assembled in her living room, she brings out a projector and shows an old home movie that was made at her wedding. The guests are taken aback. All at once they are staring at the light-scarred images of their former selves:

> Then the camera swooped and there was Sissy playing the piano, with one damp curl plastered to her forehead. Maggie and Ira, side by side, stood watching Sissy gravely. (Ira was a boy, a mere child.) They drew a breath. They started singing.

By the time we reach this section, we are reasonably well acquainted with Maggie and Ira—Maggie especially. We have seen their way with each other in the present (tolerant, alternately affectionate and irritated), we know something of their past (though the full story of their courtship has yet to be told), and we have a very strong sense about Maggie's inner life. We know what her concerns are, how her thoughts move, what kinds of connections she makes. Following along through the scene, we are not in her mind, but we are beside her. Our vantage allows us an exalting sense of intensification. The time line that we have been tracing, comprised mainly of incidents in the narrative present, is suddenly ruptured. Drawing analogies to our own confrontations with the past—as we inevitably do—we encompass the depth of Maggie's time. Her presence is immediately augmented.

Of course, we all know these intrusions of past, the irrefutable proofs that we really were once different. We are doubly stricken: We not only feel the gap from now to then, but we also grasp that there was once a then that had no inkling of its future. We glimpse ourselves "objectively," deprived of the blendings and distortions that usually soften the memory process. We are face-to-face with the truth about the passing of time, our aging; the day will come, we realize, from which our now will seem as quaint and diminished as that arrested moment of the past.

These thoughts arise in me as I read this scene, but more as sensations and intimations than as formulated ideas. I participate in Maggie's looking at the past, but it is at the same time very much my own looking. I am not merging, or losing myself, but I am identifying. The distinction is important. The contact I make with myself is not vicarious; it is direct. Maggie becomes an agent, a *medium,* for my own responses to my life. The picture is complicated when I realize that Maggie is also, in a way, a medium for conveying Tyler's own sensations about *her* past—that it is her life I am indirectly in contact with.

My experience of Tyler's characters, then, is neither the result of pure suspension of self nor the simple product of mental construction. It is something in between. While reading, I surrender parts of my customary self-awareness in order to participate in the lives created. But while I may forget that I am in a chair, I do not forget that I exist. Rather, my inner self, that chaotic bundle of emotions, longings, and memories, comes loose from its moorings. These previously latent elements circulate freely about the characters and settings. I cannot always say clearly where I stop and the fictional life begins. My thoughts swarm over the phantom selves of Maggie and Ira, occupying them in part; *their* thoughts and experiences—in the form of the language that creates them—

fill me and seem mine. The interchange brings about a kind of amalgamation.

I am living under a spell while I am reading: I am dreaming with my eyes open. In night dreams, I often feel the same familiar sense of flowing over boundaries. One person is readily combined with another, or else I feel perfectly intimate with someone I scarcely know—yet everything seems right and profound. The same familiarity and rightness move through me as I read certain novels. I keep reading because I long to perpetuate the feeling.

But this wakeful dreaming has direction and shape. The author controls me, moving the characters—and me with them—toward some determined resolution. So long as I am within the force field of the book, I am the subject of a powerful shadow reality. The phone may ring, or I may jump up to get to the store before it closes, but when I pick up the book again, I have only to wind my way back a sentence or two. Right away I locate my place in this other place; I return, and it is as if I had never left.

But novels end. The characters and the life they sustain become colored with the futurity of their imminent parting. How soon Ira and Maggie are back in their bedroom—only a few pages remain. I am going to have to finish with them just when I've come to know them most intimately. It's hard not to feel some of the twinges we reserve for real-life partings. Ira, now become so familiar, is laying out his solitaire; Maggie is looking on:

> He had arrived at the interesting part of the game by now, she saw. He had passed that early, superficial stage where any number of moves seemed possible and he had to show real skill and judgment. She felt a little stir of something that came over her like a flush, a sort of inner buoyancy, and she lifted her face to kiss the warm blade of his cheekbone. Then she slipped free and moved to her side of the bed, because tomorrow they had a long car trip to make and she knew she would need a good night's sleep before they started.

A complex, triumphant finish. Maggie, we know from that "little stir of something," has registered a metaphoric understanding of their situation: their place in life, in time, is momentarily connected to Ira's place in the game. Options have narrowed, "skill and judgment" will now be required. But the implication is that the game can be completed successfully, with nothing left over or gone to waste. As readers, we share Maggie's insight, but we also gain an added perception. We get the analogy to the fiction itself: This moment is, in effect, the last right placing of the final card. With one stroke, Tyler has flashed forth the depth of Maggie and Ira's married love and has surrounded it with the promise of a future. It is an illusionistic future—it waits off the page—but we take leave of the novel by walking a short distance into it.

The sensations we feel as we finish a novel like this are strange ones. Even as we close the covers, the mirage begins to fade; the chair, the room, everything we were insensible of, comes crowding back. It is, truly, as if we were waking from a particularly vivid dream. That feeling of fusion, of blurred boundaries, is gone. What are we left with? A set of memory traces, a lingering responsiveness to an undefined otherness of person and place, a temporary sense of completeness. We have been somewhere, and now we are back. The world has the color of our traveling.

Don DeLillo's
Underworld

The publication last fall of Don DeLillo's *Underworld* was a literary event of a kind we don't see much anymore. Of course there were reviews in all of the papers and magazines, and interviews—the notoriously reclusive author agreed to make himself available in deference to the seven figures that Scribner had ponied up to lure him away from Viking. The buzz surpassed even that surrounding the long-awaited release of Thomas Pynchon's *Mason & Dixon.* What a year for fiction! Here were two visionary extravaganzas, each of them thicker than the proverbial Manhattan phone directory. But while the Pynchon fell off the best-seller lists after a few weeks—victim, I would guess, of its own syntactical density— *Underworld* got a long ride and picked up nominations from the National Book Award and the National Book Critics Circle along the way.

This bears some pondering. Not to be asking, "Why DeLillo?" but rather "Why DeLillo now?" After all, *Underworld* is the author's eleventh novel—he is long past the stage of the breakout book. Indeed, he *had* his breakout book in *White Noise,* his 1985 postmodern classic. DeLillo's two subsequent novels, *Libra* and *Mao II,* got front-page reviews everywhere.

But something is out of sync. From Eric Konigsberg's exhaustively researched 1997 *New York* magazine story, "How to Make a Bestseller," we learn that *Mao II* sold "only in the range of 40,000 copies." A startling statistic. Most of us, naturally, would be delighted to snag those kind of sales, but for a writer of DeLillo's stature it's not much at all. The figure confirms, rather, that DeLillo was stuck fast at the upper end of the highbrow literary fiction market. Whence, then, the sudden stratospheric surge of *Underworld*? Did some canny kingmaker put a wetted finger to the wind to determine that the man's hour had come around at last;

or did his editors all see that, yes, this was the dreamed-of thing, a page-turner from a credentialed heavyweight?

I would argue that it was something else that set things into motion, something the editors may have sensed but did not really strategize for. Simply, that *Underworld* registered as it did—with critics, judges, and readers—in large part because it was understood to be a directional signal, a . . . millennium book. Dangerous word, I know. Every second product these days is shilled with a millennium twist and the only sane response is a preemptive wince. But in DeLillo's case the word—the serious concept behind the word—fits. Although *Underworld* ranges mainly over the past fifty years of American life, it points, as does everything the author writes, toward the future. Toward the capitalized Future, that is, of our various apprehensions.

From his very first books, DeLillo has had the knack of capturing on the page the odd, telling, and uneasy intimations that keep flickering through our late-modern lives. We do not go to this writer for character or plot—he frankly does not excel at either— but for what we often think of as the supporting elements of fiction: description, passages of reflection, and cunningly worded observations by his many anxious and hyperconscious mouthpiece figures. DeLillo reads the world in a special way, and he offers us a sensibility that can sound the currents of the moment. We feel that he understands the combinations, how the things we note with dread or bemusement fit together. He alone can sensibly juxtapose insights about celebrity and terrorism, or video culture and our altered sense of the materiality of things. "All plots tend to move deathward," he intones out of his authorial quasi omniscience. Or: "The future belongs to crowds." Or he will spin a riff worthy of Walter Benjamin on "the most photographed barn in America." And somehow it all fits, catches what we then believe we have been edging toward ourselves. "It's hurry up time in the West," another voice tells us.

And so it is. *Hurry up time in the West.* There *is* something urgent in the movement of the second hand, the ticking of the cursor. Our image- and data-saturated culture is pushing us toward some sort of critical mass. We are at the moment in the paradigm shift when the old has clearly given way but the new has not yet announced itself. A DeLillo world: Fundamentalists rave at us on the cable channels, while our president stars—to sensational approval ratings—in an internationally televised soap opera; the microchip ups its speed and info-gobbling power even as the fell Dr. Seed announces his intention to clone the first human; worrisome weather systems start up in the deep Pacific and track eastward . . .

Strange things have always happened, of course, but these days they come filtered through the great electronic ectoplasm so that we are at every moment filled with their vibrations. Now we start to feel the compounding pressure of the millennium—the *idea* of it—and find everything in the culture already being scored to a media fanfare of arrival and departure. Things are going to be different—new—whether they really are or not. A cynic might say that the millennial moment is just another way of shouting, "Now!" in a world that is rapidly losing the ballast weight of its sense of history.

Many of us, I suspect, feel some foreboding about the momentum of the present, that sense of change eclipsing change faster than we can make a narrative to account for everything. And we wonder how—and if—these extraordinary developments and their instantaneous collective circulation mean anything. Into this space of wondering, sturdy and dense, comes *Underworld,* and of course we sit up. For who could be better than DeLillo for finding the vantage from which to view the show? Who could more accurately capture the authentic feeling of it all? We want to understand, sure, but we also want to recognize the sensations we walk around with. We want our experience—and I steal my adjective from the late Walker Percy—"certified."

Underworld is mainly plotless; it is a loose confabulation of episodes and meditations drawn from different moments of the past half century. Unifying elements, aside from the myriad thematic echoes, are few. There is Bobby Thompson's famous home-run baseball from the 1951 National League playoff game, caught first by a young black man named Cotter Martin, which then changes hands a number of times (not unlike the battered accordion in E. Annie Proulx's *Accordion Crimes*)—but that is more a teasing link than a structural principle. Otherwise, the novel is casually threaded around the character of Nick Shay, a Bronx boy, son of a low-level mobster, who starts out bad—actually kills a man—but then straightens out, rehabilitates himself, and eventually becomes a powerful waste-management broker. But we never get inside his skin, never learn the core features of the man the way we might from another kind of writer. Nick's story, told essentially in reverse, is not the point—it gives DeLillo an armature. Around the episodically discontinuous forays into Nick's life are clumped a host of other narratives and scenes. We have bits from the life of Klara Sax, who was once, briefly, Nick's lover, and who has become a celebrated performance artist; a few interludes from the life of Nick's younger brother, who is involved with top-security nuclear physics research; a narration of Truman Capote's infamous masked ball at the Plaza Hotel from the perspective of J. Edgar Hoover, a guest; invented transcriptions of various routines Lenny Bruce did on the eve of the Cuban missile crisis, and so on.

Told this way, the architecture of this 800-plus-page behemoth looks risky: no standard continuities, a mere hint of a plot, and even less character complication. But DeLillo banks heavily on sweep and vision, and on the combinatory dynamic. If a novel is not powered by a narrative, it had better at least have a force field. Triumphantly, against high countervailing odds, *Underworld* has—is—exactly that.

The story of how DeLillo came to write *Underworld* is fairly well known by now. How lucky impulse led the author to the microfilm machine in his local library, where he studied the front page of the October 4, 1951, *New York Times* and discovered what he has called "a pair of mated headlines." "GIANTS CAPTURE PENNANT" read the first and "SOVIETS EXPLODE ATOM BOMB" the second. A potentially combustible mix, he thought. And then he found the spark. Present at the last game, the game of the famous Bobby Thompson homer—together, no less—were Jackie Gleason, Frank Sinatra, restaurateur Toots Shor, and J. Edgar Hoover. Four American icons, each in his own right an auratic figure. But it was the last name—Hoover's—that made DeLillo feel "astrologically blessed." The game became the long opening section of the novel.

Whether they love the novel or not, all of the critics agree that the scene at the old Polo Grounds is a tour de force. Shifting confidently among various perspectives, DeLillo fetches up one poetically charged detail after another. Entering the stadium, Cotter sees "that unfolding vision of the grass that seems to mean he has stepped outside his life." Walking down "into the heat and smell of the massed fans, he walks into the smoke that hangs from the underside of the second deck . . . he hears the warm-up pitches crack into the catcher's mitt, a series of reports that carry a comet's tail of secondary sound."

DeLillo wants more, though, than simply to capture the feel of the great summer game. His deeper intent is to isolate, to *create*, a historical moment. Here is the country right at midcentury, arrested as a Norman Rockwell portrait, only tinged in places with the darker intimations of a George Grosz. Call the afternoon a decisive moment, the last bright apotheosis of our vigorous—and fabled—innocence. DeLillo plants us deep in the collective psyche at a critical juncture: We are at the World Series when *home team* still signifies, when the stands are filled with boys and men from the neighborhoods around. Heroism is still viable, has not yet been vaporized by the media's ironic gaze. Sinking into the prose, feeling the afternoon gather mass around us, we allow an older set of understandings to come alive. We recognize that although America was the great global power, life for its citizens remained constrained by the immediacies of place. The local, the home-grown, still imprinted everything.

With the detonation of the A-bomb by the Soviets, however, all that changed; the world was, at a stroke, brought into the era of global consequences, of action-at-a-distance. This was the origin point of the doctrine of mutually assured destruction (MAD), which possibly more than anything else disfigured American life in the second half of the century. Here begins global paranoia.

But on this October afternoon only Hoover knows the news, and he ponders it while staring at a *Life* magazine reproduction of Brueghel's *The Triumph of Death*, which he has plucked from the avalanche of confetti all around him. The image suddenly grips his interest far more than the endgame mania surrounding him:

> He looks at the flaring sky in the deep distance out beyond the headlands on the left-hand page—Death elsewhere, Conflagration in many places, Terror universal, the crows, the ravens in silent glide, the raven perched on the white nag's rump, black and white forever, and he thinks of a lonely tower standing on the Kazakh test site, the tower armed with the bombs and he can

almost hear the wind blowing across the Central Asian Steppes, out where the enemy lives in long coats and fur caps, speaking that old weighted language of theirs, liturgical and grave.

This is what DeLillo does most commandingly, not at the expense of plot, but almost in its stead: He creates "moments," word masses that are like panels, each freestanding, but also existing in complex juxtaposition with countless other panels in the imaginary space of the novel. Meaning and intimation arise almost inevitably from the adjacencies—from the patterns that are sketched in the reader's mind. Here we have the image of the Brueghel factored through the paranoid intelligence of Hoover, the crowded death feast set counter to the swarming spectacle at the Polo Grounds. Later we will encounter other crowds, like the gathering of the powerful and fashionable at Capote's gala, and the manifestly outré paranoia of Lenny Bruce, and dozens and dozens of other sympathetically vibrating elements.

The next 800 pages perpetuate this logic of juxtaposition and suggestive combination. Having incised the October 1951 moment in our minds, DeLillo leaps forward to 1992, and then moves slowly backward, peeling away the years until we are once again back in the time period of the historic game. He concludes with an epilogue set in the near present. The impression we have as readers is that we are carrying out some sort of archaeological mission, looking back from our perch in the present to find out how and why things unfolded as they did. By the time we reach the end, we understand that Nick, our lightly shaded-in protagonist, is mainly a point of reference; he supplies the idea of witness and allows us to assume a continuous sensibility around whom the currents of the period are swirling.

Clearly DeLillo has taken an enormous risk in giving so massive a book so little endoskeleton. If he succeeds—and in significant ways he does—it is because he has mastered the sly arts of association and because he has devised a structural premise that itself resonates with thematic meaning. Form undergirds content. The novel catches so much about late-modern life because it dares to be as combinatory and—dare I say it?—paranoid as we are in our more exacerbated perceptions.

There is the impression, incessantly reinforced, that far-flung phenomena connect and that if we could but read the cipher of their connection we would have a key to meaning. Descriptions of a widely broadcast videoloop featuring an actual shooting by the so-called Texas Highway Killer are echoed, later, when we come upon an artist's installation featuring hundreds of monitors playing and replaying the Zapruder footage of the Kennedy assassination. We pause, register the pulse of energy across the synapse, and the weft of the novel tightens. Ideas about violence, media display and repetition, touched on in a half dozen other places in the novel, sift together; for a moment we feel that we understand how a nation comes to be fixated by revelations of its own darkness.

The effect of these synchronized correspondences and counterpoints is to create and then repeatedly confirm that slightly paranoid impression that events are not happening randomly but within a dense field of affinity. Seemingly unconnected things are in fact profoundly linked. For example, Nick's metaphysical interest in waste—material exhaust—has subtle links to the ethos of nuclear proliferation. The two notions can be seen to play off one another in various ways, through scenic juxtaposition as well as through the oracular pronouncements of Nick's old lover, Klara Sax. "Many things that were anchored to the balance of power and the balance of terror," she tells an interviewer, "seem to be undone, unstuck. Things have no limits now. Money has no limits. . . . Money is undone. Violence is undone, violence is easier now, it's uprooted, out of control, it has no measure anymore, it has no level of value." Suddenly we fathom our disposable culture, and the relentless consumption that underwrites it, in a new way.

DeLillo's larger point is clearly discernible: that our extraordinary growth and change over this past century have been at a cost, one spelled out in Klara's assertion. We have lost the sense of limit, the anchor line that makes it possible to grasp our values as values; we have destroyed context, the understanding of the local, the community, that used to sustain an atmosphere of meaning. The point is brought home in various ways as the novel moves into its final section. We are back in the Bronx, in the time of Nick's young manhood, the time of the now-legendary playoff game, and all at once it feels as if the world has been resolved back into its archetypal certainties. People seem to have mass; their dealings carry consequence; the horizon is placed where it ought to be, at the radius of a long day's walk. We read of kids sunning themselves on a rooftop: "The tar softened and fumed and the heat beat down and the green gnats stuck to their bodies and across the way the pigeon kid sent his birds into flight with a bamboo pole, and waved a towel at times, and whistled like a traffic cop." On it goes, not quite Molly Bloom's soliloquy, perhaps, but a genuine paean to gravity, to scale, to a world comprehensible, not yet undone by the terrible specter of action-at-a-distance.

What has this to do with history having a telos, a destination? Alas, plenty. In moving backward the way he has, bringing us at last to the Bronx of his youth, DeLillo not only induces the illusion of stepping back into ever less diffuse epochs of time, he also plants in us the suspicion that historical "progress" is in fact the opposite—that our lot is to feel things more and more as disembodied, and that this has become the salient truth about our lives. Away from the present, back at midcentury, we feel walls and roof surround our sense of unhousedness.

Finally DeLillo gives us his epilogue, titled "Das Kapital." It is the time of the present, and Nick and some of his waste-consultant colleagues are in Kazakhstan. They have been taken by their hosts to a place called the Museum of the Misshapens, a nightmarish exhibition of the human anomalies produced by radiation exposure. We naturally recall Hoover's reverie, the warping together of the Brueghel image with his imagining of the Kazakh test site. Then, quite abruptly, the scene changes. Nick is at home, in Phoenix, brooding about his life: "I walk through the house and look at the things we own and feel the odd mortality that clings to every object. The finer and rarer the object, the more lonely it makes me feel, and I don't know how to account for this." This is where—and how—the larger sweeps of history become actual in all of our lives. When, a few pages later, Nick voices his deepest longing, we very likely feel a resonant echo in our own souls: "I want them back, the days when I was alive on the earth, rippling in the quick of my skin, heedless and real."

Underworld ends—strangely, but also appropriately—in cyberspace, with what appears to be the posted account of the murder of a young woman forager in the Bronx, and the subsequent sighting of her apparition on a certain billboard—the Bronx miracle. An ancient nun, Sister Edgar, goes there to witness. Afterward, her earthly experience somehow complete, she dies peacefully in her sleep. Her afterlife, when it comes in the very last pages of the novel, is in cyberspace, where she has been magically reconstituted: "There is no space or time out here, or in here, or wherever she is. There are only connections. Everything is connected. All human knowledge gathered and linked, hyperlinked . . ."

There are only connections. We have come full and frightening circle from the crack of Bobby Thompson's bat, from the world that held that sound, and the ball, so vividly an emblem now of the prior, weighted, world:

> The ball was a deep sepia, veneered with dirt and turf and generational sweat—it was old, bunged up, it was bashed and tobacco juiced and stained by natural processes and by the lives behind it, weather-spattered and charactered as a seafront house. And it was smudged green near the Spaulding trademark, it was still wearing a small green bruise where it had struck a pillar according to the history that came with it—flaked paint from a bolted column in the left-field stands embedded in the surface of the ball.

Turned though it is to the recent past, *Underworld* begs to be read as a millennial pronouncement, a vast tone poem about the leaching away of mass and consequence from our personal and historical experience. DeLillo has given us a new way to think about cyberculture and virtuality, the next great frontiers. After reading the novel, we feel that we understand the larger context, how Sister Edgar's apotheosis—so richly symbolic—only becomes possible when we have at last escaped the gravity field of the material. When the hype has blown off, as it inevitably will, when enough readers have had a chance to weather the onslaught of its myriad perspectives, then the true buzz will start—the buzz that arises when vibrating sympathies meet and amplify each other. I hope we will then all understand that the point of the novel is emphatically cautionary.

SVEN BIRKERTS is the author of four previous collections of essays, most recently *The Gutenberg Elegies: The Fate of Reading in an Electronic Age*. He was the editor of Graywolf Forum One, *Tolstoy's Dictaphone: Technology and the Muse*. Recipient of Guggenheim and Lila-Wallace awards, Birkerts has published essays and reviews in the *Atlantic, Harper's*, the *New York Times Book Review*, the *New Republic*, and elsewhere. He teaches at Mount Holyoke College and is a member of the Core Faculty of the Bennington Writing Seminars. He lives with his wife and two children in Arlington, Massachusetts.

This book was designed by Will Powers. The typeface is ITC Baskerville, a digital version of the face cut by John Baskerville, a merchant and printer of Birmingham, England, in the 1750s. This book was manufactured by Bang Printing on acid-free paper.